About the author

Steve Wiseman runs the Norwich Citizens Advice Bureaux and this book is based on his experience of dealing with these problems on a day-to-day level.

Put It In Writing

© 2001 Law Pack Publishing Limited
Illustrations © Ros Asquith

Reprinted 2003

Published by
Law Pack Publishing Limited
76-89 Alscot Road
London SE1 3AW
www.lawpack.co.uk

ISBN 1 902646 33 9 Hardback edition

Put it in Writing

Contents

Introduction v

Part 1: How to Complain Effectively

Using this book 2
Where you can take advice 3
Ten tips 8
Taking things further 12

Part 2: Specific Problems

Accountants 26
Advertising 29
Advice services 33
Airlines and airports 36
Banking services 40
Barristers 47
Buses and coaches 49
Buying goods 57
Buying services 69
The Child Support Agency 76
Council Tax 82
Credit 86
Drivers and driving 96
Electricity services 103
Employment 107
Estate agents 117
Funeral services 120

continued ...

Gas services 123
Holidays 130
Hotels and guest houses 137
Inland Revenue 140
Insurance services 145
Investments and financial advice 152
Landlords of long leaseholders 161
Landlords and tenants 166
Local authorities 175
The media 180
National Health Services 188
The neighbourhood and the environment 201
The Police 216
Post Office and mail delivery 221
Public services – central government 225
Pubs and wine bars 229
Rail services 232
Residential care and nursing homes 240
Restaurants and cafés 245
Schools 249
Shopping from home 258
Social security 265
Social services 270
Solicitors' practices 273
Surveyors and valuers 284
Taxis and private minicabs 286
Telecommunications 289
Water and sewerage services 297

Index 303

Introduction

..........a book to inspire you, to inform you and to guide you.

So 'autumn leaves on the line' were to blame for your train stopping for an hour and a half in the middle of nowhere. You suspect that the builder you hired last week is going to charge you a lot more that his quote. You're really getting stressed out at work – you don't mind the extra responsibilities, but you think it's really unfair that you've been given no support or training to help you adjust. You're convinced the Red Lion served you short measures yesterday – again! And you can't believe the letter you received today saying you owe £325 in back tax.

Should you take all of this lying down?

We all sit and moan and worry about things like this. A lot of the time we then do nothing – OK, we might sound off to an apologetic ticket collector, or sigh deeply when the builder produces a bill that's £150 more than he said it would be. And we'll mutter 'I'll never bloody well come here again' hoping the pub landlord overhears us. We might even go as far as to 'have a word' with a manager at the office about that extra work. But that's it.

Why don't we do more? Lots of reasons – inertia, busy lives... but often we don't feel confident enough to take things further, or we are unsure as to how to go about it. Sometimes we even fear the consequences.

So here it is – a book to inspire you, to inform you and to guide you. This book will help you make that move from being a moaner to a complainer – an effective complainer no less!

Once you know how to complain effectively you'll never be a pushover again. You won't have to put up with that intermittent hissing sound when you use your mobile phone, or poor service at restaurants, or plumbers who keep you waiting for hours before turning up with the wrong parts. You'll know there is a way to challenge a solicitor's high bill, or incorrect social security entitlement, or a gas company that ups its charges just weeks after signing you up. You'll know whom to blame if the road surface caused your accident or how to make your landlord hurry to repair your leaking roof. You'll know you can do something to try to stop that new superstore you've heard is going to open down your road. That noisy aircraft flying over your house at night could become a thing of the past, and you may get your child the school of your choice after all.

Even the bank that insists you withdrew £100 from the cash machine in the High Street when you were in Barcelona may accept defeat if you complain effectively, and your aunt may get her hip replacement sooner than the three years she was told she'd have to wait.

So long as your complaint is justified, if you use the methods in the book you will have a very good chance of getting things put right – or maybe an apology, explanation or compensation. And not only will you be proud of yourself – you'll probably have benefited others who might otherwise suffer the same plight. Many organisations nowadays use complaints to keep tabs on their activity and to inform them on how they can improve their services. There are now more complaints procedures, customer charters, arbitration panels, tribunals and ombudsmen than ever before. Even the corner shop has to be more amenable to complaints knowing that their high street competitors place customer care so high on the agenda.

So go for it, use this book and make your voice heard!

Steve Wiseman

Part 1

How to complain effectively

Using this book

This book is a simple guide to ensuring that your complaint has the maximum impact. Part one gives general guidance on complaining effectively and issues to bear in mind whatever your concern. It sets the scene for Part two, which is a subject-by-subject guide to be dipped into whenever you need it. At the end of each chapter you will see how to get in touch with all the organisations mentioned in the text and sample letters outlining the best way to write to an organisation incorporating the appropriate references to the law.

Many of the organisations have websites which include a complaints form where you can either complain online or fill in the form on screen, print it off and post it.

Where you can take advice

Throughout the following chapters you will see the words take advice. But where do you go? In practice there are two sources. Firstly, places where you can get basic information so you can then act on it yourself. Secondly, places where you can get individual advice on how you stand, including having someone to assist you or act on your behalf if needed.

Getting basic information

In the reference section of your main public library there will be a range of books leaflets and internet access on the law and your rights as well as detailed local information telling you where to find local advice centres, local authority departments, local councillors and MPs.

Your local authority should provide information about council services in your area, usually combined with reception points, but some may also stock a wider range as above.

Though advice centres such as Citizens Advice Bureaux are often chocablock with queues of people seeking advice, many will have a range of leaflets available on request or on display and some may have internet access facilities in their reception areas.

Many other organisations provide a range of leaflets and forms in their receptions or at special offices in your area, for example, the Inland Revenue, the Jobcentre and the Benefit Agency. Otherwise, all have addresses to which you can write to in order to order items. **The Office of Fair Trading** is worth mentioning here, particularly as they have a public consumer information line and a range of leaflets on consumer rights.

The internet is a comprehensive (and growing) source of information about complaints procedures, charters, codes of practice and the like. Often you can print off a complaints form or complain online. Also on a chosen subject you can find out your rights, entitlements and obligations. Of particular note is www.ukonline.gov.uk, the universal local and national website which has links to most statutory bodies. To find an advice service or solicitors practice near you which can advise you on the subject in hand, try the Community Legal Service website at **www.justask.org.uk**, which links to services that have been awarded the Quality Mark in recognition of their standards. Alternatively, for basic information on your rights and entitlements on many subjects, use the National Association of Citizens Advice Bureaux website at www.adviceguide.org.uk. On consumer issues see www.tradingstandards.gov.uk or www.consumer.gov.uk, and on environmental health issues try www.hse.gov.uk.

Many organisations can provide you with basic information of this kind by telephone. Special helplines are now everywhere. **The Telephone Helplines Association** may tell you where to go. For information on your rights and entitlements many Citizens Advice Bureaux provide an automated telephone message service.

There are books in abundance at booksellers or public libraries, which explain your rights in more detail. Whether your complaint is about the way you were treated in hospital or about the purchase of a faulty bicycle, you will find a publication which explains how you stand.

Getting advice and help

Some of the following organisations may give you basic information, but they also offer advice and help if needed.

Citizens Advice Bureau (CAB)

You can telephone, visit or write to any CAB in your area. Some also deal with email enquiries. They are so popular that they often have large queues in their reception areas and their telephone lines get jammed. If possible, see if you can make an appointment or get there early!

Citizens Advice Bureaux offer free information on your rights, obligations and entitlements and may also help you with your complaint by putting you in touch with people and organisations you can write to, helping you draft a letter or making a telephone call on your behalf. In addition, many bureaux offer specialist help, such as representation at appeal tribunals, which is usually to the same level as a solicitor specialising in that area.

The bureau will also suggest other organisations or services that may be able to offer you further assistance with your case. Bureaux are independent organisations and their service is confidential. The address of your nearest Citizen's Advice Bureau will be listed in the phone book or you can find out from the National Association of Citizens Advice Bureaux at **www.nacab.org.uk**.

Other advice services

There are many other advice services. Some are only available nationally, usually by phone or email, others may be found in your town or neighbourhood. Most concentrate on certain areas of advice or advocacy, for example, debt, housing, welfare rights, particular health problems, or advice to particular age groups. Some are voluntary organisations, others are provided by local authorities or commercial bodies. Some are law centres, staffed by solicitors as well as advice workers. You will need to check out whether they are appropriate to you by getting information as above, or in the case of the latter contact the **Law Centres Federation for England and Wales**, the **Scottish Association of Law Centres** or **Law Centre Northern Ireland**.

Solicitors' practices

In some areas of law there may be no difference in terms of quality whether you use a solicitor or an advice service. Use the **Community Legal Service** website at www.justask.org.uk or the other sources above to help you choose. It is particularly important to ensure that they specialise in the area of law you need. Also bear in mind that unless you are eligible for Legal Help or Publicly Funded Legal Services you will have to pay commercial rates, although many solicitors offer contingency fee schemes where most fees are paid only if you win your case.

Some solicitors do what is called 'pro bono' work – providing free advice sessions at other advice services offices. Some may see you for a quick interview at their offices for half an hour or so without charge, or for a token payment.

Other sources of legal advice

You may be entitled to free advice, usually by phone, if you have legal expenses insurance, are a member of a trade union, staff or professional association, or other bodies such as the **AA, RAC** or **the Consumers Association**.

Trading Standards

Your local authority Trading Standards Service is a useful source for information and advice on consumer rights and the legal obligations of traders. Although they cannot compel a trader to compensate you they can intervene where they suspect the trader is committing a criminal offence, and this may put the trader under pressure to settle with you. They can be located in the phone book under the name of your County Council (or Unitary Authority, or Borough in London). Also the Institute of Trading Standards has a useful website which explains the work of their members and links you to all the offices around the country at www.tradingstandards.gov.uk.

Useful addresses

Law Centres Federation
Duchess House
18-19 Warren Street
London W1T 5LR
Tel: 020 7387 8570
Fax: 020 7387 8368
Email: info@lawcentres.org.uk
Website: www.lawcentres.org.uk

Law Centre Northern Ireland
124 Donegall Street
Belfast BT1 2GY
Tel: 028 9024 4401
Fax: 028 9023 6340
Email: admin.belfast@lawcentreni.org
Website: www.lawcentreni.org

The Office of Fair Trading
Fleetbank House
2-6 Salisbury Square
London EC4 8JX
OFT enquiries line: 0845 722 4499
Other tel: 020 7211 8800
Email: enquiries@oft.gov.uk
Website: www.oft.gov.uk

Scottish Association of Law Centres
Paisley Law Centre
65 George Street
Paisley PA1 2JE
Tel: 0141 561 7266

Telephone Helplines Association
3rd/4th Floor
9 Marshalsea Road
London SE1 1EP
Tel: 0845 120 3767
Fax: 020 7089 6320
Email: info@helplines.org.uk
Website: www.helplines.org.uk

Ten tips

1. Know what you want

It helps to have thought through what you want to achieve by complaining.

You may just want to sound off, in the hope that someone will listen and another person will not be a victim of what you have just gone through. Perhaps you would like to see a complete policy change to benefit everyone. Or maybe all you want is for things to be put right and for a decent service. Is it compensation you are after, or at least a refund? Perhaps you want them to be punished, either by reprimand or disciplinary action. Maybe just an apology will suffice?

You may want several of these outcomes at once, but if you know what you are looking for you may save time barking up the wrong tree.

2. Show you know

Unless your complaint is minor it is worth knowing where you stand. You do not need to be a lawyer but it helps to show you know your basic rights and entitlements, and that you are familiar with any relevant code of practice or customer charter. Most staff do not want to be seen to be breaking their own rules unless it is to your benefit.

There is another advantage of knowing your rights, if it turns out you have none, at least you will know you only have your charm to rely on.

3. Go by the book

Follow the complaints procedures as outlined in the following chapters. Also make sure you complain to the right person. Unless your complaint is very serious, if you jump the earlier stages and complain directly to someone very high up in the organisation, your protests will probably be ignored and you may antagonise the people lower down for complaining over their heads.

4. Dig in for a long battle

Do not expect overnight results. You might be lucky and find that your complaint can be resolved quickly and easily at the first stage but if you have to take the complaint further it may take weeks, even months, before a final decision is made. Success cannot be guaranteed. You may follow all the correct procedures and still find yourself up against a brick wall. The effective complainer must be persistent and patient.

5. Prove your point

You will need to back up your complaint with relevant information such as details of the incident, identities of anyone involved if known, any reference numbers, times, dates, receipts, bills. Have any witnesses to hand in case they are needed. For some long running problems keep a journal of events. Other evidence such as photographs may well help. Also, if you are pursuing a complaint via new avenues you will need to present evidence of how your complaint has been dealt with so far, so keep a file.

6. Put it in writing

A phone call or personal visit is often the most effective way of lodging a complaint but unless that resolves the problem instantly, you should always follow this up in writing. This serves as evidence that you have complained and it might help in the event of your case going further, or to court or arbitration. Keep copies of all your letters or emails, and keep a diary of all phone conversations.

7. Control your anger

Well-directed anger can be effective, but getting involved in a slanging match will not help your case. You will make a personal enemy of the staff member, and they may not be to blame anyway. You will need to judge when to be angry. Sometimes charm works all the way but at other times people need to know you are not a soft touch. The point is to always give the impression of utter reasonableness, taking a 'you know it makes sense' line.

8. Phone a friend

Some complaints procedures can be gruelling: you may have to fill in endless forms and provide evidence, and in some cases attend a hearing or two, and perhaps be put on the spot. You should not have to go through all this alone – get help from a friend, if only as moral support or as a sounding board. Alternatively, use one of the advice services, as they may be able to act on your behalf. On occasion, you will need a solicitor.

9. Keep to time

You may lose your right to complain if you leave it too late. The best advice is to complain immediately when you realise there is a problem, but always check on any time limits because it is easy to miss them if you are waiting on something else, for example a reply to a letter. In some cases time limits can be extended, but it is best to avoid wasting time arguing for such concessions.

10. Think before saying yes

You may be made an offer, but is it really too good to refuse? Are there any hidden implications? Could you get any more by complaining further? Once you have accepted such an offer you cannot normally go back and ask for more. If you have any doubts take advice before accepting.

Take care not to jeopardise your case unwittingly by agreeing to do something, which you could later be bound by. Put in writing that you are taking a course of action (for example making a payment) 'under protest' and ' without prejudice to my legal rights.' This will safeguard you in case you decide to take legal action later.

In the next two chapters *Taking things further*, there are some general points to bear in mind, which will apply in many situations.

TAKING THINGS FURTHER
Taking legal action

If you cannot pursue your complaint any other way you may need to take legal action in court. This can be done to claim compensation or damages but also to make the person or organisation do something or stop them doing something (called getting an injunction).

Taking legal action may be costly if you use a solicitor (see *Where you can take advice*) but you may be able to do this yourself using the Small Claims Track as this is designed for people to use without solicitors. Of course, it may be pointless taking legal action for financial compensation or money owed against an individual if they have not got the means to pay you if you won.

A word about the Small Claims Track

In England and Wales, most financial claims, unless they are particularly complicated, are allocated by the County court to the Small Claims Track if the claim is for £5,000 or less. Here, the costs you have to pay the other side if you lose are limited. Before you apply you will need to send a final warning letter to the other party saying that unless your claim is settled satisfactorily within a given time, say seven days, you will take court action. See sample letter 1.

You will need to work out what the other person or organisation reasonably owes you, and get evidence together. This could include all or some of their original charges, but also any extra costs you incurred. For example getting someone else to do the work, loss of income, maybe damage to your property or injury to yourself or family. You can also include other costs such as stress, trauma or inconvenience. Take advice on quantifying this.

To apply complete a claim form (summons) available from your local County court or the **Court Service** websites. Then send, or preferably take, this to the County court, which has jurisdiction to hear the case. This will be the court in whose area the contract was agreed or the incident took place so it may or may not be your local court. The court will give the opportunity for the other party to reply to your summons. A judge will then consider the case, a hearing may be held (you could ask the judge to consider the case in your absence if you wish) and a decision will be made. Take advice.

NB In Scotland and Northern Ireland there are differences in procedures and the limit for claims is lower – take advice.

Types of legal action

Here are the types of legal action most relevant to complaining.

Breach of contract

Put simply, the law of contract says that if two people reach an agreement about something, they must honour that agreement. This is a common law which has existed for centuries but nowadays there is a lot of legislation to back it up, for example the Supply of Goods and Services Act (see *Buying goods* and B*uying services*). With many complaints there is usually a breach of contract in that the other party has not gone along with what was agreed. What was decided upon may appear in written form, but it does not have to in most cases, much is implied. Breach of contract usually applies when you buy from a private company, but is not common if you receive services from the state.

If you have already paid you can sue the trader in the County court for breach of contract, but if you have not you could refuse to pay all or part of the bill on these grounds. Usually you would be expected to give the trader reasonable warning that you intend to do this, to give them the chance to put things right. The amount you deduct should be your reasonable costs as above. The trader may try to sue you for the balance so you may have to defend your actions in court.

If you cannot avoid paying even though you know there is a problem, do say in writing that you are paying 'under protest' and ' without prejudice to my legal rights.' This will safeguard you in case you decide to take legal action later.

Negligence

You can sue for negligence whether or not you have a contract with the other party, so you can sue a government agency, an incompetent bank or a maker of dodgy meat pies. The principle is the same but take advice because claims can be complex.

Common law imposes a general obligation on all of us to take reasonable care not to injure anyone or damage his or her property. Failure to exercise this care is called negligence. It is supported by legislation such as the Consumer Protection Act 1987 where, for example, you can take action against a company selling unsafe products or services. You can take legal action for negligence if the person or organisation could have reasonably expected to foresee that their behaviour would cause you injury or loss. If someone acts on the basis that they have a particular skill, then their duty of care includes the responsibility to use that skill. So a solicitor, water company or chef could not defend a claim for negligence on the grounds that they 'did their best.'

Discrimination

In many cases your complaint may be that you have been unfairly treated. If you feel this is due to your sex, marital status, race, colour, nationality, ethnic origin or any disability or illness you may be a victim of unfair discrimination, which is illegal. You may therefore be able to take legal action by going to a tribunal (for example an Employment Tribunal) or a court. The Human Rights Act prohibits discrimination on wider grounds so if you feel unfairly treated for some other reason take advice to see if legal action could be taken.

In the case of sexual discrimination you could seek the advice and support of the **Equal Opportunities Commission (EOC)**; with disability discrimination contact the **Disability Rights Commission (DRC)** and in the case of race discrimination, the **Commission for Racial Equality (CRE)**. There may also be a local Race Equality Council in your area. The CRE will tell you, or take advice.

Human Rights Act

With many kinds of complaints you may be able to take legal action under the Human Rights Act, not only to further your complaint but in some cases to challenge some of the procedures for dealing with your complaint as well. Take advice or you could consult Liberty or one of the bodies that deal with discrimination, above. The Act stems from the European Convention on Human Rights, which sets out 16 basic human rights as Articles. Some are very relevant to complaining.

- Article 6 says you have the right to a fair and public hearing within a reasonable period of time. You might be able to cite this Article if you are denied a hearing; if there is a long delay in arranging one; if there is a question mark over its independence or if you think it was biased.

- Article 8 says you have a right to have your private and family life respected, so use this to complain about any unwanted intrusion or harassment.

- Article 10 upholds your right to freedom of expression so complain if your voice is prevented from being heard.

- Article 14 prohibits discrimination.

Judicial review

You may be able to make one more challenge in the form of a judicial review, if you have exhausted the complaints procedures and appeals to no effect and if your complaint is about any public service, including appeals tribunals. The judicial review is not a new appeal or a re-hearing of your complaint; instead what you will be doing is bringing into question the procedures that you had to go through. You can do this on a number of grounds, for example that the decision made was unreasonable, or the public body, or official, exceeded their powers, or there has been a breach of natural justice, i.e. you were denied a fair and impartial hearing.

Permission has to be made to the **High Court**. If they agree they will review the public body's decision at a hearing. Sometimes even the threat to seek a judicial review can be enough to change things. However, the judicial review is a very complicated procedure and specialist legal help will always be needed, so take advice.

Defamation

You can take legal action for defamation. This is where an organisation or individual has published or broadcast accusations about you, or stated them about you to someone else, which are untrue and you feel damage your character, reputation or credit worthiness. Libel is written and slander is spoken defamation, but libel can also be conveyed in other ways such as photographs and cartoons. There are, however, certain exceptions, which include reports of court proceedings, or debates in Parliament.

Cases can be complex to pursue, although sometimes a letter saying you have been libelled or slandered might get an immediate response (see *The media*).

TAKING THINGS FURTHER
Alternatives to legal action

Going to court is not the only way to resolve a dispute. Here are some alternatives to those mentioned in the chapters.

Mediation

Mediation is a way of dealing with disputes in which a third party, known as the mediator, helps the people involved to reach an agreement which each considers acceptable. There may be community mediation schemes in your area to help with such problems as neighbour disputes or school conflicts. Take advice or contact **Mediation UK** for details. Also, if you are in dispute with an organisation, for example a trader, you may be able to suggest that they consider trying to arrive at a mediated settlement with you. If they are agreeable you could contact one of the bodies that offer mediation (for a fee) in the commercial and business sectors such as the **Centre for Effective Dispute Resolution**, the **ADR Group**, the **Academy of Experts**, the **Chartered Institute of Arbitrators**, the **Royal Institution of Chartered Surveyors' Dispute Resolution Service**.

Using an arbitrator

You may be able to get the other party to agree to allow an independent arbitrator to adjudicate on the case. Many organisations belong to arbitration schemes, indeed building them into their customer charters or codes of practice. Professional and trade associations also use them. Take advice, or contact the **Department for Constitutional Affairs**.

Each party will probably have to pay a smallish registration fee, and usually the loser has to reimburse the winner. The loser will not have to pay any other costs except those incurred in collecting the evidence, which you get back from the other party if you lose The arbitrator (arbiter in Scotland) receives all the evidence, considers the facts impartially, and, taking the law into account, decides who is in the right and what form any compensation could take.

The decision is legally binding on you and the other party. If the other party ignores the decision you can go to court. Take advice. If you disagree with the decision you cannot then take legal action to try to get a different decision. To find out more, or to see if the organisation you are complaining about belongs to a scheme consult the Chartered Institute of Arbitrators.

Use your elected representatives

If your complaint is a major one, and particularly if it concerns a general principle or government policy that affects other people, you could raise the matter with either your **MP, Member of the Scottish Parliament** or the **Welsh Assembly**. Take advice to find out where the local MP can be contacted (many have surgeries where you can call for help). Otherwise write to him or her at the House of Commons, the Scottish Parliament or Assembly for Wales. At a local level, your ward councillors may help you push your complaint if it is within their sphere of influence.

Taking group action

If you know of other people with similar complaints or if your complaint raises an issue of general public concern, you could consider forming a group to campaign for changes – perhaps to improve road safety in your area or possibly to protest about a proposed airport expansion. Setting up a group and helping to organise its activities does, of course, require a great deal of effort, planning and time but it may lead to success where all else has failed.

Existing campaign groups

There may already be a campaign group prepared to lend you support by providing technical expertise or guidance on how to make the best of your case. If your complaint concerns something they feel strongly about, say environmental pollution caused by a local company, such a group may even be prepared to take the case over, representing you and any other people affected. Take advice.

Using the media

If you take group action this is bound to be of interest to the local press, TV, or radio and possibly to the national media as well. The media are also interested in individual complaints if they are unusual or interesting enough, particularly when they illustrate problems that may affect many people. Whether it is a case of

bureaucracy gone mad, a health or a safety hazard, airing your complaint publicly may embarrass the government, company or individual into doing something about it, especially if public opinion is on your side. For local coverage, telephone or write to a reporter on your local newspaper, radio or TV station. For national coverage, write to the editor of a newspaper or the producer of a television or radio consumer programme.

Useful addresses

The Academy of Experts
3 Gray's Inn Square
London WC1R 5AH
Tel: 020 7430 0333
Fax: 020 7430 0666
Email: admin@academy-experts.org
Website: www.academy-experts.org

ADR Group
Grove House, Grove Road
Redland
Bristol BS6 6UN
Tel: 0117 946 7180

Family helpline: 0800 970 6969
Fax: 0117 946 7181
Email: info@adrgroup.co.uk
Website: www.adrgroup.co.uk

Centre for Effective Dispute Resolution (CEDR)

Exchange Tower
1 Harbour Exchange Square
London E14 9GB
Tel: 020 7536 6000
Fax: 020 7536 6001
Email: info@cedr.co.uk
Website: www.cedr.co.uk

Chartered Institute of Arbitrators

International Arbitration Centre
12 Bloomsbury Square
London WC1A 2LP
Tel: 020 7421 7444
Fax: 020 7404 4023
Email: info@arbitrators.org
Website: www.arbitrators.org

City Disputes Panel

International Dispute Resolution Centre
8 Breams Buildings, Chancery Lane
London EC4A 1HP
Tel: 020 7440 7373
Fax: 020 7440 7374
Email: info@citydisputespanel.org
Website: www.disputespanel.com

Commission for Racial Equality

St Dunstan's House
201-211 Borough High Street
London SE1 1GZ
Tel: 020 7939 0000
Fax: 020 7939 0001
Email: info@cre.gov.uk
Website: www.cre.gov.uk

Court Service

England and Wales
Southside, 105 Victoria Street
London SW1E 6QT
Tel: 020 7210 2266
Email: cust.ser.cs@gtnet.gov.uk
Website: www.courtservice.gov.uk

Northern Ireland
Bedford House, Bedford Street
Belfast BT2 7DS
Tel: 028 9032 8594
Fax: 028 9023 6361
E-mail: informationcentre@courtsni.gov.uk
Website: www.courtsni.gov.uk

Scotland
Hayweight House, 23 Lauriston Street
Edinburgh EH3 9DQ
Tel: 0131 229 9200
Fax: 0131 221 6890
Email: enquiries@scotcourts.gov.uk
Website: www.scotcourts.gov.uk

Department for Constitutional Affairs
Selborne House
54-60 Victoria Street
London SW1E 6QW
Tel: 020 7210 8500
Email: general.queries@lcd.gsi.gov.uk
Website: www.lcd.gov.uk

Disability Rights Commission
Freepost MID02164
Stratford upon Avon CV37 9BR
Helpline: 0845 7622 633
Fax: 0845 7778 878
Text: 0845 7622 644
Email: ddahelp@stra.sitel.co.uk
Website: www.drc-gb.org/drc

Equal Opportunities Commission

England
Arndale House, Arndale Centre
Manchester M4 3EQ
Tel: 0845 601 5901
Fax: 0161 838 1733
Email: info@eoc.org.uk
Website: www.eoc.org.uk

Equality Commission for Northern Ireland
Equality House
7-9 Shaftesbury Square
Belfast BT2 7DP
Tel: 028 9050 0600
Fax: 028 9024 8687
Textphone: 028 9050 0589
Email: information@equalityni.org
Website: www.equalityni.org

Scotland
St. Stephen's House
279 Bath Street
Glasgow G2 4JL
Tel: 0845 601 5901
Fax: 0141 248 5834
Email: scotland@eoc.org.uk
Website: www.eoc.org.uk

Wales
Windsor House, Windsor Lane
Cardiff CF10 3GE
Tel: 029 2034 3552
Fax: 029 2064 1079
Email: wales@eoc.org.uk
Website: www.eoc.org.uk

House of Commons
London SW1A 0AA
Tel: 020 7219 3000
Website: www.parliament.uk

Liberty
21 Tabard Street
London SE1 4LA
Tel: 020 7403 3888
Fax: 020 7407 5354
Email: info@liberty-human-rights.org.uk
Website: www.liberty-human-rights.org.uk

London Court of International Arbitration (LCIA)
The International Dispute Resolution Centre
8 Breams Buildings, Chancery Lane
London EC4A 1HP
Tel: 020 7405 8008
Fax: 020 7405 8009
Email: lcia@lcia-arbitration.com
Website: www.lcia-arbitration.com

Mediation UK
Alexander House
Telephone Avenue
Bristol BS1 4BS
Tel: 0117 904 6661
Fax: 0117 904 3331
Email: enquiry@mediationuk.org.uk
Website: www.mediationuk.org.uk

The National Assembly for Wales
Cardiff Bay
Cardiff CF99 1NA
Tel: 029 20 825111
Website: www.wales.gov.uk

National Association of Citizens Advice Bureaux (NACAB)
Myddelton House
115-123 Pentonville Road
London N1 9LZ
Tel: 020 7833 2181
Fax: 020 7833 4371
Website: www.nacab.org.uk

Northern Ireland Assembly
Parliament Buildings
Stormont
Belfast BT4 3XX
Tel: 028 9052 1333
Fax: 028 9052 1961
Email: info.office@niassembly.gov.uk
Website: www.niassembly.gov.uk

The Royal Institution of Chartered Surveyors' Dispute Resolution Service
Surveyor Court
Westwood Way
Coventry CV4 8JE
Tel: 0870 333 1600
Email: contactrics@rics.org.uk
Website: www.rics.org

The Scottish Parliament
Edinburgh EH99 1SP
Tel: 0131 348 5000
Website: www.scottishparliament.uk

Sample letter 1: Letter before action

1, Any Street
Anytown
Anyshire
AN1 2YZ

25th June, 2003

Dear Sirs

Re: *Reference Number: 2156 – Holiday*

Further to our telephone conversations and my letter of *17th June* to which you failed to reply, I am still dissatisfied with your response.

In view of this, I am writing to let you know that unless I receive satisfactory proposals for settlement of my claim within the next seven days from the date of this letter, I will issue a claim against you in the County court without further notice.

Yours faithfully,

David Chambers

David Chambers

Part 2

Specific problems

Accountants

First ask for an explanation from the accountant; see if they can put things right. If this fails, write to the senior partner. If you have suffered a loss due to the accountant's negligence or breach of contract, take legal action. If sample letter 2 does not work, see *Taking things further* (also see *Buying services* as the principles are the same).

If this does not resolve things check whether the accountant belongs to a professional body. All chartered accountants are members of the Institute of Chartered Accountants in England and Wales (or its counterpart the Institute of Chartered Accountants in Scotland). The Institute will investigate claims that a member has been incompetent or inefficient, as well as complaints alleging professional misconduct. If your complaint is upheld the accountant may be reprimanded or even expelled.

Other accountants may be members of the **Association of Chartered Certified Accountants**, the **Chartered Institute of Management Accountants**, the **Chartered Institute of Public Finance and Accountancy** and, for bookkeepers, the **Institute of Chartered Secretaries and Administrators**. All of these bodies will investigate and may take disciplinary action against the accountant if your complaint is upheld.

If you have suffered a loss at the hands of an accountant you will have to take legal action for damages. Take advice.

Useful addresses

The Association of Chartered Certified Accountants
64 Finnieston Square
Glasgow G3 8DT
Tel: 0141 582 2000
Fax: 0141 582 2222
Email: info@accaglobal.com
Website: www.acca.org.uk

The Chartered Institute of Management Accountants
26 Chapter Street
London SW1P 4NP

Tel: 020 7663 5441
Fax: 020 7663 5442
Website: www.cimaglobal.com

The Chartered Institute of Public Finance and Accountancy
3 Robert Street
London WC2N 6RL
Tel: 020 7543 5600
Fax: 020 7543 5700
Website: www.cipfa.org.uk

The Institute of Chartered Accountants in England and Wales
Chartered Accountants' Hall
PO Box 433
London EC2P 2BJ
Tel: 020 7920 8100
Fax: 020 7920 0547
Website: www.icaew.co.uk

The Institute of Chartered Accountants of Scotland
CA House
21 Haymarket Yards
Edinburgh EH12 5BH
Tel: 0131 347 0100
Fax: 0131 347 0105
Email: enquiries@icas.org.uk
Website: www.icas.org.uk

The Institute of Chartered Secretaries and Administrators
16 Park Crescent
London W1B 1AH
Email: info@icsa.co.uk
Website: www.icsa.org.uk

Sample letter 2: Complaint to an accountant

1, Any Street
Anytown
Anyshire
AN1 2YZ

25th June, 2003

Accountant

Dear Mr *Thomas,*

I am writing to express my dissatisfaction with your service.

Together we reviewed my files on *17th April, 2003* and I explained to you my financial situation. It is evident from the accounts you prepared that you failed to follow the requirements I described and neglected to give me adequate advice.

The Supply of Goods and Services Act 1982 requires you to conduct your services as an accountant with reasonable skill and care. Your failure to do so has resulted in you breaching our contract and I have suffered a loss in the amount of £300.

I demand your cheque for the reasonable sum of £300 and anticipate recovery of the same by *7th July.*

I remind you that according to the above referenced Act, you may not ignore this complaint but are required by law to deal with it. If you fail to abide by your legal obligations, I am prepared to refer this matter to the Institute of Chartered Accountants.

Yours sincerely,

David Chambers

David Chambers

Advertising

If you find an advertisement offensive, perhaps for example you found it sexist or racist, or presented certain other people unfairly, you may need to enlist the aid of bodies that tackle discrimination. See *Taking things further*. There are various bodies you can complain to depending on where the advertisement appeared, but also you may be able to take legal action.

If you were mislead by an advertisement into buying goods or services you have legal grounds for complaint because what is sold by a trader or private individual must be 'as described' under the Sale of Goods Act 1979 (as amended). See *Buying goods*, *Shopping from home* and *Buying services*. You may be able to take legal action, but not if the trader warned you the advertisement was wrong before you purchased.

Advertising in the non-broadcast media

Complain to the **Advertising Standards Authority (ASA)** about advertisements in magazines, newspapers and posters, cinema advertisements, advertisements on computer games, videos and non-broadcast electronic media (such as the internet). They enforce the British Codes of Advertising and Sales Promotion. If they decide the Codes have been broken they have a number of sanctions but they cannot order any compensation to be paid or start any legal proceedings. You can, if you wish, complain on a special form you can print off from their website.

The broadcast media

If your complaint relates to a broadcast advertisement you can write to the **Radio Authority** if it appeared on any radio station or the **Independent Television Commission** for advertisements on television including cable or satellite channels (see sample letter 3). At the same time, and depending on the nature of the complaint, you can write to the **Broadcasting Standards Commission** (see *The media*).

Other courses of action

Your local **Trading Standards Office** may prosecute traders who give false or misleading information about a product, also any trader who masquerades as a private individual to try to get round the law. Advertisements in catalogues are also covered by the **Mail Order Traders Association** code of practice and telephone advertising is monitored by the **Independent Committee for the Supervision of Standards of Telephone Information Services (ICSTIS)** so you can complain to these bodies. Also you may want to restrict your unsolicited advertising by phone, fax, email or post (see *Shopping from home*).

If your complaint is about an advertisement that comes from another European country contact the appropriate body in the UK as above. The complaint will be passed on to the member of the **European Advertising Standards Alliance (EASA)**, which covers the country in question.

Useful addresses

Advertising Standards Authority (ASA)
2 Torrington Place
London WC1E 7HW
Tel: 020 7580 5555
Fax: 020 7631 3051
Email: inquiries@asa.org.uk
Website: www.asa.org.uk

Broadcasting Standards Commission (BSC)
7 The Sanctuary
London SW1P 3JS
Tel: 020 7808 1000
Fax: 020 7233 0397
Email: bsc@bsc.org.uk
Website: www.bsc.org.uk

European Advertising Standards Alliance (EASA)
Website: www.easa-alliance.org

Independent Committee for the Supervision of Standards of Telephone Information Services (ICSTIS)
4th Floor, Clove Building
4 Maguire Street
London SE1 2NQ

Tel: 020 7940 7474
Fax: 020 7940 7456
Email: secretariat@icstis.org.uk
Website: www.icstis.org.uk

Independent Television Commission (ITC)

33 Foley Street
London W1W 7TL
Tel: 0845 601 3608
Textphone: 020 7306 7753
Website:www.itc.org.uk

Mail Order Traders Association (MOTA)

Drury House
19 Water Street
Liverpool L2 0RP
Tel: 0151 227 9456
Fax: 0151 227 9678
Website: www.adassoc.org.uk

Radio Authority

Holbrook House
14 Great Queen Street
Holborn
London WC2B 5DG
Tel: 020 7430 2724
Fax: 020 7405 7062
Email: prog&ad@radioauthority.org.uk
Website: www.radioauthority.org.uk

Sample letter 3: Complaint to the Independent Television Commission about an advertisement on television

1, Any Street
Anytown
Anyshire
AN1 2YZ

25th June, 2003

Independent Television Commission
33 Foley Street
London W1W 7TL

Dear Sirs,

Re: 'Beer' Advertisement

I am writing to the ITC to complain about the above advertisement. I have taken the matter up with *Channel 6* and the programme *Sitcom*, but to date I have not received a satisfactory response/no response at all.

I would greatly appreciate it if you would use your regulatory powers to investigate my complaint because I feel there has been a breach of the ITC Advertising Code. I enclose my correspondence, together with the reply I have received (*if there has been a reply!*),for your information.

I saw the advertisement on 12th June at 8:30pm and the product being advertised was 'Beer.'

I am unhappy about the advertisement because *I consider it offensive in that it was far too explicit for that time of night. I believe that the ITC Code states that no such material should be shown before the 9pm watershed.*

I hope that once you have investigated this matter you will consider it fitting to take action against the company concerned. Please may I be kept informed of the progress of this complaint.

Yours faithfully,

David Chambers

David Chambers
Enc.

Advice services

There are many advice services. Most are voluntary organisations (e.g. **Citizens Advice Bureaux**, Law Centres), some are Local Authority services, some are commercial and some are adjuncts of larger statutory bodies such as health authorities and government departments. Voluntary as well as paid staff often staff the voluntary organisations, but this should make no difference if you need to complain. Some of the staff are, in fact, professionals such as solicitors, barristers or accountants.

If your complaint is about such issues as poor service, inappropriate behaviour by staff, inaccurate or insufficient advice or representation, put your complaint in writing to the most senior manager in the organisation, but it would be best if you first established the complaints procedure (see sample letter 4).

Most advice services have one – indeed it is obligatory for those that have the Community Legal Service Quality Mark. This will be indicated at the offices, on their headed notepaper, and on the **Community Legal Service** website. Citizens Advice Bureaux are also monitored by the National Association of Citizens Advice Bureau (NACAB). Copies of their complaints procedure and form for making a complaint can be obtained from any Bureau or from NACAB. Many other advice services are members of the Federation of Information and Advice Centres (FIAC) so it may be worth bringing a complaint to their attention.

If the advice service has been awarded a Quality Mark for its services you could also complain to the awarding body, the **Legal Services Commission**, once you have exhausted the above procedures (see *Solicitors' practices*). If the advice service is part of a Local Authority see *Local authorities*, if it is a commercial service see *Buying services*, if the service is part of a government department see *Taking things further*. None of these procedures are likely to get you financial redress. Most likely, the outcome could be an apology, an assurance that the incident(s) will not be repeated, an explanation or maybe an opportunity to have further advice.

If you can establish that the person who advised you was a solicitor, barrister or accountant, see *Solicitors' practices*, *Barristers* or *Accountants*. For other professions take advice because most professional bodies have a means of dealing with complaints about members.

Claiming damages

If advice given was negligent (for example inaccurate, unclear, misleading or insufficient) and you suffered a loss as a result, you may be able to take legal action for damages – take advice.

Useful addresses

Community Legal Service
Website: www.justask.org.uk

Federation of Information and Advice Centres (FIAC)
12th Floor
New London Bridge House
25 London Bridge Street
London SE1 9ST
Tel: 020 7407 4070
Fax: 020 7407 4071
Email: general@adviceuk.org.uk
Website: www.fiac.org.uk

National Association of Citizens Advice Bureaux (NACAB)
Myddelton House
115-123 Pentonville Road
London N1 9LZ
Tel: 020 7833 2181
Fax: 020 7833 4371
Website: www.nacab.org.uk

Sample letter 4: Complaint about advice service

1, Any Street
Anytown
Anyshire
AN1 2YZ

25th June, 2003

Manager
Advice Service

Dear Sir/Madam,

Re: *Visit on 2nd June, 2003 – Adviser Mrs Evans*

I am writing to make a formal complaint about two aspects of the service that I received from your advice service on the above date.

Firstly, I had to wait more than an hour to be seen by an adviser, who then informed me that I could have made an appointment, if I had wished, to avoid waiting now. Why wasn't this option suggested to me when I arrived at your offices rather than after I had queued for that length of time? I feel I have completely wasted time waiting, causing me inconvenience, when I could easily have avoided this by making an appointment.

Secondly, and more importantly, I have to complain that I was given inadequate advice when I did see the adviser. She advised me on my rights in respect of my recent dismissal from my job, but she neglected to tell me that if I wished to complain to an Employment Tribunal I must do so within three calendar months of my losing the job. I did not realise this omission until last week, by which time it was too late for me to take action.

Through your negligence I have lost my day in court, in addition to the compensation I would have been awarded had I won my case.

In the light of this I look forward to receiving your offer of compensation, failing which I will issue a summons against your organisation in the County court. With regard to the other matter of complaint, I look forward to a full explanation.

Yours faithfully,

David Chambers

David Chambers

Airlines and airports

For airlines, before complaining have a look at the airlines customer charter (most will have one). This will set their standards and complaints procedures. You could write to their head office, though if it is abroad you may be able to address your concern to their UK branch. If you are at the airport you could lodge your complaint with the airlines duty officer – there should be one available round the clock. See also *Holidays*.

The next step is to write to the **Air Transport Users Council**. They will investigate your case and try to conciliate.

- Under international law you can receive compensation when your fight is delayed if the airline could reasonably have avoided the delay. As ever some companies will have more generous arrangements than others when things go wrong. The customer charter will advise (see sample letter 5). Most airlines will pay for hotel charges and meals if necessary. If you feel you receive more compensation than you are offered you may have to consider legal action. Take advice.

- If you are turned away because your flight is overbooked, you can claim compensation if, for example you have to stay overnight in a hotel. Most airlines have compensation schemes for this. Indeed all flights from European Union airports and those in Austria, Finland, Iceland, Norway and Sweden have booking compensation rules whereby they will pay you compensation if they fail to get you to your destination within four hours (overseas flights) or two hours (domestic flights) of your original arrival time.

- Under the terms of the Warsaw Convention, you can claim compensation for lost or damaged luggage, unless the airline can show they took all reasonable precautions. If your luggage is delayed by the airline on your outward flight you can claim to cover the cost of replacement items such as toiletries and nightclothes. If your luggage is damaged you must complain within seven days of collecting the items. See sample letter 6.

Other airport services

Ask to speak to the manager of the relevant department. If your complaint concerns a **British Airports Authority (BAA)** airport (Heathrow, Gatwick, Stansted, Glasgow, Prestwick, Aberdeen and Edinburgh) you can speak to BAA staff at the information desk in the arrival area or fill in one of their special 'comment cards.' You can also write to the Public Relations Officer at the airport. If you still get no satisfaction write to the General Manager of the airport and then to the secretary of the Airport Consultative Committee. Of course many facilities at an airport may only be renting space (e.g. restaurants, shops) so see *Buying goods* and *Buying services.*

Aircraft noise

If your complaint is about noise made by civil or military aircraft see *The neighbourhood and the environment.*

Useful addresses

Air Transport Users Council
CAA House
45-59 Kingsway
London WC2B 6TE
Tel: 020 7240 6061
Fax: 020 7240 7071
Website: www.auc.org.uk

British Airports Authority
Head Office
Gatwick Airport
Gatwick
West Sussex RH6 0NP
Tel: 0870 000 2468
Website: www.baa.co.uk

Sample letter 5: Complaint to an airline about a flight delay

1, Any Street
Anytown
Anyshire
AN1 2YZ

25th June, 2003

Airline

Dear Sirs,

Re: Flight No. *BS214* to *Frankfurt* on *12th May, 2003*

I am writing to complain about the above flight, in that it was scheduled to depart at *10:15am* but did not actually leave until *six* hours later at *4:15pm*. This meant that instead of arriving at my destination at *1:15pm* (local time) I did not arrive until *7:15pm*. This caused me considerable inconvenience and although I complained to your staff at the airport at the time all I received was an apology and a voucher for coffee and sandwiches.

I have since found out that *refuelling* caused the delay. In my view your company could reasonably have avoided this problem. It was a term of the contract between your company and myself that you get me to my destination within a reasonable time of the scheduled arrival time. By not doing so, you are quite clearly in breach of contract.

Moreover, I understand that under international law I am entitled to compensation. Indeed your company's customer charter states that in these circumstances I should receive £10 *for every hour I was delayed, totalling £60.*

I await a reasonable offer of compensation within the next 14 days. Should this not occur, I will consequently take legal action.

Yours faithfully,

David Chambers

David Chambers

Sample letter 6: Requesting compensation for lost luggage

1, Any Street
Anytown
Anyshire
AN1 2YZ

25th June, 2003

Airline

Dear Sirs,

Re: Flight No. *VW 324*

I took the above flight on *22nd June, 2003.* I notified your staff of the loss of my luggage after I arrived at *Amsterdam* airport and filled out and submitted a report as requested. It has now been *three* days since then and I have still not received any response from you.

Under the terms of the Warsaw Convention I am legally entitled to compensation for the loss of my luggage. This is calculated on the current rate of £15 per kilogram of luggage, as laid down in the terms of the Convention.

I look forward to hearing from you shortly with any news on my luggage or your offer of compensation.

Yours faithfully,

David Chambers

David Chambers

Banking services

This chapter covers the services provided by banks and building societies (see also *Credit*, and *Investments and financial advice*). The Banking Code, a voluntary code of practice, which sets out the standards to be observed in providing personal banking services, regulates their activities. If you have a complaint it may be worth seeing if the Code has been breached, if so you could make reference to this in your letter.

If a local branch administers your account you could visit them and try to resolve things informally, otherwise contact the relevant department. If this fails you will need to follow the complaints procedure – details will be given to you on request (you may have been given them also when you opened the account). Usually if a branch administers your account your starting point will be to write to the branch manager enclosing any evidence such as cheque stubs and statements. For internet and telephone access accounts you will need to find out whom to contact.

If you exhaust the internal complaints system and get no joy you will need a letter confirming this from the bank or building society – called a 'deadlock letter.' Once you have this you may be able to complain either to the **Banking Ombudsman Scheme** or the **Building Society Ombudsman Scheme**. You can do this if your bank or building society is a member of the scheme, and your complaint is about unsatisfactory service rather than policy matters such as interest rates, or decisions about whether to grant you an overdraft or loan. See sample letter 7.

At first they will attempt to resolve the complaint internally, but if this fails adjudication will be made. You will be asked to comment on this, as will the bank or building society. If you do not accept the adjudication your comments will be considered and the Ombudsman will make a final decision. They can award as much as £100,000 in compensation. Though the bank or building society will be bound by the decision, you do not have to accept it.

If your bank or building society has caused you to suffer a financial loss you may be able to take legal action for breach of contract or negligence. It may also be possible to sue for defamation if your cheque was wrongly bounced. However, you will not be able to take legal action if you accepted the Ombudsman's final decision.

As well as or instead of the Ombudsman schemes, if the bank is a member you could take your complaint to arbitration by the **Finance and Leasing Associates Conciliation and Arbitration Scheme**, or the **Consumer Credit Trade Association Arbitration Scheme** (see *Credit*).

- If you feel you have been **overcharged**, first check the bank's charging policy, which should form part of your contract for their services. You have grounds for complaint if the policy is not being applied or if you have not been given sufficient explanation or notice (usually 14 days). See sample letter 8. You must have advanced details of any cash machine charges and you should not be double charged.

- In respect of **cash machines**, you may wish to complain immediately, firstly if you did not receive the cash you asked for yet it was debited from your account, secondly if the same withdrawal may have been debited twice, or thirdly if money may have been withdrawn without your knowledge. Your case will be helped if you provide supporting evidence such as witness statements, receipts, and (in the case of phantom withdrawals) evidence that you were elsewhere. See sample letter 9.

- If you suspect fraud you will need to report this to the issuing bank or building society immediately, as well as the police, then usually your liability will be limited to a maximum of £50.

- If the interest rates on your investments are varied without sufficient notice you should not have to pay a penalty if you wish to close the account (so say the Office of Fair Trading guidelines).

- If you stop a cheque (take advice on when you can do this) and the bank still goes on and pays it out, complain – the bank must reimburse you.

- If you are victim of a bounced cheque and you have not got the address of the account holder ask their bank to forward your demands for payment!

- With direct debit, if the wrong amount is taken out of your account, or at the wrong time, your bank or building society must make an immediate refund to you if you complain. This is the Direct Debit Guarantee. If you cannot resolve things through complaining contact **Bankers Automated Clearing System Ltd** for further advice. If a payment is not paid into your account on time, for example your salary, the bank or building society must refund any charges and other expenses you incur if they were to blame.

- Complain if your bank divulges your confidential details as this breaches the Banking Code, except in certain limited circumstances (for example court proceedings).

- If your cheque book is stolen and the thief goes on a spending spree with the funds, the bank must refund your account as soon as you report the theft under the Cheques Act 1992, even if the signature is a perfect imitation of yours. Complain if they refuse to do so.

Useful addresses

Bankers Automated Clearing System Ltd.
3 de Haviland Road
Edgware
Middlesex HA8 5QA
Tel: 0870 010 0698

Consumer Credit Association

Suite 8, The Wool Exchange
10 Hustlergate
Bradford BD1 1RE
Tel: 01274 390 380
Fax: 01274 729 002
Email: info@ccta.co.uk

Finance & Leasing Association

2nd Floor, Imperial House
15-19 Kingsway
London WC2B 6UN
Tel: 020 7836 6511
Fax: 020 7420 9600
Email: info@fla.org.uk

The Office of the Banking Ombudsman

South Quay Plaza
183 Marsh Wall
London E14 9SR
Tel: 020 7964 1000
Helpline: 0845 080 1800
Fax: 020 7964 1001
Email: complaint.info@financial-ombudsman.org.uk
Website: www.obo.org.uk

The Office of the Building Society Ombudsman

South Quay Plaza
183 Marsh Wall
London E14 9SR
Tel: 020 7931 0044
Fax: 020 7931 8485
Email: bldgsocombudsman@easynet.co.uk

Sample letter 7: Requesting Ombudsman to investigate

1, Any Street
Anytown
Anyshire
AN1 2YZ

25th June, 2003

The Office of the Banking Ombudsman
South Quay Plaza
183 Marsh Wall
London, E14 9SR

Dear Sirs,

Re: Bank of London, Holborn Branch, Account Number 8787

I am writing to ask you to investigate and take action in respect of my complaint against the above bank.

Enclosed please find all the relevant documentation regarding my ongoing and to date unresolved dispute with them.

In summary, my complaint is that they honoured a forged cheque for the amount of £250 but they do not accept that the cheque was a forgery.

I have pursued my claim as far as the company's headquarters without satisfaction, and I enclose evidence of this in the form of a deadlock letter from the bank.

I look forward to your reply and wish to be kept informed of the progress of my case.

Yours faithfully,

David Chambers

David Chambers

Enc.

Sample letter 8: Disputing banking charges

1, Any Street
Anytown
Anyshire
AN1 2YZ

25th June, 2003

Bank/Building Society

Dear Sirs,

Re: Account Number *054454354*

I am writing to you in reference to the above-mentioned account number. Your statement number *54354*, dated *12th June, 2003* shows you have incorrectly charged a fee in the amount of £50 for a dishonoured cheque.

I have been a customer of your bank for *15* years. A study of your records will show that I did not write the dishonoured cheque as you claim.

Additionally, you have failed to follow the recommendations of the Banking Code of Practice, which clearly mandates you provide a minimum 14 days' notice prior to any charges being deducted from a customer's account. I have not received such a notice.

Enclosed please find a copy of your statement. Please credit my account in the amount of £50 plus the loss of any interest that would have been due me.

Yours faithfully,

David Chambers

David Chambers

Sample letter 9: Complaint to Head Office about phantom withdrawal from cash machine

1, Any Street
Anytown
Anyshire
AN1 2YZ

25th June, 2003

Bank/Building Society Head Office

Dear Sirs,

Re: Account Number *054454354*

This letter is in regards to an unauthorised cashpoint withdrawal to my account of the amount of £50 on *17th June, 2003.* Please refer to the enclosed correspondence with your branch.

I was *on holiday in France* at the time of the supposed transaction, and I can provide names of witnesses if required. Since I have not written down my PIN number nor told it to anyone, I have no reason to believe that it has fallen into the wrong hands. Therefore I am sure that this is a case of a computer malfunction or procedural defect.

Please send me notice of your resolution of this matter within 14 days.

Yours faithfully,

David Chambers

David Chambers

Enc.

Barristers

You would have instructed a barrister via a solicitor, or in some cases via an advice service, so if you are dissatisfied with their service you first of all need to establish whether the fault is the barrister's or that of the solicitor or advice service which instructed them. (For example, maybe all the relevant information was not passed on correctly). See *Solicitors' practices* and *Advice services*. The next step, if you think the barrister is to blame, is to get the views of the solicitor or advice service.

Claiming damages

Did the barrister fail in his/her duty to show reasonable care and skill in doing work for you? Did you suffer loss as a result? If the answers to these two questions are yes then you may be able to take legal action for damages – take advice.

Professional misconduct

If your complaint is about professional misconduct, such as inappropriate behaviour, failing to properly master a brief, unreasonable delay or pulling out of a court hearing at short notice, then your complaint should be directed to the **General Council of the Bar** (use sample letter 10 or they can supply a complaints form). A breach of any of the rules of professional conduct can lead to disciplinary action against the barrister.

Still dissatisfied?

If you are not satisfied with the way in which your complaint has been dealt with you can go to the **Legal Services Ombudsman** – see *Solicitors' practices*.

Useful addresses

General Council of the Bar – Complaints Department
3rd Floor, Northumberland House
303-306 High Holborn
London WC1V 7JZ
Tel: 020 7440 4000
Website: www.barcouncil.org.uk

Sample letter 10: General complaint to Bar Council

1, Any Street
Anytown
Anyshire
AN1 2

25th June, 2003

General Council of the Bar
Complaints Department
Northumberland House
303-306 High Holborn
London WC1V 7JZ

Dear Sirs,

Re: *Mr Wood, Palace Chambers, Lincoln*

Please regard this letter as a formal letter of complaint about the above barrister. He was representing me in respect of legal action I am taking against my local hospital for medical negligence. My complaint is that *Mr Wood* not only arrived 45 minutes late on the day of my court hearing but it was also quite clear to me that he had failed to master his brief. He seemed to be in a tearing hurry and left me with the overwhelming impression that he could not be bothered with my case. My solicitor was clearly embarrassed and it was she who suggested I complain to you.

Fortunately I have not suffered a loss; otherwise I would have been requesting a large amount of compensation. However, this was only due to my solicitor's presence of mind in pressing the barrister to get the court to agree to an adjournment.

I seek from you an apology and a full explanation, and an assurance that this barrister be reprimanded for his unprofessional conduct.

I look forward to being advised on the progress of your investigation. My solicitor, who is *Miss Clifford* of *Clifford Solicitors, High Street, Lincoln* would be pleased to provide evidence. Please advise if you require further information.

Yours faithfully,

David Chambers

Buses and coaches

You will need to phone or, preferably, write to the operator, giving the route number, the destination of the bus and the time and date of the incident (see sample letter 11). See also *Holidays*. The operators name and address should appear in or on the vehicle itself, otherwise this should be available from the bus station or the local authority (some run bus information centres with local operators). Find out if the operator has a Passenger Charter or a Code of Practice as it may be worth referring to it in your complaint, saying it has been breached in some way. In London, London Transport Buses will advise you who the operator is, or whether it was one of their own services. If it is London Transport you should first write to the General Manager of the district where the complaint arose (see the phone book).

For buses outside of London your next stop is to write to the **Bus Appeals Body (BAB)**. Say why you think the operator has not dealt with your query properly. The BAB will try to reach an amicable settlement. Failing this if they agree with your complaint they will make recommendations to the operator, and if these are ignored they will inform the Traffic Commissioner. In London you can complain to **Transport for London – Buses** as they have wider responsibility than their own services. If you are still dissatisfied write to the **London Transport Users Committee (LTUC)**. They may try to mediate or act on your behalf and they can recommend the operator to take action, but not compel them.

Before proceeding further, check with the local authority whether the bus service is subsidised. If it is you can complain to them (see *Local authorities*) or the **Passenger Transport Executive** (if the service is in Greater Manchester, Merseyside, Tyne and Wear, West Midlands, West Yorkshire, South Yorkshire or Strathclyde). These authorities may threaten to withdraw the subsidy if they get enough complaints.

If this did not resolve the matter or if the service is not subsidised, complain to the **Traffic Commissioner** for your area. If they agree with your complaint they can sanction the operator.

- Only London Transport Buses can levy penalty fares. You can appeal to **Transport for London Customer Services Department** within 21 days. If you lose the appeal and still refuse to pay London Transport will have to sue you in the County court so you could consider disputing the fare at the court hearing.

- If you have a general complaint, for example about inadequate service or no service at all, use the above procedures. Letters to the press may influence the operator and may encourage others to complain as well. Operators may feel it is not commercially viable to run a service but some lobbying may persuade them to run a trial service. You could also lobby the local authority or **Passenger Transport Executive** for the route to be subsidised; evidence of need would have to be gathered. There may be a bus users' group in your area, which is already campaigning to improve services, or you could help set one up. **London Transport Users Committee, Transport 2000** or the **National Federation of Bus Users** will advise.

- Disability access concerns should be taken up as above. Your local authority or a local disabled peoples' group may support you. Under the Disability Discrimination Act buses brought into service after 31 December 2000 are supposed to be accessible but this is not necessarily the case for wheelchair users! In London contact **Transport for London Access & Mobility**.

Useful addresses

Bus Appeals Body (BAB)
PO Box 320
Portsmouth PO5 3SD
Tel: 023 9281 4493
Fax: 023 9286 3080
Email: enquiries@nfbu.org
Website: www.nfbu.org

London Transport Users Committee (LTUC)
6 Middle Street
London EC1A 7JA
Tel: 020 7505 9000
Fax: 020 7505 9003
Email: enquiries@ltuc.org.uk
Website: www.ltuc.org.uk

National Federation of Bus Users
PO Box 320
Portsmouth PO5 3SD
Tel: 023 9281 4493
Fax: 023 9286 3080
Email: enquiries@nfbu.org
Website: www.nfbu.org

Passenger Transport Executives

Greater Manchester PTE
9 Portland Street
Piccadilly Gardens
Manchester M60 1HX
Tel: 0161 242 6000
Email: publicity@gmpte.gov.uk
Website: www.gmpte.gov.uk

Merseyside PTE (Merseytravel)
24 Hatton Garden
Liverpool L3 2AN
Tel: 0151 227 5181

Fax: 0151 236 2457
Website: www.merseytravel.gov.uk

South Yorkshire PTE
P.O.Box 801
Sheffield S2 5YT
Tel: 0114 221 1333
Email: comments@sypte.co.uk
Website: www.sypte.co.uk

Strathclyde PTE
Consort House
12 West George Street
Glasgow G2 1HN
Tel: 0141 332 6811
Website: www.spt.co.uk

Tyne and Wear PTE (Nexus)
Nexus House
St. James' Boulevard
Newcastle upon Tyne NE1 4AX
Tel. 0191 203 3333
Fax. 0191 203 3180
Website: www.nexus.org.uk

West Midlands PTE (Centro)
Centro House
16 Summer Lane
Birmingham B19 3SD
Tel: 0121 214 7214
Fax: 0121 214 7033
Website: www.centro.org.uk

West Yorkshire PTE
Wellington House
40-50 Wellington Street
Leeds LS1 2DE
Tel: 0113 251 7272
Website: www.wymetro.com

Traffic Commissioners
Website: www.tan.gov.uk

Eastern
For the counties of Bedfordshire, Buckinghamshire, Cambridgeshire, Hertfordshire, Essex, Leicestershire, Lincolnshire, Norfolk, Northamptonshire & Suffolk
City House
126-130 Hills Road
Cambridge CB2 1NP
Tel: 01223 531 060
Fax: 01223 309 684

North
For Metropolitan boroughs in Greater Manchester, Merseyside, South Yorkshire, Tyne and Wear & West Yorkshire and the counties of Cheshire, Cumbria, Derbyshire, Durham, Lancashire, Northumberland, Nottinghamshire & North Yorkshire
Hillcrest House
386 Harehills Lane
Leeds LS9 6NF
Tel: 0113 254 3291
Fax: 0113 248 9607

Scotland
Argyle House
3 Lady Lawson Street
Edinburgh EH3 9SE
Tel: 0131 200 4955
Fax: 0131 529 8501

South Eastern and Metropolitan area
For Greater London and the counties of Kent, Surrey, East Sussex & West Sussex
Ivy House, 3 Ivy Terrace
Eastbourne BN21 4QT
Tel: 01323 452 473
Fax: 01323 721 057

Wales
Cumberland House, 200 Broad Street
Birmingham B15 1TD

Tel: 0121 609 6805
Fax: 0121 608 1001

West Midlands
For Metropolitan boroughs in the West Midlands and the counties of Shropshire,
Staffordshire, Warwickshire & Worcestershire
Cumberland House
200 Broad Street
Birmingham BR15 1TD
Tel: 0121 609 6813
Fax: 0121 608 1001

Western
For Cornwall, Devon, Dorset, Gloucestershire, Hampshire, Oxfordshire, Somerset &
Wiltshire
2 Rivergate, Temple Quay
Bristol BS1 6EH
Tel: 0117 900 8577
Fax: 0117 929 8352

Transport 2000
The Impact Centre
12-18 Hoxton Street
London N1 6NG
Tel: 020 7613 0743
Fax: 020 7613 5280
Website: www.transport2000.org.uk

Transport for London
Windsor House
42-50 Victoria Street
London SW1H 0TL
Tel: 020 7941 4500
Website: www.transportforlondon.gov.uk

Transport for London – Access & Mobility
Windsor House
42-50 Victoria Street
London SW1H 0TL

Tel: 020 7222 1234
Textphone: 020 7918 3015
Email: travinfo@tfl.gov.uk
Website: www.londontransport.co.uk/buses/phb_mobility.shtml

Transport for London – Buses

Customer Services Department
172 Buckingham Palace Road
London SW1W 9TN
Tel: 020 7918 4300
Fax: 020 7918 3999
Textphone: 020 7918 4435
Email: customerservices@tfl-buses.co.uk
Website: www.transportforlondon.gov.uk/buses

Sample letter 11: Complaint about a bus operator

1, Any Street
Anytown
Anyshire
AN1 2YZ

25th June, 2003

Bus operator

Dear Sirs,

Re: Complaint about your Company's Bus Service

I am writing to complain about your company's bus service in *Anytown*. The bus journey in question was on *14th April at 8:30am from Slack Street to the Anytown Rotunda on bus number 245*. I enclose a copy of my bus ticket as proof of purchase.

My complaint is as follows. *The bus driver, for no apparent reason, left the bus at the Donkey Road stop and did not return until 15 minutes later. This severely made me late for work and caused great inconvenience.*

I would like a full explanation, together with an apology and compensation for the inconvenience caused. You will be aware that your company is in breach of its own Code of Practice – in particular Section 3 – reliability of service.

If I do not get a satisfactory response I will refer the matter to the Bus Appeals Body. *(NB You cannot do this in London or Northern Ireland).*

I look forward to hearing the outcome of your investigation.

Yours faithfully,

David Chambers

David Chambers

Enc.

Buying goods

With disputes about goods you have bought, complain to the seller. If it is a trader it is best to see either a supervisor or manager, or the customer services department if there is one. You will need to take the goods back, or if they were delivered arrange for their collection. Before complaining take advice to see how you stand legally. If the law is not on your side you will be appealing to the seller's goodwill so know how far you can push it. On the other hand if you have rights it is good tactics to refer to them when complaining! If you have got rights having the receipt is not legally essential but it helps.

Know your rights

In essence, once you buy goods there is a contract between you and the seller, if the seller is a trader, which assumes they must be of satisfactory quality, fit for the intended purpose and as described on the package or display sign or by the trader in person. This is the Sale of Goods Act 1979 (as amended) except in Scotland where these rights are covered by Common Law. You have the same rights buying in a sale as at other times. You also have the same rights with second hand goods

but the quality expected will be lower the older they are! Take advice. (See also *Shopping from home*). If the seller is a private individual the goods do not have to be free of faults, but they must be as described.

You usually have more redress if you have only just bought the goods. If you tell the trader promptly that the goods are faulty or not fit for the purpose etc and you do not want them you should be entitled to your money back. As long as you have not legally "accepted" the goods you can still "reject' them – that is refuse to accept them. Of course, you can insist on a free repair instead – see sample letters 12 and 13. One of the ways you 'accept' goods is by keeping them, without complaint, after you have had a reasonable time to examine them. What is reasonable is not fixed but depends on the goods and all the other circumstances. Normally you can at least take your purchase home and try it out. The same might apply if you bought on hire purchase (see sample letter 14) or see also *Credit*.

If you have had use out of the goods and some time later they go wrong you still have the above legal rights, at least to a free repair or maybe a replacement, and perhaps compensation to cover the time you are without the goods.

In complaining whether you have an easy ride or a great battle depends on the seller's attitude or policy. Some will refund or replace without question, others will send the goods away for rigorous tests before deciding whether they are faulty.

Complaining further

If you get no joy you could take the matter further up within the firm – for example, a manager or supervisor. If this gets nowhere, many high street stores have a customer relations office to whom you can complain.

Other possibilities

Find out if the trader is a member of a relevant trade association for the product. Some may pursue a complaint for you, particularly if they have a code of practice setting out the standards expected (see *Taking things further*). Note, however, this may preclude you from then taking legal action. Take advice. Some also have facilities for testing goods if there is a dispute over whether they are faulty. If the product carries a seal of approval of some kind, the organisation concerned may help you with your complaint (for example, the **British Standards Institution** may investigate if the goods carry their Kitemark).

As well as advising your local authority, the **Trading Standards Service** may take up your case, if they think criminal trading offences are being committed. In some circumstances, suggesting to the trader that you may involve trading standards may be enough for the trader to reach a settlement with you. Trading Standards will also investigate misleading advertising (see *Advertising*).

If you bought the goods on credit for more than £100 you may be able to complain to the creditor and get money back from them. See *Credit.*

Guarantees (or warranties) give you an additional complaining route – to the manufacturer. First check the terms of the guarantee, for example it may only cover replacement parts not labour, especially if it is an extended guarantee you have purchased. The trader may agree, in this case, to send the goods to the manufacturer.

- If you buy unfit food or drink you could write to the manufacturers who may offer you something as a goodwill gesture. Also complain to your local authority **Environmental Health Department**. They may order the removal of goods from sale; possibly prosecute the trader and give you evidence if you wanted to take legal action (for example, if you were made ill). Take advice to help work out your damages claim and whether your claim should be against the manufacturer or the shop. See also *Restaurants and cafés.*

- Was a firm delivery date agreed? Was it made clear that if the goods did not arrive on that date, then the deal was off? If yes, in legal terms you are making it part of the contract that 'time is of the essence' so if there was a delay in delivery you could normally cancel and claim a refund. If there is not a deadline, the trader will only be obliged to refund you if their delay is unreasonable. But you could write and have one added, and then any delay after that would allow you to cancel. Take advice.

- If you buy a car or other motor vehicle that turns out to be seriously faulty, for example steering or brakes, it may be in an unroadworthy condition. Complain to the police. They will investigate and may prosecute the seller.

- In the case of other unsafe goods complain to **Trading Standards**. There are a number of safety regulations that apply specifically to certain items such as furniture (fire safety) and toys.

- If goods you buy cause you injury or illness, or damage to your property you also may wish to take legal action for damages from the seller – see *Taking things further*, but first try sample letter 15. Also, the manufacturer or importer could also be liable. You could ask the seller in writing who supplied them. If they fail to reply in a reasonable time they themselves become wholly liable under the Consumer Protection Act 1987 (see sample letter 16). You may also have a claim for negligence against either the trader or manufacturer if goods injured you that you did not buy yourself. All claims of this nature should normally be made within three years of the date the damage was caused, unless it was hidden for a time after this. Take advice.

- If you bought goods in Britain as a result of seeing an advertisement from a trader in another European Union country UK law would usually apply, but otherwise that country's law would apply. The **European Consumer Centre** for the country concerned may advise or assist you if things go wrong. Also you can ask **Law Society** to refer you to a solicitor who is familiar with the law of that country.

- Purchases made outside of the European Union are subject to the law in the country concerned.

Useful addresses

British Standards Institution
389 Chiswick High Road
London W4 4AL
Tel: 020 8996 9000
Fax: 020 8996 7001
Email: info@bsi-global.com
Website: www.bsi-global.com

European Consumer Networks

Athens
European Consumer Centre Athens
7 Akadimias Street
10671 Athens
Tel: +30 210 363 2443
Fax: +30 210 363 3976

Email: info@ecca.gr
Website: www.ecca.gr

Austria
Europaïsche Verbraucherberatungsstelle Wien
Mariahilfer Strasse 81
A-1060 Wien
Tel: +43 1 588 77 342
Fax: +43 1 588 77 71
Email: europainfo@vki.or.at
Website: www.europakonsument.at

Brussels
Centre Européen des Consommateurs Rue des Chevaliers18, Riddersstraat 18
1050 Bruxelles
Tel: +32 (0) 87 59 18 50
Fax: +32 (0)87 59 18 51
Email info@cec-ecc.be
Website: www.cec-ecc.be

Finland
City of Helsinki
Environment Centre
Helsinginkatu 24
FIN - 00530 Helsinki
Tel: +358 9 7312 2610
Fax: +358 9 7312 2605
Email: ymk@ymk.hel.fi

France
Agence Européenne d'Information sur la Consommation (AEIC)
Centre Régional de la Consommation
47 bis, rue B. Delespaul
F - 59000 Lille
Tel: +33 3 28 82 89 00
Fax: +33 3 28 82 89 05
Email: aeic@crc-conso.com
Website: www.euro-conso.org/

Germany
Europisches Verbraucherzentrum
Enscheder Straße 362
D - 48599 Gronau
Tel: +49 2562 70 207
Fax: +49 2562 70 247
Email: verbraucher@euregio.de
Website: www.verbraucher.euregio.de

Europäisches Verbraucherzentrum
Willestraße 4-6
D-24103 Kiel
Tel: +49 4319 71 9350
Fax: +49 4319 71 9360
Email: evz@evz.de
Website: www.evz.de

Ireland
European Consumer Centre
13A Upper O'Connell Street
Dublin 1
Tel: +353 1 809 06 00
Fax: +353 1 809 06 01
Email: info@eccdublin.ie
Website: www.eccdublin.ie

Italy
Centro Europeo Consumatori
Via Brennero 3
39100 Bolzano
Tel: +39 0 471 980 939
Email: info@euroconsumatori.org

Luxembourg
Union Luxembourgeoise des Consommateurs
55 rue des Bruyeres
L - 1274 Howald-Luxembourg
Tel: +325 49 60 22 1
Fax: +352 49 49 57

Email: ULC EGC@pt.lu
Website: www.ulc.lu

Portugal
Centro Europeu do Consumidor Praça Duque de Saldanha
31 1° P 1069-013 Lisboa
Tel: +351 21 356 46 60/351 21 356 46 57
Fax: +351 21 358 25 73
Email: euroconsumo@ic.pt
Website: www.ic.pt

Spain
Centro Europeo del Consumidor
Institut Català del Consum
Gran Via Carles III, 105, lletra B-I
E-08028 Barcelona
Tel: +34 93 330 98 12
Fax: +34 93 411 06 78
Email: cec@cecbarcelona.org
Website: www.cecbarcelona.org

Centro Europeo del Consumidor
Dpto. de Industria, Comercio y Turismo
Gobierno Vasco
Donositia-San Sebastian, 1
E - 01010 Vitoria-Gasteiz
Tel: +34 945 01 99 48
Fax: +34 945 01 99 47
Email: cec@ej-gv.es
Website: www.euskadi.net/consumoinfo

Law Society
The Law Society's Hall
113 Chancery Lane
London WC2A 1PL
Tel: 020 7242 1222
Email: info.services@lawsociety.org.uk
Website: www.lawsociety.org.uk

Sample letter 12: Requesting refund as goods unsuitable

1, Any Street
Anytown
Anyshire
AN1 2YZ

25th June, 2003

Trader

Dear Sirs,

Re: *Food Processor* purchased on *19th May, 2003*

At the suggestion of one of your sales staff, I purchased the above item on *19th May, 2003*.

I have since discovered that it does not match the purpose or description for which I bought it, as described by your member of staff. The reasons for my dissatisfaction are:

1. *It does not include a liquidiser.*
2. *It cannot beat eggs successfully.*

Under Section 14 of the amended Sale of Goods Act 1979, all goods sold must match the purpose or description indicated by the retailer at the time of purchase. The unsuitability of this product constitutes your breach of contract, and I wish to exercise my rights under the Sale of Goods Act.

I am therefore returning the food processor and claim from you a full refund of the purchase price (£79.99) as per the enclosed receipt, plus delivery costs.

Please send me a cheque for this sum within 10 days. Otherwise, I shall have no alternative but to issue a County court claim for recovery of the amount owed to me without further notice.

Yours faithfully,

David Chambers

David Chambers

Enc.

Sample letter 13: Requesting a free repair

1, Any Street
Anytown
Anyshire
AN1 2YZ

25th June, 2003

Trader

Dear Sirs,

Re: *Dishwasher* purchased on *17th June, 2003*

I purchased the item described above on *17th June, 2003*. On *21st June*, I discovered the following serious defects:

1. *The door did not fit properly.*
2. *It leaked water whenever you turned it on.*

Under the amended Sale of Goods Act 1979, all goods sold must be of reasonable quality. The fact that the product became faulty only *four* days after purchase proves that the item was inherently defective at the time of purchase, which constitutes your breach of contract.

I offer you the opportunity to repair the item free of charge and pay for all delivery costs, while maintaining my rights to a full refund under the Sale of Goods Act should you not repair the item or your repairs prove faulty.

Please send me a written response detailing your proposal within 10 days.

Yours faithfully,

David Chambers

David Chambers

Sample letter 14: Rejecting goods bought on hire purchase due to fault

1, Any Street
Anytown
Anyshire
AN1 2YZ

25th June, 2003

Hire Purchase Company

Dear Sirs,

Re: HP Reference Number *2425 – 'Sleepwell' Bed*

After following through on a hire purchase agreement with you, I received a bed from *Sleepwells* on *11th June, 2003*. On *18th June*, I discovered serious problems with the product.

Because the product became unusable after just *seven* days in my possession, it is safe to conclude that it was unsatisfactory at the time of purchase. I hereby exercise my rights to reject the product under the amended Supply of Goods Act 1979 and to terminate our agreement.

I demand that you collect the above-mentioned bed and return to me the sum of *£500*, which includes the deposit and all instalments to date. As of the date of this letter, I will make no further installment payments and am not amenable to any suggestions that the faulty product be repaired.

I trust you will inform me of your arrangements to pick up of the faulty goods and reimburse the sums I have paid.

Yours faithfully,

David Chambers

David Chambers

Sample letter 15: Requesting refund as goods unsuitable and compensation due to damage caused

1, Any Street
Anytown
Anyshire
AN1 2YZ

25th June, 2003

Trader

Dear Sirs,

Re: *Washing Machine purchased on 19th May*

I bought the above item on *19th May*. On *25th May* it became apparent that the *washing machine* had a serious defect *with regard to the piping*, as it caused damage to my property by *leaking throughout my kitchen* (see enclosed photographs). The damage cost *£250* to repair.

Under the amended Sale of Goods Act 1979 all goods sold must be of satisfactory quality and as retailer you are liable for any damage caused by faulty goods. The very fact that the product developed a fault only *six* days after purchase means that the item was inherently faulty at the time of purchase and not of satisfactory quality, which constitutes your breach of contract.

I therefore wish to exercise my rights under the Sale of Goods Act. I am returning the goods and claim from you a full refund of the purchase price, as per the enclosed receipt plus *£250* for damage to my property.

If I do not receive a cheque within 10 days I shall have no alternative but to issue a County court claim for recovery of the amount owed to me without further notice.

Yours faithfully,

David Chambers

David Chambers

Enc.

Sample letter 16: *Warning manufacturer of a damages claim due to defective goods*

1, Any Street
Anytown
Anyshire
AN1 2YZ

25th June, 2003

Manufacturer

Dear Sirs,

Re: *Hairdryer* purchased on *31st May* from *Simon Electricals, Wimbledon*

I purchased the item described above from *Simon Electricals* of *Wimbledon, London*.

On *5th June*, it became evident that the appliance had a serious defect in that *as soon as I plugged it in I received a severe electric shock*.

As *manufacturer* of this product you are liable under the Consumer Protection Act 1987 for this injury, caused by your inherently defective goods.

I am taking legal advice on the amount of compensation I should claim based on the pain and suffering I suffered and will keep you informed regarding this matter.

Yours faithfully,

David Chambers

David Chambers

Buying services

Use this chapter if your complaint is about builders, plumbers, hairdressers, television or shoe repairers, electricians, dry cleaners, carpet fitters, heating engineers, photographers, gas fitters, motor mechanics ...or indeed any other service for which you have to pay.

As with sale of goods (see *Buying goods*) before complaining consider how you stand legally. Is the trader in breach of contract? Have they broken their agreement (the contract) with you when you bought the service? If there is a written agreement, check this. It may simply be on display in the trader's premises (e.g. a dry cleaner). Does the agreement set out what the trader will do if you have a complaint?

In addition to all this, whatever the contract says, the Supply of Goods and Services Act states you have legal grounds for complaint if the service has not been provided with reasonable care and skill, the service has not been carried out in the time

agreed (or within a reasonable time) or you have been charged more than the price agreed. If no price was agreed it should be reasonable for the work done.

Usually you should give the trader a chance to put things right first. If you are still not happy, put the complaint in writing to the appropriate manager, saying what you want done, and set a deadline. If the trader has clearly broken an agreement, for example by not keeping to a promise to repair your computer in two hours, you could cancel the agreement and go elsewhere. Ask for the job to be done again without charge if the work is unsatisfactory. If you have suffered a loss you will need to work out how much financial compensation to ask for (see sample letters 17, 18 and 19).

If you get no joy you could take the matter further up in the firm (if it is large enough!). If this gets nowhere, many larger companies have a procedure for handling complaints and perhaps a customer services office so you can find out how to complain further.

Small print

Small print in an agreement can tie you down, but you may be able to challenge it, so take advice. For example, a trader may have penalty clauses and terms that give them the right to vary the contract (perhaps by increasing the price!) without you having the right to withdraw. Or they may use exclusion clauses, for example a dry cleaning ticket saying 'No responsibility for loss or damage to garments, however caused.' These can be challenged under the Unfair Contracts Terms Act 1977.

Other complaining routes

If a trader causes you to suffer a loss in carrying out a service, such as injury, trauma, damage to property, take advice, as you may be able to take legal action for damages.

If you cannot get anywhere with the trader and you bought the service on credit for more than £100, you may be able to complain, and get money back from the creditor. See *Credit.*

See if the trader is a member of a trade association as some have drawn up codes of practice and will investigate complaints (see *Taking things further*). However, note, this may preclude you from taking legal action.

If you have not already paid, you could deduct the cost to you of getting someone to finish the job properly or compensation that you feel is due to you. Give the trader reasonable warning that you intend to do this, and the chance to put things right unless your trust in them has completely broken down. See *Taking things further.* The trader may try to sue you for the balance so you may have to defend your actions in court.

If it is impossible to make a deduction from the bill, say because the trader will not let you have your car back until you have paid in full for the service, put it in writing that you are paying 'under protest' and 'without prejudice to my legal rights'. This will safeguard you in case you decide to take legal action later.

- If a trader breaks an appointment and this causes you to lose money or a day's holiday from work, you may be able to claim compensation. Usually this will only be   possible if you had made it clear to the trader in advance that you would lose money if she or he failed to turn up. If the trader continually breaks appointments you may be able to cancel the agreement altogether. Take advice.

- If you feel you have been mislead, for example if the service was falsely described or the price was higher than you were lead to believe, contact your local **Trading Standards Service** as a criminal offence may have been committed. If the trader's advertisements were misleading see *Advertising.*

- If your case hinges on a technical dispute, for example whether a job has been carried out to a reasonable standard or not, you may need the opinion of a technical expert. If the relevant trade association cannot help, there are testing services available. There will be fees, however, but you may be able to add such expenses to any damages claim you make. Take advice first. If you are a member of one of the motoring organisations such as the RAC or AA you may be able to get an independent test done on a motor vehicle.

- If the trader breaks the contract you may have a claim for a refund of your deposit or any advance payment made. If you yourself cancel you cannot normally claim for the return of a deposit, unless the agreement allows this. If you made an advance payment, which was not a deposit, you may be able to claim part of this but the trader would usually keep some back for expenses suffered.

- There may be little you can do if your trader has gone bust or cannot be traced.

If the trader was a member, a trade association may have a guarantee scheme. In some cases, other firms take over the contract if a trader goes bust – the local **Official Receiver's Office** will advise.

- If you buy services outside the UK the advice is the same as for *Buying Goods*.

- If you are concerned about the standards of work on a new home check whether the builders are registered with the **National House Building Council (NHBC)**, and whether they have issued a Notice of Insurance Cover for the property. If so, the builders should put right without charge any defects, which arise in the first two years due to their failure to comply with NHBC standards. (In the case of installations such as central heating, however, this applies to the first year only). If there is a dispute, the NHBC will arbitrate. If the builders still refuse to comply or have gone out of business, they will pay up to 90 per cent of the cost of repairs. If damage is caused by structural defects that occur over the next eight years, again complain to the NHBC where the builders are to blame.

Useful addresses

National House Building Council (NHBC)
Buildmark House
Chiltern Avenue
Amersham
Bucks HP6 5AP
Tel: 01494 735 363/369
Website: www.nhbc.co.uk

Sample letter 17: General letter seeking compensation

1, Any Street
Anytown
Anyshire
AN1 2YZ

25th June, 2003

Trader

Dear Sirs,

On *27th May*, I used the services of your firm for the following:

Dry-cleaning of my duvet and cashmere sweater.

Under the Supply of Goods and Services Act 1982, you are under a duty to carry out your services with reasonable skill and care using materials of suitable quality, at reasonable cost and in reasonable time. However, I consider that the service you provided me was deficient for the following reasons:

1. *The cleaning failed to remove the black marks on my duvet.*
2. *My cashmere sweater shrunk.*

I therefore hold you in breach of contract and am entitled to compensation for the damage I have suffered and consider £75 to be a reasonable sum.

I look forward to receiving your cheque for the above amount within 10 working days.

Yours faithfully,

David Chambers

David Chambers

Sample letter 18: Complaint about a trader's delay in getting the job completed

1, Any Street
Anytown
Anyshire
AN1 2YZ

25th June, 2003

Trader

Dear Sirs,

Re: Reference Number *210 – House Decoration*

I am putting in writing my concern about your firm's delay in completing the work you have contracted to do for me.

When I accepted your quote for the work, you promised me that all would be finished by *25th May, 2003.* That is now *four* weeks ago, and still the following has yet to be done:

1. Kitchen painted
2. Hall completed (it is presently half finished)
3. Skirting boards in lounge painted

In view of your delays I am making time of the essence in the contract between us. If your firm fails to complete the outstanding work within 14 days of the date of this letter, I shall consider the contract between us to be at an end. I am within my rights to do this.

If this happens I will only pay you for the work you have done, minus any extra expense I suffer, and I will contract with another firm to complete the work.

Yours faithfully,

David Chambers

David Chambers

Sample letter 19: Asking a trader to put things right

1, Any Street
Anytown
Anyshire
AN1 2YZ

25th June, 2003

Trader

Dear Sirs,

Re: Reference Number *001 – Replacement Boiler*

You completed the above work for me on *10th June, 2003.*

Unfortunately I have experienced defects in the work. *Since the boiler has been fitted it has lost pressure on two occasions and has failed to provide me with hot water.*

I would be pleased if you could contact me within the next seven days to arrange a visit to rectify the problem without further charge.

You will be aware that under the Supply of Goods and Services Act 1982 you are obliged to carry out your work with reasonable care and skill, and to use materials of a reasonable quality. Indeed this is implied in the contract between us. I will reserve my rights to claim from you for breach of contract should the defect not be attended to satisfactorily, or indeed if you fail to attend to it at all. In this case I will exercise my legal right to arrange for another contractor to carry out the work at your expense.

I look forward to hearing from you.

Yours faithfully,

David Chambers

David Chambers

The Child Support Agency

You may want to complain about the Child Support Agency (CSA) if, for example, they divulged your whereabouts without your permission, they wrongly sought child maintenance from you, or you suffer delays in getting your child maintenance assessed. Alternatively, you may want to dispute or appeal against a CSA decision.

Dissatisfied with the service?

The first step will be to find out what procedures the CSA have to follow. Take advice or phone the **CSA National Enquiry Line**. Obtain a copy of the Child Support Agency Charter, which sets out the standards for their service.

Next, phone or write to the Customer Service Manager at the Child Support Agency Centre in the region dealing with your case. This will be the region where the parent with the child or children lives. If you are not sure which is the right Centre, contact the **Enquiry Line** or the local **CSA office**, or your local **Benefits Agency** office. In complaining say if you feel you have suffered a financial loss or gross inconvenience.

Claims for compensation will be referred to the **CSA Special Payments Section**. As an alternative you can just write to them direct and they will look into whether you should receive compensation but pass the rest of your complaint to the CSA Centre.

If you are still not satisfied write to the manager at the Child Support Agency Centre and they will investigate further. If you get no joy, next go to the CSA's Chief Executive at the Child Support Agency Head Office.

The next step may be for you to write to the **Independent Case Examiner**. You can complain about the way the CSA used its discretion, but not about the law itself. You can also complain if there were long delays or mistakes in handling your complaint (see sample letter 20). The Examiner will only consider your case after you have received written replies from both the Child Support Agency Centre and the Chief Executive as above. Write within six months of receiving the latter letter. As an alternative to this you could complain via your MP to the **Parliamentary Ombudsman** (see *Public services*).

Challenging a maintenance assessment

If you are unhappy with a maintenance assessment, whether or not you are the parent living with the child, take advice as a complicated formula is used. There may be a mistake, or the CSA may have wrong information about you, for example your income level. Even if all this is correct you may be able to apply for a departure direction, that is for an exception to be made in your case, for example if you have high travel, housing costs or ill health. Also you may have had an interim assessment, which is usually higher than the final assessment you will have later, or some of the assessment may include arrears.

To dispute a decision contact the **Personal Case Team** at the CSA Centre dealing with your case by phone, personal visit, email or letter, explaining your reasons – take advice to help you with this. In most cases there is a time limit of one month. If you phone, the officer will go through your assessment with you and things may be resolved there and then. If not, make it clear that you wish to continue with the disputes procedure. After reconsidering your case the officer will advise you whether or not they have revised the original decision. The revised decision would normally take effect from the date of the original decision so your maintenance allowance would be altered retrospectively. If you are dissatisfied you may be able to appeal, or, if you have new information, apply to dispute this decision – take advice.

Instead of being revised a decision may be superseded. Here the original decision still stands from the time it was made but a new decision has been made to take into account the current situation, for example, your circumstances have changed. In this case there will be no retrospective change.

Appeals

To appeal to a Unified Appeal Tribunal you will need to fill in an appeal form supplied by the CSA office, stating the decision you are appealing against, why you think it is wrong, and if anyone is representing you (see *Taking things further*). Send it to the **Child Support Agency Appeal Centre** or (for Northern Ireland) the **NI Child Support Agency Appeal Section**. Take advice on whether it is worth appealing and how best to present your case. The time limits and procedure are the same as for social security appeals including applying for a tribunal decision to be set aside and going to the **Social Security and Child Support Commissioners** (see *Social security*).

Arrears

If you look after the children and you are losing out because you feel the CSA is not doing its job properly in recovering arrears then you may be able to claim compensation as above.

Under what is called the Deferred Debt Scheme, if you are the person held liable for the maintenance you can apply to the CSA for part of the arrears to be waived but only if there is more than six months worth, and at least three months worth are because of CSA delays. If they do waive some arrears, they will cancel this decision if you fail to pay the remaining arrears over an agreed time period, or if you fail to meet your regular payments.

If they cannot reach agreement with you to pay arrears, the CSA may order your employer to deduct weekly or monthly amounts from your salary. You can appeal against this to your local magistrates court (or Sheriffs court in Scotland) if you apply within 28 days, but nothing will be altered unless a mistake has come to light. If the CSA uses other recovery methods, such as bailiffs or an order to sell your property, or applies to have you disqualified from driving or committed to prison then take advice before complaining.

Useful addresses

Child Support Agency Appeal Centre
'R' Block
Government Buildings
Moorland Road
Lytham St. Annes FY8 3ZZ
Tel: 0845 610 0943/0845 610 0764
Email: csa-cau@dwp.gsi.gov.uk

Child Support Agency Centres
Website: www.csa.gov.uk

Belfast
Great Northern Tower
17 Great Victoria Street
Belfast BT2 7AD
Tel: 0845 713 2000
Email: belfast-customer-helpline@dwp.gsi.gov.uk

Birkenhead
2 Weston Road
Crewe CW98 1BB
Tel: 0845 713 8000
Email: birkenhead.csa@iclwebkit.co.uk

Dudley
2 Weston Road
Crewe CW98 1BB
Tel: 0845 713 1000
Email: dudley-csa@dwp.gsi.gov.uk

Falkirk
Parklands, Callendar Business Park
Callendar Road
Falkirk FK1 1XT
Tel: 08457 136 000
Email: falkirk@dwp.gsi.gov.uk

Hastings
Ashdown House
Sedlescombe Road North
St Leonards on Sea
East Sussex TN37 7NL
Tel: 0845 713 4000
Email: hastings-csa@dwp.gsi.gov.uk

Plymouth
Clearbrook House
Towerfield Drive
Bickleigh Down Business Park
Plymouth PL6 7TN
Tel: 0845 713 7000
Email: plymouth-csa@dwp.gsi.gov.uk

Child Support Agency National Enquiry Line
PO Box 55
Brierley Hill
West Midlands DY5 1YL

Tel: 08457 133 133
Email: csa-nel@dwp.gsi.gov.uk

Child Support Agency Appeal Section – Northern Ireland

Great Northern Tower
17 Great Victoria Street
Belfast BT2 7AD
Tel: 0845 713 9896
Email: belfast-cust-helpline@dwp.gsi.gov.uk
Website: www.dsdni.gov.uk

Child Support Agency Special Payments

Central Appeals Unit
'R' Block
Government Buildings
Moorland Road
Lytham St. Annes FY8 3ZZ
Tel: 0845 7133 133
Email: csa-cav@ms24.dss.gsi.gov.uk

Independent Case Examiner

PO Box 155
Chester CH99 9SA
Tel: 0151 801 8800
Helpline: 0845 606 0777
Minicom: 0151 801 8888
Email: ice@ukgov.demon.co.uk
Website: www.ind-case-exam.org.uk

Sample letter 20: Complaint to the Independent Case Examiner re Child Support Agency

1, Any Street
Anytown
Anyshire
AN1 2YZ

Independent Case Examiner
Child Support Agency
PO Box 155
Chester CH99 9SA

Dear Sir,

Re: *David Chambers, born 11/07/70,* Reference Number *04324, Birmingham CSA*

I am writing to ask you to investigate my complaint about the way the above CSA office has dealt with my case (see above reference number). There has been a history of problems, including lost papers and long delays in processing my claim for Child Support. This has left me having to support myself and *two* children aged *three and five* on a very low income for *five* months.

The details of my complaint are as follows:
Since being granted child support on 15th January, 2003, due to errors at the Birmingham office it appears that it has taken them nearly five months to arrange the payment from my ex-wife and now that I have received it, it seems to be £300 less per month than what was agreed.

I have taken the complaint as far as I can within the CSA, even to Chief Executive level, but so far all I have had is a long explanation that I do not fully understand, and which scarcely amounts to an apology.

I understand that you have the power to recommend that compensation be paid to me for the problems I have experienced. I look forward to receiving such an offer together with an unconditional apology and an assurance that I will suffer no repetition of these events.

I enclose copies of all correspondence between me and the CSA and myself to date on this complaint. Please keep me informed of the progress of your investigation.

Yours faithfully,

David Chambers

David Chambers

Council tax

Complaints about council tax mostly centre around the amount of the bill.

Changing the bill

If you think your bill is wrong, check that it has been calculated with up to date information about your circumstances – for example, if you live alone have you been allowed the second adult rebate, does the bill include arrears you dispute? Are you actually liable at all? Take advice.

If you complain (see sample letter 21), the council should review the bill. If that does not get you anywhere, you can appeal to your local **Valuation Office Agency (VOA),** (this is part of the Inland Revenue) within two months of the decision being notified to you. A Valuation Tribunal will hear your case. If all else fails and you do not pay the bill, the council will seek permission from the Magistrates Court to take out enforcement proceedings, for example, deductions from earnings or bailiffs. There is a hearing you can attend at that point to dispute liability. If you disagree in limited circumstances you can ask for a review of their decision. Take advice.

Changing the valuation band

You may feel you are paying too much Council Tax because your property has been put in the wrong valuation band. Most properties were put in this band between December 1991 and July 1992, unless it was built since then. To complain apply in writing to the listing officer at the VOA, see sample letter 22. This is called 'making a proposal'. Examples of valid reasons are where the property has been reduced in size or physically deteriorated so its value should be lower, or the area has gone downhill, perhaps a factory has been built next door. Alternatively, perhaps the property has been adapted to make it suitable for a person with disabilities. Take advice.

If the VOA does not agree with your proposal your application automatically becomes an appeal to the Valuation Tribunal as above after six months.

Offsetting the bill

You may be able to offset the bill by claiming Council Tax Benefit – see *Social security*.

You may want to complain about the way your Council Tax has been dealt with. If so, see *Local authorities*. If you disagree with a decision not to award you Council Tax Benefit, see *Social security*.

Sample letter 21: Appealing against a Local Authority decision

1, Any Street
Anytown
Anyshire
AN1 2YZ

25th June, 2003

Treasurer's Department
Local Authority

Dear Sirs,

Re: *3, High Street, London, SW21*

I am the sole owner of the above dwelling and I am writing to challenge the decision of the Council to levy Council Tax on my abode for the period *3rd March, 2003* onwards.

The reason is as follows. *I did live there alone as the owner-occupier, and was consequently the liable person. However, as from 3rd March, 2003 I ceased to occupy the dwelling as I had to move in with my son and his family in order to receive care, as unfortunately I have severe arthritis and have very restricted mobility. The dwelling is now thus empty.*

As evidence of this I enclose *a statement from my son, and a letter from my doctor. As further evidence of my care needs, please note that I have been deemed eligible for Attendance Allowance. If you wish to inspect the dwelling to verify that it is unoccupied please let me know and I will arrange for my son to show you around.*

I look forward to your revised decision in respect of my liability for Council Tax. If I do not hear from you within two months from receipt of this letter, or if I disagree with your revised decision, I will appeal to the Valuation Tribunal.

Yours faithfully,

David Chambers

David Chambers

Enc.

Sample letter 22: Proposing to alter the valuation list

**1, Any Street
Anytown
Anyshire
AN1 2YZ**

25th June, 2003

The Listings Officer
Valuation Office Agency

Dear Sirs,

Re: *3, High Street, London, SW21*

Please regard this letter as a proposal to alter the valuation list in respect of the above dwelling.

I am both the owner and the person liable to pay Council tax on the dwelling, which is currently listed in Band D.

My proposal is that the valuation list be altered to place the dwelling in a lower valuation band – Band C – on the grounds that there have been changes to the dwelling which have reduced its value.

When it was valued the property was situated in a quiet country lane (see the photographs attached). Now, as you will discover should you inspect, the surrounding area has changed markedly – the once green fields at the back have been replaced by a housing estate, the country lane is now a busy through road and the land opposite which was formerly occupied by a period country pub is now given over to distribution warehouses.

I would further propose that the reduction in valuation takes place from the time that the circumstances which caused the change first arose – this would be on 5 May, 1997 when the building work began on the new housing estate, as all the other changes followed on from this.

The owners of two neighbouring dwellings have today also submitted two similar proposals to the above, as their dwellings have been similarly affected.

I hope very much that you will agree with this proposal, and I will be happy to discuss the matter with you if required to help you reach a decision. Please keep me informed of the progress of my case.

Yours faithfully,

David Chambers

David Chambers

Enc.

Credit

Disputes with creditors can be pursued in the same way as all complaints against a trader, using any customer services offices and complaints procedures where they exist (see *Buying goods, Buying services* and *Shopping from home*). Also, if the credit was obtained from a bank or building society, see *Banking services.*

- You may be chased for a debt for which you can dispute liability. Perhaps you have already paid, the goods or services were not received or the debt is not in your name. Perhaps you were pressurised into signing the agreement without fully understanding the implications ('undue influence'), or possibly the lender did not conform to regulations, e.g. the Consumer Credit Act. Complain as above and contact **Trading Standards**. Failing this you could ignore them and let them sue you for the money, and then you can dispute liability in court. Take advice. See also *Taking things further.*

- If you have a complaint about the way your mortgage application has been handled you could check if the lender (or the intermediary) has broken a term in the Mortgage Code of Practice. The **Mortgage Code Compliance Board** will advise you if they subscribe to this. If you cannot resolve things you can refer the matter to the **Mortgage Code Arbitration Scheme**.

- If you think a term in a mortgage agreement is unfair, for example, a disproportionately high redemption penalty, ask the **Office of Fair Trading** to obtain a ruling (see *Taking things further*). If it was in your favour you would then not be bound by the term.

- If you are being pursued by a creditor for an old debt you may be able to ignore this on the grounds that it has time lapsed. This is six years, except in Scotland where it is five, but this only applies if no legal action has been taken against you on the debt, and you have not acknowledged it during the time. If you do now acknowledge it as a result of the creditor contacting you, you will reactivate the debt; so take advice before doing anything.

- If you think you are being charged an extortionate rate of interest you may be able to get the debt written off or the interest rate reduced by applying to a

County court (Sheriff court in Scotland), see sample letter 23. Take advice or contact **Trading Standards**.

- You may be dissatisfied with goods or services you bought and try to get a refund – see *Buying goods* or *Buying services*. If you bought on credit you may be able to claim a refund from the creditor instead, for example, if the trader is being difficult, cannot be traced, or has gone bust. This only applies to certain types of agreements for single purchases of £100 to £ 30,000. Take advice. Write to the credit company giving details of your complaint, the steps you have taken to claim against the trader, and the redress you are seeking. See sample letter 24.

- If you have goods on hire purchase and the company is threatening to take them back because you have fallen behind with payments, take advice. If you have paid more than one third of the price they will have to take legal proceedings against you in County court, and the court may not agree to them having the goods back.

Are you being harassed?

It is a criminal offence for creditors, debt collecting agencies or private bailiffs, or bailiffs acting on behalf of the court, to harass you, that is to cause alarm, distress or humiliation. This includes repeated phone calls, contacting you at work or making enquiries of your neighbours. Complain as above pointing out that a criminal offence is being committed. (In England and Wales you can refer to Section 40 of the Administration of Justice Act 1970). See sample letter 25.

If the problem persists, complain to **Trading Standards**. Sanctions could include prosecuting the firm or revoking its credit licence. If the offender is a debt collection agency it may be a member of the **Credit Services Association**. They have codes of practice and may investigate if you complain. If a solicitor acting for creditors writes to you making threats that are not enforceable by the courts you could report the matter to the **Office for the Supervision of Solicitors** (see *Solicitors' practices*). In the case of bailiffs you can complain to the **Association of Civil Enforcement Agents**, which represents the larger firms, or the **Certificated Bailiffs Association**, which aids mostly smaller firms and individuals. If the bailiffs were acting on behalf of the court, you could complain to the court and the **Sheriff Officers Association**.

If the bailiffs caused trauma to yourself or your family in acting incorrectly, or use violence or damage to your property you could sue for damages, or report to Trading Standards and the police. You may be able to claim compensation from the **Criminal Injuries Compensation Authority** (see *The Police*). Take advice.

Credit refused?

You can complain as above about being refused credit. The lender is not obliged to give you reasons for refusal unless credit scoring was used but they must tell you which credit reference agency was used, if any (see sample letter 26).

The lender should send you an explanation of how credit scoring works and the main reason for turning you down. You can ask them for a review, sending in any additional information you feel might help you, though you may want to get the credit reference agency report first (see below). A different staff member should carry out the review. If you are still unhappy complain as above.

Write to establish whether a Credit Reference Agency was used within 28 days of being refused and the lender must reply within seven days. Then write to the agency – it will be either **Experian** or **Equifax** – to ask for a copy of any files they have on you (the search fee is £2). Give your name and address and any previous names and addresses over the past six years. Within seven days you should receive the copy of the file if there is one. Then ask the agency to alter any incorrect

information. However, if the lender provided the information you will have to ask them to get it altered. The agency should tell you what they have done within 28 days.

If you want to explain or expand the information on your file you can at any time send in a statement, called a Notice of Correction (not more than 200 words). For example, you might wish to say that you got into debt problems because of an unexpected occurrence such as divorce or redundancy. This may help lenders see you in a better light in future. Send this to the agency to put on your file. You must do this within 28 days. The agency is legally bound to send details of any correction to anyone who has requested information about you in the previous six months. This could mean that the lender who refused you credit may review their decision.

If you are dissatisfied with any way this has been handled complain to the **Office of the Information Commissioner** who will investigate.

Your credit file may reveal that you have one or more County court judgements against you. You can then search the **Registry of County Court Judgements** (or the **Enforcement of Judgements Office** in Northern Ireland) and amend your entry if it is wrong or out of date. If you have a record of a judgement against you but you paid the debt within one month you can ask the court, which made the judgement to issue a certificate (cost £10). Send this to the Registry and they will delete the record. For any judgements where you paid the debt after one month you can ask the court in question for a Certificate of Satisfaction (again £10). If the debt was not paid through the court you will need to provide evidence that it was paid (e.g. an acknowledgement from the creditor) and send this to the registry so they will amend your record.

Any changes you succeed in making this way will be fed to the credit reference agencies thus improving your credit rating.

Useful addresses

Association of Civil Enforcement Agents
Chesham House
150 Regent Street
London W1R 5FA
Tel: 020 7432 0366
Fax: 020 7432 0516
Email: sec@acea.org.uk
Website: www.acea.org.uk

Certificated Bailiffs Association
Ridgefield House
14 John Dalton Street
Manchester M2 6JR
Tel: 0161 839 7225
Fax: 0161 834 2433
Email: director@bailiffs.org
Website: www.bailiffs.org.uk

Credit Services Association
3 Albany Mews
Montague Avenue, Gosforth
Newcastle Upon Tyne NE3 4JW
Tel: 0191 213 2509
Fax: 0191 284 5431
Email: mail@csa-uk.com
Website: www.csa-uk.com

Enforcement of Judgements Office (Northern Ireland)
Bedford House
Bedford Street
Belfast BT2 7DS
Tel: 028 9024 5081
Fax: 028 9031 3520

Equifax Europe Ltd.
Credit File Advice Centre
PO Box 1140
Bradford BD1 5US
Tel: 0870 010 0583
Email: contactcis.uk@equifax.com
Website:www.equifax.co.uk

Experian Limited
Consumer Help Service
PO Box 8000
Nottingham NG1 5GX
Tel: 0870 241 6212
Website:www.experian.co.uk

The Mortgage Code Arbitration Scheme
Chartered Institute of Arbitrators
12 Bloomsbury Square
London WC1A 2LP
Tel: 020 7421 7444
Fax: 020 7404 4023
Email: info@arbitrators.org
Website: www.arbitrators.org

Mortgage Code Compliance Board
University Court
Stafford ST18 0GN
Tel: 01785 218 200
Fax: 01785 218 249
Email: enquiries@mortgagecode.org.uk
Website: www.mortgagecode.com

Office of the Information Commissioner
Wycliffe House, Water Lane
Wilmslow
Cheshire SK9 5AF
Tel: 01625 545 745
Fax: 01625 524 510
Email: data@dataprotection.gov.uk
Website: www.dataprotection.gov.uk

Registry of County Court Judgements
Registry Trust Limited
173-175 Cleveland Street
London W1P 5PE
Tel: 020 7636 5214
Email: info@registry-trust.org.uk

Sheriff Officers Association
Ashfield House, Illingworth Street
Ossett
West Yorkshire WF5 8AL
Tel: 01924 279 005
Fax: 01924 280 114

Sample letter 23: Complaint about extortionate credit

1, Any Street
Anytown
Anyshire
AN1 2YZ

25th June, 2003

Creditor

Dear Sirs,

Re: Account Number *7876876*

This letter is with regard to the notice you sent on *14th June, 2003* informing me of the APR increase from *14%* to *20%* on our credit agreement referenced above.

Before I opened the account, you assured me that the APR would not likely rise above *14.5%*. As our agreement is governed by the Consumer Credit Act 1974, the rise in APR to an unacceptable rate qualifies as extortionate under the terms of Sections 137-40.

Please consider lowering my APR to its initial rate, or at least to a reasonable rate. Failure to respond will leave me with no option but to take up the matter with Trading Standards and the County court.

There shall be no further notice.

Yours faithfully,

David Chambers

David Chambers

Sample letter 24: Claiming from Credit Company for defective goods

1, Any Street
Anytown
Anyshire
AN1 2YZ

25th June, 2003

Credit Card Company

Dear Sirs,

Re: *4854124* Credit Card Reference Number

On *1st May, 2003*, I purchased a leather jacket, value £250, supplied by *Canterbury Leather Goods* using the above credit card.

However the *jacket* has proved to be defective in that *all the lining has come undone and the jacket is falling apart.*

Under the equal liability provisions of the Consumer Credit Act 1974, creditors can be held liable by customers for breach of contract if the value of the purchase was over £100. I am holding your company in breach of contract and I am legally entitled to seek compensation from you as well as the supplier.

I look forward to receiving your offer of compensation.

Yours faithfully,

David Chambers

David Chambers

Sample letter 25: Complaint about harassment by a creditor

1, Any Street
Anytown
Anyshire
AN1 2YZ

25th June, 2003

Creditor

Re: Credit Account Number *88374*

Dear Sirs,

As you know, I am *£1,274* in arrears on the above account. I have already explained the reason for this – *three months ago my wife lost her job and as a result our family income dropped by £275 per week.* When I agreed to take out the above loan from your company I had not anticipated this.

You will also know that I fully intend to make proposals to you on how we intend to repay the loan, including the arrears, by reduced instalments. I will do this just as soon as I have been able to reschedule all our outgoings in the light of our changed financial circumstances. *To help us, I have applied for Working Families Tax Credit as I understand we are now eligible, and I have been advised I should receive payment in the next three weeks.*

I fail to understand why is it necessary for your debt recovery department to contact me every other day (sometimes at around 10.30pm)? Even worse, *I have received complaints from my boss that they have often tried to phone me at my place of work – Facia Photocopiers Ltd , 372, Anytown High Road – when I have been away on business. Moreover, my neighbour reports that a 'shady character' who said he was from your company, called on him on Monday this week and quizzed him about my whereabouts and my private life.* You should be aware that not only do I and my wife find your tactics very upsetting and disturbing, they also constitute harassment and this is a criminal offence under Section 40 of the Administration of Justice Act 1970.

Unless your company's action ceases with immediate effect, I will report the episode to the Trading Standards Service and urge that they prosecute.

Yours faithfully,

David Chambers

David Chambers

Sample letter 26: Requesting Credit Reference Agency and credit scoring details

1, Any Street
Anytown
Anyshire
AN1 2YZ

25th June, 2003

Credit Company

Dear Sirs,

Re: Credit Application

Having just received your letter rejecting my application for credit with your company, I am baffled as to how you arrived at your decision. Did you use a credit reference agency? Did you use credit scoring?

If you used a credit reference agency, I am legally entitled under sections 157-60 of the Consumer Credit Act 1974, to know the name and address of the agency in question. I intend to contact this agency in order to determine the nature, origin and truthfulness of the information supplied to you.

If you used credit scoring, you are obliged to send me an explanation of how credit scoring works and the main reason for turning me down. I would be pleased if you could let me have this information.

I look forward to your prompt response to these requests.

Yours faithfully,

David Chambers

David Chambers

Drivers and driving

Complaints here may be wide ranging...

Accidents

If you have an accident and it is someone else's fault...

Take advice, in particular if you have suffered an injury, unless the harm to your person is very minor. Evidence and often witnesses are essential.

- If the other road user is to blame you claim from their insurance company (or to them in person if they do not want the company involved) – see sample letter 27. If the police prosecute the offender this would assist your case.

- If the person refuses to give you their contact details so long as you have their vehicle registration number ask the **Driver and Vehicle Licensing Agency (DVLA)** in writing, giving your reasons. Current fee is £2.50. In Northern Ireland you go through a solicitor or your insurance company to the **DVLNI**.

- If the road user was an uninsured or unidentified motorcyclist or motorist you may be able to claim for damages from the **Motor Insurers Bureau**, but only for personal injuries. Take advice.

- If a child caused the accident usually you would have to claim from the adult who was supposed to be looking after them, but you would have to show they were negligent. Take advice.

- The owner of an animal could be liable if you can prove negligence, but not if the animal was a cat or poultry!

- If an object in the road was to blame you will need to identify and claim from the person or body who put it there (e.g. an unlit skip).

- Where the road or road system itself is the cause (for example, damaged surface or poor lighting) liability rests with the local authority if they could reasonable have done something about it. For trunk roads and motorways the responsibility rests with the **Highways Agency**. For roads in Northern Ireland, liability rests with the Department of the Environment for Northern Ireland. It is best to photograph the damage as you may need it, because it is not uncommon for local authorities etc to quickly carry out repairs after receiving a complaint, thus removing evidence!

- If mud or grease has been left on the road without adequate warnings, the offender, for example a contractor, would be liable. This would also be the case if he had failed to replace the road surface after carrying out works.

Traffic pain

If your concern is about an accident black spot, the need for a new bypass, traffic calming measures or a pedestrian crossing, put your case to the local authority (and the Highways Agency if its about a trunk road). A campaign might achieve more (see *Taking things further*). You will need evidence, for example, accident statistics, to support the case. See also *The neighbourhood and the environment.*

The local authority or the Highways Agency could also be the place to complain to if you are inconvenienced by road works. See sample letter 28.

Disputing parking penalties

To dispute a parking penalty, how you complain depends on who enforces them in your area. If it is the local authority you could refuse to pay and after 28 days you will get a notice demanding payment. At that point you could make representations in writing (the notice tells you who to send them to) – take advice and see sample letter 29. If your representations are rejected you can appeal to the **Parking Appeals Service** for the area. If you fail here and you still do not pay the local authority will sue you, so you could try to defend the action in court.

If the police – usually via traffic wardens – enforce the penalties, you could refuse to pay the parking ticket fixed penalty but complain in writing to the chief executive at the ticket office – the address is on the ticket. If they do not let you off write to relevant senior officer in the police force. A police officer will then investigate. The Magistrates Court will then consider your case. If they disagree you may be found guilty and thus probably fined. (This may be two or three times the penalty plus costs.)

Other motoring complaints

- If you are dissatisfied about the service you have had from DVLA or DVLANI first write to the person you have been dealing with. Next, take your complaint to the **Customer Complaints Manager**.

- You can appeal if you have been refused an MOT test certificate. Complete form VT17 and send it to the **Vehicle Inspectorate Area Office** (usually this is at a Heavy Goods Vehicle Testing Station). The form can be obtained from this office or any MOT testing station. The fee is the same as the maximum MOT test charge. Another test will then be arranged.

- If you are concerned about the standard of someone else's driving, or if you have been a victim of road rage, you could report the offender to the police, but they will only take action if there is good evidence and/or witnesses.

Useful addresses

Driver and Vehicle Licensing Agency (DVLA)
Customer Enquiries (Drivers Unit)
Longview Road
Swansea SA6 7JL
Tel: 0870 240 0009
Fax: 01792 783 071
Email: drivers.dvla@gtnet.gov.uk
Website: www.dvla.gov.uk

DVLNI
County Hall
Castlerock House
Coleraine
Co. Londonderry BT51 3TA
Tel: 028 7034 1469
Fax: 028 7034 1398
Email: dvlni@doeni.gov.uk
Website: www.dvlni.gov.uk

Highways Agency
Traffic, Safety and Environment Division
St. Christopher's House
Southwark Street
London SE1 0TE
Tel: 08457 50 40 30
Email: ha_info@highways.gsi.gov.uk
Website: www.highways.gov.uk

Motor Insurers Bureau (MIB)
Linford Wood House
6-12 Capital Drive
Linford Wood
Milton Keynes MK14 6XT
Tel: 01908 830 001
Website: www.mib.org.uk

Sample letter 27: Notice lodging an accident claim

1, Any Street
Anytown
Anyshire
AN1 2YZ

25th June, 2003

Third party

Dear Mr *Tarrant*,

You are hereby notified of a claim against you for damages arising from the following accident or injury, to which I believe you are liable.

Description of Accident: *Collision of your vehicle into my rear bumper*

Date: *1st June, 2003*

Time: *8am*

Location: *Junction 5 going clockwise on the M25 at Woking*

Please ask your insurance company or solicitor to contact me as soon as possible, unless you wish to settle with me direct.

Yours sincerely,

David Chambers

David Chambers

Sample letter 28: Complaint to the Highways Agency about trunk road

1, Any Street
Anytown
Anyshire
AN1 2YZ

25th June, 2003

Chief Executive
Highways Agency
Traffic, Safety and Environment Division
St. Christopher's House
Southwark Street
London SE1 0TE

Dear Sir,

Re: *Road works on A24 at Kingston*

I have made a complaint to the Area Manager concerned, but I have not received a satisfactory response. Therefore, I am following the next stage of the complaints procedure in writing to you. My complaint is as follows. I am a regular traveller along the *A24*. Travelling North, for four miles just before the *A243* turn-off, every day I am faced with long traffic queues due to lane closures. A major road-widening programme started *two* months ago and still it shows no sign of being completed – most days no work seems to be being carried out on the road at all. All I want to know is the timetable for the completion of the works so that I can at least have a day to look forward to when my travel misery is at an end. I would also like an explanation why your Area Manager could not let me have this information.

I look forward to your reply.

Yours faithfully,

David Chambers

David Chambers

Sample letter 29: Representation against a Local Authority Penalty Charge Notice

1, Any Street
Anytown
Anyshire
AN1 2YZ

25th June, 2003

Local Authority

Dear Sirs,

Re: Penalty Charge received on *17th June* at *4:05pm in the High Street, Chesham*
      Registration: *S243 WPO, Honda Accord*

I have yesterday received a Penalty Charge Notice (PCN) for allegedly illegally parking the above vehicle in *the High Street, opposite the supermarket*. Please regard this letter as my representation against the imposition of this penalty.

My grounds are that *I had no choice but to stop my vehicle, it had broken down and I was waiting for the AA to attend. I left the vehicle for five minutes to buy a newspaper, and during that brief time your parking attendant arrived and wrote the ticket before I was able to explain.*

I believe my reason for stopping is exempted from the local traffic order, so I would be pleased if you would cancel the PCN. If not, I will exercise my right to appeal.

I look forward to your reply.

Yours faithfully,

David Chambers

David Chambers

Electricity services

Your electricity supply is organised on a regional basis by **Public Electricity Suppliers (PES)** you may receive your supply direct from them on tariff terms or under contract, or from a supplier company, called a **2TS (Second Tier Supplier company)**.

Use the supplier's complaints procedure and request compensation if you feel they have fallen short of their standards as set out in their publicity or contract with you. If you are not happy with the company's response you can use the same procedures as for Gas, including Energywatch and the **Office for the Regulation of Electricity and Gas (OfGEM)** – see *Gas* and sample letter 30.

You have a right to a supply. If you are not connected at all ask the PES to connect you, they should do this within two working days for a fee. They may refuse if the wiring is in a dangerous condition, where your supply has been disconnected or you refuse suitable security. However, you should not be asked for security such as a deposit or a guarantor unless you have refused a prepayment meter. To challenge

a refusal contact Energywatch (see *Gas*) or the OfGEM in Northern Ireland (see *Gas*).

The arrangements for giving notice to a supplier to end your contract with them are the same as for gas suppliers. Procedures for dealing with pushy sales methods, disputing bills, faulty meters and price increases are also the same, except that if the PER is also your supplier you may have a tariff arrangement with them rather than a contract. In addition, the supplier can test faulty meters themselves, but you can go direct to **OfGEM** (see *Gas* and sample letter 31).

If there is a problem with the electricity supply up to your meter complain to the PES. If it is the meter itself and you own the property you are responsible, but if you are a tenant your landlord has an obligation to ensure any electrical appliances or wiring is safe. Anyone supplying you with an electrical appliance must ensure it is safe (see *Buying goods*).

Sample letter 30: Asking OfGEM to investigate

1, Any Street
Anytown
Anyshire
AN1 2YZ

25th June, 2003

OfGEM
9 Millbank
London SW1P 3GE

Dear Sirs,

Re: Account Number 56742

I am writing to request your intervention in my dispute with Acme Electricity Company that remains unresolved.

Please refer to the enclosed bills and correspondence relating to this case. As you will see, the amount of the bill in dispute does not appear to be in line with previous bills, despite the fact that the use of my electrical appliances has remained virtually unchanged. I also tested the meter with all appliances turned off and it was still running. Thus, I have ample reason to believe the meter is no longer accurate.

I should be grateful if you would look into my claim and send an independent Meter Examiner to complete a further inspection. It is my understanding that during your investigations my services will not be interrupted nor any legal action be taken regarding the non-payment of the bill.

Please keep me informed on the progress of this investigation.

Yours faithfully,

David Chambers

David Chambers

Sample letter 31: Disputing a bill

1, Any Street
Anytown
Anyshire
AN1 2YZ

25th June, 2003

Electricity Company

Dear Sirs,

Re: Account Number 56742

I have received my bill dated 14th June, 2003, regarding the above account.

I am writing to question the accuracy of the meter reading, as the units of electricity consumed appear to be far above my normal usage for this time of year. I have tested the meter with all electrical appliances in the property turned off and observed the meter still running. There must either be a leakage to earth or the meter is faulty.

In order to settle the matter, please arrange for an engineer to test the meter so we can determine its accuracy and advise me of any charge for doing this. I would also like confirmation that the costs for meter testing are refundable should the meter indeed prove faulty, and that I may be entitled to compensation.

I look forward to hearing from you with a proposed appointment date.

Yours faithfully,

David Chambers

David Chambers

Employment

You may want to complain to your employer while you are in the job, or complain about your employer if you have left the job. You may wish to complain about the attitude of a colleague or colleagues, your pay or your work conditions, being overlooked for promotion, poor working practices, or to appeal against being disciplined. In addition, you may wish to appeal against a dismissal or redundancy.

How to proceed with your complaint

If the concern is relatively minor you could raise the matter with your immediate supervisor or line manager, either informally or as part of a formal session with them (maybe an appraisal). Alternatively, with a complaint about a particular issue you could speak to the person responsible, for example the heath and safety officer.

For more serious matters before you proceed, find out how you stand legally because this can strengthen your position. Also if you discover you have no legal rights this might affect how you go about things – then it's more a matter of negotiation.

If you want to complain formally find out what procedure exists, usually referred to as a grievance procedure – see sample letter 32. Possibly this is written down in your written statement of employment particulars. This is the written part of your contract of employment you are legally entitled to after working for the company for at least 13 weeks. It may also be in a Staff Handbook, or on a staff notice board. If there is a personnel (or human resources) department, they will advise you.

Failing this ask colleagues what normally happens, as there could be an unwritten procedure (custom and practice). If you are still none the wiser write to your line manager unless the complaint is about them, when you may prefer to write to his or her manager. In small firms you may have to write direct to the boss.

Sources of advice and support

If your legal rights are being bypassed take advice or contact the Advisory Conciliation and Arbitration Service (ACAS). ACAS will offer to conciliate on any complaint that is made by a group of employees.

Take advice or consult your union or staff association representative if you are a member, or consider joining. Also useful is the **Department of Trade and Industry's website, TIGER** (Tailored Interactive Guidance on Employment Rights), the **Commission for Racial Equality, Equal Opportunities Commission** and the **Disability Rights Commission** may also assist in case where your complaint is about discrimination or harassment. See *Taking things further.*

With any health and safety matter, including harassment and bullying, you may also get advice and possible intervention from the **Health and Safety Executive** or the health and safety section of your local authority's environmental health department. Note that your company should have a health and safety policy and health and safety precautions and notices must be displayed.

If you are paid less than the National Minimum Wage hourly rate you can complain to an Employment Tribunal but you could also report the matter to **National Minimum Wage Enquiries**. They may contact the employer or send a compliance officer to inspect records.

Know your legal rights

Take advice as Employment law is complex, you could well have statutory rights you were unaware of, which might generate further complaints from you!

You can complain, for example, if your employer fails to provide pay statements, a fixed amount of notice of dismissal, time off for antenatal care, time off for study and training if you are under eighteen-years-old, up to four weeks paid holiday, paid maternity leave and the right to return, time off to deal with an emergency involving one of your dependants and 13 weeks parental leave for each child. These latter rights are unpaid at the time of writing. You are also likely to have the law on your side if you complain that you suffer deductions from your pay (see sample letter 33), or if you are paid less than the National Minimum Wage hourly rate. You also have other rights in relation to health and safety in the workplace.

These are only some of your rights – take advice for a fuller account. Also you should establish what other rights and obligations you have as part of your contract of employment (see above). Your employer may be more generous (but not less generous) than the statutory provision.

If you are injured or made ill by conditions at work you may be able to claim damages from the employer. Take advice. You may also be able to claim certain benefits such as Industrial Disablement Benefit from the **Benefits Agency**. Take advice.

The possible downside to complaining....

Making a serious complaint at work is often not easy. Although you have some legal protection you could still end up losing your job or finding it difficult to remain working there. If you uncover major concerns about what is going on in your company but you fear for your job if you complain take advice or contact **Public Concern at Work**.

Employer altering your job?

It is especially important to take advice immediately if you are dissatisfied because your employer is proposing to alter your job in some way, alter your working hours or reduce your pay. If you carry on working for the company after changes have been made you may jeopardise your right to complain unless you make it clear you are doing so under protest.

Complaining to an Employment Tribunal

You can complain to an **Employment Tribunal** for a wide variety of reasons but here are the main ones:

- If you have exhausted all the complaints (grievance) procedures and nothing has changed, you could appeal to a Tribunal to request that the employer grants your statutory rights (take advice on what these are – some appear above).

- If the complaint is very serious and you feel it is intolerable for you to work for the company anymore it is possible to resign and appeal to the Tribunal. You would be arguing that you were 'constructively dismissed' i.e. you were forced to quit.

- If you have been dismissed because you asked for your statutory rights (some of which appear above).

- If you have been unfairly dismissed for some other reason (usually, though, you will have had to have worked continuously for the company for at least the last twelve months).

- You were made redundant but the procedure was not carried out properly, for example you were not consulted (again twelve months employment required).

- You were made redundant but were not paid your full entitlement (two years employment).

- You are a woman and are being paid less than a man for doing the same job (or vice versa).

- You have faced discrimination at work because of your sex, race or disability.

Apply for your case to be considered by the tribunal on form IT1. This appears in the leaflet 'How to apply to an Employment Tribunal' available from job centres, an Employment Tribunal office and advice services. For complex cases it is best to be represented because a solicitor or a barrister could represent the employer. It is very

important to cite all the statutory rights that you feel have not been granted, as the Tribunal may not be able to rule on those that you do not mention. You must usually ensure the application gets to the Tribunal office for your area within three months of the incident you are complaining about; only if there are exceptional reasons will they consider your case otherwise. In some circumstances the time limit is six months for appeals on redundancy.

Your employer will be sent a copy of your application and invited to respond. In most cases ACAS will also be sent a copy and they will try to facilitate a settlement of your claim. If such an agreement is reached, no tribunal hearing takes place, but if your employer does not honour the agreement, you can enforce it in the County court – take advice.

If no agreement is reached the Tribunal will hear your complaint and make a ruling. If you lose your case you can appeal to an **Employment Appeal Tribunal** within 42 days but usually only on points of law. Take advice.

If your complaint is upheld the tribunal will either order the employer to pay you compensation, for example, in the case of unfair dismissal, or will order the employer to grant you certain rights, for example, paid holiday. If you win an unfair dismissal case, you have an option to be reinstated in your job if this is practicable. If your employer still refuses to pay as directed by the Tribunal you have to take out a court order to get the order enforced. Take advice.

Alternative complaining routes

If your feel you have been unfairly dismissed you may be able have your case referred to an arbitrator under the **ACAS Arbitration Scheme,** but your employer would have to agree to this as well. This would not be allowed if your case were legally complex. If you have a number of complaints you can elect to have the unfair dismissal one dealt with under the Scheme and the rest dealt with by a tribunal.

To apply, contact ACAS at the outset, or discuss this with ACAS when they contact you after you send in the Employment Tribunal application form IT1. The arbitrator will consider the facts of both sides of the case on a more informal basis than at an Employment Tribunal and try to arrive at a fair decision. If you disagree with the decision, you cannot then go to an Employment Tribunal and you can only challenge or appeal to a court in very limited circumstances. Take advice.

In some circumstances where you cannot use other routes, you can claim damages for breach of contract via the **County court** (see *Taking things further*). This includes where you are dismissed but you are owed money because you did not receive the correct notice.

You may also be able to sue your employer for negligence say because you were injured at work. See *Taking things further*, and take advice.

If you are owed money such as wages, notice pay, redundancy pay or compensation ordered by a tribunal and your employer has gone bust, you can claim from the Department of Employment's Insolvency Fund. Take advice on the procedures.

Disputes about Statutory Maternity Pay or Statutory Sick Pay

If you disagree with your employer over your entitlement to Statutory Maternity Pay or Statutory Sick Pay and you cannot get anywhere by complaining, ask the employer for a written statement. This should set out their reasons and how much they think you are entitled to (if anything) and for what dates. Within six months of the dispute, write, sending the statement to your local **National Insurance Contributions Office** (NICO – part of the Inland Revenue) to ask them to make a formal decision.

If this is in your favour and the employer then still refuses to pay up the Inland Revenue will pay you instead, unless the employer decides to appeal in which case you will have to wait until the result of that is known. If the decision goes against you, you can appeal within 30 days by sending an appeal form to the NICO (see also *Inland Revenue*). While this is all going on, you may be entitled to social security (see *Social security*).

If you have been off work ill for 23 weeks, your employer should send you the form SSP1 so you can claim other social security when your Statutory Sick Pay ends after 28 weeks. If they refuse, complain. Failing that you can ask the local NICO to intervene on your behalf.

Useful addresses

ACAS Public Enquiry Points
Birmingham – 0121 456 5434
Bristol – 0117 946 9555

Cardiff – 029 2076 2636
Fleet – 01252 816 650
Glasgow – 0141 248 1400
Kent – 01892 837 273
Leeds – 0113 205 3800
Liverpool – 0151 728 5600
London – 020 7396 5100
Manchester – 0161 833 8500
Newcastle upon Tyne – 0191 269 6000
Nottingham – 0115 985 8253
Suffolk – 01284 774 500

Advisory Conciliation and Arbitration Service (ACAS)
Head Office
Brandon House
180 Borough High Street
London SE1 1LW
Tel: 020 7210 3613
Helpline: 0845 747 4747
Textphone: 0845 606 1600
Website: www.acas.org.uk

Department of Trade and Industry's Website, TIGER
Website: www.tiger.gov.uk

Employment Tribunals Service
Website: www.employmenttribunals.gov.uk

England and Wales
100 Southgate Street
Bury St. Edmunds IP33 2AQ
Tel: 01284 762 171
Fax: 01284 706 064
Email: buryet@ets.gsi.gov.uk

Scotland
Eagle Building
215 Bothwell Street
Glasgow G2 72S
Tel: 0141 204 0730

Fax: 0141 204 0732
Email: glasgowet@ets.gsi.gov.uk

Health and Safety Executive
HSE Infoline
Caerphilly Business Park
Caerphilly CF83 3GG
Information line: 08701 545 500
Fax: 029 20 859 260
Email: hseinformationservices@natbrit.com
Website: www.hse.gov.uk
There is a network of regional and local offices – see your phone book

National Minimum Wage Enquiries
Freepost PHQ1
Newcastle upon Tyne
NE 98 1ZH
Helpline: 0845 600 0678
Email: team.nmw@irdv.dti.gov.uk
Website: www.dti.gov.uk/er/nmw

Public Concern at Work
Suite 306
16 Baldwins Gardens
London EC1N 7RJ
Tel: 020 7404 6609
Fax: 020 7404 6576
Email: whistle@pcaw.demon.co.uk
Website: www.pcaw.demon.co.uk

Sample letter 32: Invoking grievance procedure

1, Any Street
Anytown
Anyshire
AN1 2YZ

25th June, 2003

Employer
Human Resources Manager

Dear Sir,

Re: *Marketing* Department, Payroll number *123*, National Insurance No. *PF 121 212 522*

I am very concerned that I have been put under pressure to do work, which is not only outside my job specification but also for which I have received no prior training. This work involves *designing the company's website, despite the fact that I have no experience in HTML or Java whatsoever.*

I have raised the matter informally with my line manager but he says there is nothing he can do. Therefore I feel I have no alternative but to invoke the formal grievance procedures as set out in the Staff Handbook. I understand from the procedures that you are the person I should write to in the first instance. I further understand that I have the right to a hearing under the procedure, and the statutory right to be accompanied under the Employment Protection Act 1999.

I look forward to attending such a hearing to explain my grievance within the next five working days as set out in the procedure.

I look forward to your reply.

Yours faithfully,

David Chambers

David Chambers

Sample letter 33: Complaint about unauthorised deduction from wages

1, Any Street
Anytown
Anyshire
AN1 2YZ

25th June, 2003

Employer

Dear Sir,

Re: *Marketing* Department, Payroll number *123*, National Insurance No. *PF 121 212 522*

My contract of employment states that on *1st July* each year my pay should increase in line with inflation (see Section 10.2 of my written statement of employment particulars). I have received *two* monthly salary payments (*15th July and 15th August*) and to date such a pay increase has yet to be awarded.

I telephoned your office and have been told the matter is being looked into, but as yet nothing has happened. I am writing to inform you that failure to pay my contractual pay increase constitutes an unauthorised deduction from my wages and this is illegal under Section 13 of the Employment Rights Act 1996.

I would be pleased if you would include the increase backdated to *1st July* in my next salary payment due *15th September*. If you fail to do so I have been advised that I have a right to appeal to an Employment Tribunal.

I would be pleased if you would confirm that you will grant the pay rise to which I am entitled.

Yours faithfully,

David Chambers

David Chambers

Estate agents

Initially try to get an explanation informally from the member of staff dealing with you. If you are still dissatisfied complain to the manager and then the Head Office or a director of the firm. Larger firms will have complaints procedures set out. Where the agent is acting as an accommodation or managing agent and you are a tenant see *Landlords*.

You could also take your complaint to **Trading Standards,** as they have statutory responsibilities for monitoring estate agents. Additionally you could go to the **National Association of Estate Agents** if either the company itself is a member or if a principal in the firm is a member. You will have grounds for complaint if there has been a breach of the Rules of Conduct, which are rules covering the selling, buying and letting of property. Also you can complain to the **Ombudsman for Estate Agents** if the Estate Agent is a member of the Corporate Estate Agents Scheme.

- If you suffer inconvenience or loss as a result of an inaccurate or misleading description of a property, for example you wasted your time by visiting the property, complain as above. In serious cases Trading Standards may prosecute. If you can prove loss, you may be able to take legal action, even if there is a written disclaimer denying responsibility for inaccuracies – take advice.

- To dispute a bill, first get a breakdown of the costs. Then check whether you have to pay for anything other than what it says in your agreement, or other information you may have received from the agent. If you are a seller you may have signed an agreement, which binds you to pay a fee even if you found the buyer yourself, ('sole selling rights') or if you changed to another agent ('sole agency'). If you still dispute   charges, seek an explanation from the agent dealing with you. Next, complain as above, see sample letter 34, paying that part of the bill that you agree with. If the agent sues you, you will have to dispute liability in court. See *Taking things further*.

- If you are dissatisfied and want to switch to another agent check the agreement you have with the present agent as above. You may be tied into using this agent for a time period and end up having to pay them as well as the new agent if the latter achieved a sale.

- If you think you did not get the best deal, for example your property was sold for less than it should have been because of the agent failed to pass on a higher offer, or set the price too low in the first place, you will need evidence to back up your complaint or take legal action for negligence.

Useful addresses

National Association of Estate Agents (NAEA)
Arbon House
21 Jury Street
Warwick CV34 4EH
Tel: 01926 496 800
Fax: 01926 400 953
Email: info@naea.co.uk
Website: www.naea.co.uk

Ombudsman for Estate Agents
Beckett House
4 Bridge Street
Salisbury
Wiltshire SP1 2 LX
Tel: 01722 333 306
Fax: 01722 332 296
Email: admin@oea.co.uk
Website: www.oea.co.uk

Sample letter 34: Disputing an estate agent's claim for commission

1, Any Street
Anytown
Anyshire
AN1 2YZ

25th June, 2003

Estate Agent

Dear Sirs,

Re: Reference Number *025 – 25, Barons Road, West Wittering*

I am in receipt of your invoice dated *19th June* for *£1,075* commission but I am writing to inform you that I do not accept liability for these charges.

You advise me that you have invoiced me because you introduced *Miss Jones* to me as a buyer who was 'able and willing to complete the transaction'. However, the agreement between us states that you would only be paid commission if you introduced me to someone who actually bought the property. As I have not sold the property to *Miss Jones*, I do not believe that commission is due to you. The reason I did not sell it is that I *have taken the property off the market, as your agency staff should know because I informed them two weeks ago on 11th June.* I enclose a copy of my letter instructing you to do this.

Please confirm that you no longer hold me liable. If you pursue the matter further I will continue to resist, if necessary in the County court. I will also draw the matter to the attention of the Ombudsman for Estate Agents.

Yours faithfully,

David Chambers

David Chambers

Enc.

Funeral services

You may be dissatisfied with the way in which a funeral service was organised, or you may be in dispute about their charges or monies held.

First raise the concern informally with the company, preferably the person you discussed the funeral with in the first place. Possibly it may turn out that the complaint should be directed to another party, for example, the crematorium if a service overran and the funeral was held up as a result. If this approach fails, complain in writing to the owner or most senior manager of the company (large firms will probably have a complaints procedure). See sample letter 35.

The Funeral Ombudsman Scheme closed on September 2002. However, the majority of the 4,000 or so funeral directors in the UK belong to one of three trade associations. These are the **Funeral Standards Council**, the **National Association of Funeral Directors** and the **Society of Allied and Independent Funeral Directors**. Each association has its own complaints and resolution arbitration scheme, which should be your first port of call if you have a complaint.

Crematoria and burial grounds

To complain first establish who provides the facilities. If it is a private company find out their complaints procedures (See *Buying services*). If it is the local authority see *Local authorities*. If it is a church or religious organisation you will need to contact the church incumbent and, failing this, take the matter up with the church hierarchy (for example, in a Church of England Church you would go to the vicar, then the Bishop via the Diocesan Register)

Legal action

As with all services you can take legal action for breach of contract or negligence if you have suffered a loss. Take advice but with funeral companies if you do this you

cannot then go to the Ombudsman. You could take legal action if you do not want to accept the Ombudsman's award.

Useful addresses

The Funeral Standards Council
30 North Road
Cardiff CF10 3DY
Tel: 029 2038 2046
Fax: 029 2034 3557
Website: www.funeral-standards-council.co.uk

The National Association of Funeral Directors
618 Warwick Road, Solihull
West Midlands B91 1AA
Tel: 0121 711 1343
Fax: 0121 711 1351
Email: info@nafd.org.uk
Website: www.nafd.org.uk

The Society of Allied and Independent Funeral Directors
SAIF Business Centre
3 Bullfields, Sawbridgeworth
Herts CM21 9DB
Tel: 0845 230 6777
Fax: 01279 726 300
Email: info@saif.org.uk
Website: www.saif.org.uk

Sample letter 35: Complaint to a funeral company

1, Any Street
Anytown
Anyshire
AN1 2YZ

Funeral company

Dear Sirs,

Re: 3pm on *12th April, 2003, Holy Trinity Church,* deceased *Ethel Snodgrass*

When my *Aunt Ethel (Ethel Snodgrass)* died I, and indeed most people in the village where she had lived *for forty years,* wanted her funeral to be a fitting and moving tribute to this dear lady*'s sterling and dedicated good work for the community through her longstanding membership of the local WI, the Holy Trinity Church and the Parish Council.*

I was advised by the villagers that I could do no better than contract your company to make all the necessary arrangements.

Your staff will confirm that I was less than happy with the way you organised the funeral. *Not only was the funeral cortege 25 minutes late in arriving at the church, but after the service, it travelled direct to the crematorium, despite the fact that I had specifically requested that the cortege take the route past the parish council offices and drive slowly past them in recognition of her long association with them. Moreover we were all very disappointed to discover that only three of the floral tributes were placed at the crematorium as instructed. Your Mr Smith said the other four had 'vanished'; yet he was able to locate them in the boot of one of your limousines two hours later.*

This was always going to be a sad day for all concerned but I and all who attended the funeral never expected the event to be marred by your company's apparent incompetence.

Doubtless you will be sending me your invoice shortly – I would expect you to make an adjustment to this to my satisfaction before I consider making any payment to you. I look forward also to your full apology for the additional distress caused, so that I might communicate these to all those who mourned *Ethel's* passing. Failing this, I will not hesitate to make a formal complaint to the Funeral Standards Council.

Yours faithfully,

David Chambers

David Chambers

Gas services

Your gas supply will be under contract with a gas supplier company or with British Gas Trading Ltd. A separate company, **British Gas TransCo** is the only public gas transporter and is responsible for gas pipelines, gas storage and dealing with emergencies such as leaks. Use the company's complaints procedure (they all have to have one) and also ask for compensation where you feel they have fallen short of their standards as set out in their publicity or contract with you.

- If you are not happy with the company's response, take your complaint on to **Energywatch** – see sample letter 36. They can negotiate with the supplier after investigation and, depending on your case, recommend that the supplier compensate you. Energywatch cannot force a company to take action but they may advise you to take your complaint to the **Office of Gas and Electricity Markets (OfGEM)** if they think the company is breaking one of its licence conditions. For Northern Ireland, contact the **General Consumer Council** and the **Office for the Regulation of Gas and Electricity**.

- If you are unhappy with a supplier's sales methods, for example, misleading you or being too pushy, complain to the supplier initially. Next, contact the **Association of Energy Suppliers** if the supplier is a member as they enforce a code of practice on marketing. See sample letter 37.

- You have a right to a supply though you may have to pay British Gas TransCo or an independent engineer to connect you to the main. There are exceptions, for example where the pipes are in a dangerous condition, where your supply has been disconnected or you refuse to provide suitable security if requested (e.g. a deposit, a guarantor, joining a regular payment plan). To complain about a refusal contact Energywatch. If your complaint is about the level of a deposit requested they may refer the matter to OfGEM.

- Call out **British Gas TransCo** if there is a gas leak. They will repair pipes on the mains side of the gas meter, but beyond this it will be the property owner's responsibility so they may just disconnect the supply until the repairs are carried out if this is the only way of solving the problem, or, in the case of a faulty appliance, either carry out a minor repair or prohibit its usage. If you are a pensioner, disabled or in poor health they should ensure you have alternative heating and cooking facilities if they cut you off so complain to them if they fail to do this.

- If you are a tenant your landlord has an obligation to ensure any gas appliances provided are safe, and any appliances you purchase should be safe (see *Buying goods*).

- If your complaint is against a gas installer see *Buying services*. Also contact the **Council for Registered Gas Installers (CORGI)**.

- If you are dissatisfied with a supplier usually you can end your contract with them by giving 28 days notice (48 hours if you are moving house). You may be able to complain that terms in your contract with the supplier are unfair and challenge them in court (see *Buying services*).

- Whether you can complain about a price increase depends on the contract. If it is not allowed for, complain. If you give notice to end the contract the price increase will not apply.

- If instead of a credit meter you want a prepayment meter installed the company should oblige, unless they think it is not safe or practical to do so. Again, complain if you disagree with them on this.

- If you think your bill is too high, read your meter and compare it with what is on the bill. It may be wrong either because the meter was misread or because it is an estimate, and the estimate is too high, or previous bills have been estimates that were too low. If there is a major discrepancy send in the correct reading immediately and you will be sent a new bill.

- Your bill may be too high because of a faulty meter. If you complain the supplier can arrange for your meter to be independently tested by the **OfGEM Technical Directorate** (see sample letter 38). You will have to pay a fee if the meter turns out to be OK, but if it is overcharging by more than two per cent, the supplier will pay this fee and refund the amount overpaid since the penultimate meter reading.

Useful addresses

Association of Energy Suppliers (AES)
30 Millbank
London SW1P 4RD
Tel: 020 7963 5700
Fax: 020 7963 5959
Website: www.aes.org.uk

British Gas Transco
31 Homer Road
Solihull
West Midlands B91 3LT
Tel: 0121 626 4431
Emergency number: 0800 111 999
Website: www.transco.uk.com

British Gas
Website: www.gas.co.uk

Council for Registered Gas Installers (CORGI)
1 Elmwood
Chineham Business Park
Crockford Lane
Basingstoke RG24 8WG
Tel: 01256 372 200
Email: enquiries@corgi-gas.com
Website: www.corgi-gas.com

Energywatch
4th Floor, Artillery House
Artillery Row
London SW1P 1RT
Tel: 0845 906 0708
Fax: 020 7799 8341
Textphone: 0845 7581 401
Email: enquiries@energywatch.org.uk
Website: www.energywatch.org.uk

General Consumer Council for Northern Ireland

Elizabeth House
116 Hollywood Road
Belfast BT4 1NY
Tel: 028 9067 2488
Complaints line: 0845 601 6022
Fax: 028 9065 7701
Email: info@gccni.org.uk
Website: www.gccni.org.uk

Office for the Regulation of Electricity and Gas

Brookmount Buildings
42 Fountain Street
Belfast BT1 5EE
Tel: 0845 764 3643
Website: www.ofreg.nics.gov.uk

OfGEM

Website: www.ofgem.gov.uk

England & Wales
9 Millbank
London SW1P 3GE
Tel: 020 7901 7217/7003
Fax: 020 7901 7378
Email: library@ofgem.gov.uk

Scotland
Regents Court
70 West Regent Street
Glasgow G2 2QZ
Tel: 0141 331 2678
Fax: 0141 331 2777

Sample letter 36: Asking Energywatch to intervene in a dispute

1, Any Street
Anytown
Anyshire
AN1 2YZ

25th June, 2003

Energywatch
4th Floor, Artillery House
Artillery Row
London SW1P 1RT

Dear Sirs,

Re: Account No. 1725 – Acme Gas Company

I am writing regarding my dispute with the above gas company, which has yet to be resolved.

Please refer to the enclosed bills and correspondence relating to this case, which concerns the fact that *they have overcharged me for the amount of £150.*

I should be grateful if you would please look into this case on my behalf. I understand that during your investigation my gas supply will not be interrupted.

Please keep me informed on the status of my case.

Yours faithfully,

David Chambers

David Chambers

Sample letter 37: Complaint about sales methods

1, Any Street
Anytown
Anyshire
AN1 2YZ

25th June, 2003

Association of Energy Suppliers
30 Millbank
London SW1P 4RD

Dear Sirs,

Re: *Acme* Company

I am writing to complain about the sales methods of the above company, which I feel has been in breach of your Code of Practice for Marketing. The problem I have experienced is as follows:

In recent marketing literature, Acme stated that if one's monthly household charges were over £70 per month and one joined their 'Savers' scheme, one could receive a 15% discount. I joined this scheme on 25th March but have not received any discount on my past three bills.

I have attempted to resolve this matter by complaining to the company, but to no avail. I enclose a copy of my correspondence with the company.

Please could you investigate this complaint and order the company to compensate me. I look forward to your reply.

Yours faithfully,

David Chambers

David Chambers

Sample letter 38: Disputing the bill

1, Any Street
Anytown
Anyshire
AN1 2YZ

25th June, 2003

Gas Company

Dear Sirs,

Re: Account No. *1725*

I have received my bill dated *12th June, 2003* regarding the above account.

The amount of the bill appears to be far above my normal usage for this time of year, and I can only think that either the gas meter is faulty or you have made a billing error.

Please respond with an appropriate adjustment on the bill or a proposed date for an Office of Gas and Electricity Markets (OfGEM) engineer to come and test the meter.

Yours faithfully,

David Chambers

David Chambers

Holidays

This chapter covers package and non-package holidays abroad and in the UK.

Non-package holidays

British law may apply if you booked in Britain as a result of the trader advertising here (for example a hotel). But otherwise the law of the country concerned will apply. Of course if your entire holiday was in Britain, British law applies throughout, but there may be some variations if you live in England and you travel to Scotland or vice versa.

If you are on holiday complain direct to the person responsible, for example, the manager. Also, unless things are completely resolved, keep a log of events including any photographic evidence you can get, for example a dirty swimming pool. If your complaint is about accommodation, and you are offered an alternative, which you consider unsatisfactory, you must decide whether to carry on complaining, to reject the offer and go elsewhere, to go home or to accept the offer 'under protest.' If you decide on the latter course of action put this in writing, preferably in the language of the country, reserving your right to claim damages later on.

Use this evidence to complain when you get home. If British law does not apply, a **European Consumer Centre** may help if it was a European Union country, or if you need to take legal action, the **Law Society** will refer you to a specialist solicitor (see *Buying goods*). Take advice. See also *Hotels, Airlines and airports* and *Buying services.*

Package holidays

If you booked a holiday abroad from the UK as a package, UK law will apply if you have a complaint about anything included in the package, such as flights, accommodation, food and trips.

For a package, your complaint is against the tour operator, even though a travel agent may have handled your booking, except in cases where the travel agent operated the tour itself. You have cause for complaint if the tour operator has not kept to their side of the agreement or if you feel you have been mislead in any way.

Details of the agreement will be found in the booking conditions in the holiday brochure, together with any other publicity such as photographs, advertising, and so on. The Package Travel Regulations state that the brochure must contain clear details of what you should expect including arrangements that will apply if you are delayed.

First see the courier or local representative of the tour operator or contact their local office if there is one. Otherwise phone the customer service people at their head office. Keep a diary for non-package holidays.

When you get back write directly to the tour operator referring to any evidence, witnesses etc (see sample letter 39) – they will have a customer services section. Alternatively, the travel agent may be prepared to take the complaint up for you. Any evidence you have collected, including your 'diary of events,' will help you with your case. Also **Trading Standards** may intervene and pave the way for you to get compensation if there has been a breach of the Package Holiday Regulations or related legislation.

If you are dissatisfied with what you are offered you could take the matter further within the company. If this does not work either take your case to the Association of British Travel Agents (ABTA) or the **Association of Independent Tour Operators (AITO)** if the tour operator is a member. They will investigate free of charge and you could use their arbitration service. Alternatively, you could take legal action (see *Taking things further*). Take advice.

- The tour operator may try to dispute liability by citing clauses in the booking conditions that say they do not accept responsibility if your holiday is disrupted by something like bad weather or an airport strike which is outside their control. If this happens you could take advice to see if you could take legal action on the basis that the clauses were unreasonable. However, you may be able to claim on your holiday insurance or against another party, for example the airline. Take advice.

- If your holiday is cancelled, you can ask for your money back if the operator is unable to offer you a satisfactory alternative. If it is too late for you to book another holiday you can claim compensation for disappointment as well as your money back. If the only other holidays available are more expensive, you may be able to claim the extra from your tour operator. Take legal advice.

- You will have to pay surcharges if they are to cover unforeseen events unless the operator has guaranteed prices, but you should make sure the operator could justify the charges. If you are not happy try to pay 'under protest' and reserve your right to claim a refund later.

- If your travel agent goes bust, so long as the booking has been confirmed with the tour operator your holiday is safe.

- If it has not been confirmed, or if the tour operator goes bust, contact the **Association of British Travel Agents (ABTA)** if the operator is a member. You will, if necessary, be offered an alternative holiday or else be given a refund. If your tour operator goes bust while you are on holiday, ABTA will help get you home. If you bought the holiday on credit, you may be able to claim compensation from the credit company (see *Credit)*.

- If your holiday airline goes bust your flight will be guaranteed under a bonding scheme covered under the Air Travel Organisers Licence (ATOL) held by your tour operator. If you have any difficulties, contact the **Civil Aviation Authority (ATOL)** section. The tour operator will make alternative plans for you if the airline goes out of business before you fly out.

- Similar schemes exist for journeys on ferries and ships and coach holidays, if the company is a member of the **Passenger Shipping Association** or the Bonded Coach Holidays Section of the **Confederation of Passenger Transport** respectively.

- If you paid for the package or any element of the holiday on credit you may be able to claim money back from the creditor. See *Credit*.

- With delays, missed connections or overbooking complain as above (see sample letter 40). The representative of the tour operator should ensure you are properly attended to and if necessary give meal vouchers and find accommodation for the night. If you suffer a very long delay in setting out you may be able to cancel the holiday and claim a refund, as well as other compensation. The Package Holiday Regulations say that you are entitled to compensation or an alternative holiday if the package is cancelled due to overbooking. Alternatively your holiday insurance cover may compensate you.

If you were booked on a scheduled, as opposed to a chartered flight, you may be able to claim under the denied booking compensation rules. See *Airlines and airports*.

Useful addresses

Association of British Travel Agents (ABTA)
68-71 Newman Street
London W1T 3AH
Tel: 020 7637 2444
Fax: 020 7637 0713
Email: information@abta.co.uk
Website: www.abtanet.com

Association of Independent Tour Operators (AITO)
133A St. Margaret's Road
Twickenham
Middlesex TW1 1RG
Tel: 020 8744 9280
Fax: 020 8744 3187
Email: info@aito.co.uk
Website: www.aito.co.uk

Civil Aviation Authority
CAA House
45-59 Kingsway
London WC2B 6TE

Tel: 020 7379 7311
Website: www.caa.co.uk

Confederation of Passenger Transport
Imperial House
15-19 Kingsway
London WC2 6UN
Tel: 020 7240 3131
Fax: 020 7240 6565
Website: www.cpt-uk.org

Passenger Shipping Association
Walmar House
288-292 Regent Street
London W1R 5HE
Tel: 020 7436 2449
Fax: 020 7636 9206
Email: admin@psa-psara.org
Website: www.psa-psara.org

Sample letter 39: Complaint to a tour operator about a misleading description

1, Any Street
Anytown
Anyshire
AN1 2YZ

25th June, 2003

Tour Operator

Dear Sirs,

Re: Reference Number *330, Club Kosos, 24th April – 7th May, 2003*

I am writing to express my disappointment regarding the above holiday I took with your company costing £650.

The description of the hotel in your catalogue was misleading for the following reasons:
1. The hotel was still in the process of being built
2. There were no crèche facilities

On *25th April* I made a complaint about this to your local courier *Mr Tim Stewarts* but to no effect. I enclose photographs and copies of testimonials from other disgruntled holidaymakers for your information.

The brochure description and photographs form part of the contract between us. As they were misleading this amounts to misrepresentation and a breach of the Trade Descriptions Act 1968 and the Package Holiday Regulations. I am therefore holding you in breach of contract and am claiming compensation for the disappointment and loss of enjoyment suffered, and for the additional expenses incurred for which I am enclosing receipts. In the circumstances, I consider £300 to be a reasonable compensatory sum.

I look forward to receiving your offer within 10 days. Failing that I will pursue the matter in the County court without further notice, and will also complain to the Trading Standards Service.

Yours faithfully,

David Chambers

David Chambers

Enc.

Sample letter 40: Complaint to a tour operator about change of hotel at short notice due to overbooking

1, Any Street
Anytown
Anyshire
AN1 2YZ

25th June, 2003

Tour Operator

Dear Sirs,

Re: Reference Number *330, Club Kosos,Greece, 30th June to 13th July, 2003*

I am writing to express my disappointment in the fact that the hotel you arranged for me to stay in has been overbooked. You have advised me of this today at *5pm*, just *five* days before I am due to travel. I note that you have offered me a hotel at a different resort or alternatively will allow me to cancel and receive a full refund.

You will be aware that in failing to find me accommodation at the above hotel you are in breach of an express term of the contract between us. I confirm I will accept your offer of alternative accommodation since it is now too late for me to book a holiday elsewhere but I do so under protest. Please note that my acceptance does not affect my legal rights to claim compensation from your company upon my return for any losses I incur, including the loss of enjoyment I suffer.

In respect of this I will write to you on my return.

Yours faithfully,

David Chambers

David Chambers

Hotels and guest houses

There may be complaints procedures if, for example, the hotel or guest house is part of a chain – see *Buying services*. Otherwise you may need to deal with the manager or owner direct. If you get no joy you can complain to Trading Standards who may investigate. Also the tourist authorities publish information on hotel standards, so they may be interested to know if a hotel has fallen short of these standards.

Disputing the bill

Complain if you are charged more than the charges agreed at the time you booked the room, provided the hotel confirmed the booking. If you book on arrival, complain if the hotel charges more than the prices displayed in reception or at the entrance. Prices must include VAT. If you have to pay do this under protest, but if possible pay what was originally agreed as the correct price, then the balance would have to be disputed in court (as for *Restaurants and cafés*).

There is a **Code of Booking Practice**, which requires hotels to be specific about what is available for the price in question so take advice. If your hotel subscribes to this but has still mislead you or has been unclear about what you have booked you have extra grounds for complaint.

- If the room is not available due to overbooking you can complain if you are not offered a reasonable alternative or a refund. You may also be entitled to compensation to cover extra costs including inconvenience and loss of enjoyment.

- If your property is lost, stolen or damaged while in a hotel premises you can normally claim compensation from the hotel at certain fixed rates. This will not usually include your car parked outside a hotel or any valuables left in it. Hotels can limit the amount of compensation they must pay if they display a notice at reception to this effect. However you can claim more than these limits if you can prove that the hotel has been negligent, say if you had specially asked the hotel to look after the goods – take advice. With other establishments the above compensation scheme does not apply, so legal action (or the threat of it) is the only option here.

- If you have booked accommodation in a hotel specifying certain requirements and they turn out not as described, for example, you were told it would be room with a double bed and sea view, and you are given a room with twin beds facing a cement factory, first ask to be transferred to a more suitable room. If the proprietor cannot do this, take the action on disputing the bill as above (see sample letter 41), and go to **Trading Standards**. See also *Advertising*.

- In a hotel you may have grounds for complaint if no food or drink was available on request. Hotels by law should offer travellers food, alcoholic drink and sleeping accommodation at a reasonable time. In the case of other establishments you would only have grounds if an agreement to provide food and drink had been broken.

- Whether a hotel or a guest house, the standard of accommodation must be reasonable bearing in mind the type and price of the establishment. If you are dissatisfied and cannot sort things out with the management you could consider disputing the bill as above. With noise you should complain straight away but whether you have strong grounds will depend on how loud it was in the circumstances, whether you were warned in advance, and whether the hotel describes itself in the brochure as 'quiet' or 'exclusive.' Take advice.

- If the hotel is outside the UK, British law may apply in some circumstances or, in Europe, a **European Consumer Centre** may help you pursue your complaint. See *Buying goods*. If you booked as part of a package holiday, see *Holidays*.

Sample letter 41: Complaint about misdescription

1, Any Street
Anytown
Anyshire
AN1 2YZ

25th June, 2003

Hotel Manager

Dear Sir,

Re: Reference Number 4554 – Room *101* booked for *four nights*

I am writing to make a formal complaint about your hotel. We raised this issue at the time of my stay, but your duty manager said that he had no authority to make a decision and that I should complain in writing.

My complaint is that we booked *a double room via your Internet website and in your description you clearly stated that the room in question contained a double bed and 'panoramic views of the beautiful coastline' – one of the 12 in your 'deluxe' range in fact. Imagine our disappointment on our arrival therefore to find that the room did not face the coast at all but a large car park fronting what appeared to be some kind of cement factory. The coastline was only visible if I leaned perilously far out of the window and twisted my neck to the right - a manoeuvre only remotely safe if my wife held me tight by the legs to stop me falling. We asked to be transferred to another room but we were informed that they were all fully booked.*

You have failed accurately to describe the facilities available at the hotel, and you have grossly misled us about *the view*. This amounts to misdescription. As the description on your website was embodied in our contract, you are also in breach of contract. Please note that I have reported the matter to the local Trading Standards Service.

You will be aware that I only paid the hotel bill under duress, reserving my right to take legal action against your hotel. Note that I am legally entitled to receive compensation from your hotel for the disappointment and loss of enjoyment suffered. In consequence, I am claiming the sum of £100.

Please let me have your decision within 14 days. If I am still dissatisfied I will not hesitate to sue your hotel in the County court.

Yours faithfully,

David Chambers

David Chambers

Inland Revenue

Here we cover the Inland Revenue's responsibility for taxation, particularly Income Tax but also the National Insurance Contribution system. To find out about appealing to the Inland Revenue about Statutory Sick Pay and Statutory Maternity Pay, see *Employment.*

There are two complaining routes – one if you are dissatisfied with the way your affairs are treated, another if you are disputing liability. Of course your complaint may mean you have to pursue both routes at once! Whatever your route, first see if you can resolve the matter informally by phoning or visiting the office for your tax district. Your correspondence should tell you where this is. Alternatively, there should be an **Inland Revenue Enquiry Office** you could contact in your area.

Treated badly?

If you feel you are getting poor service, not being treated fairly, or not being given enough time to pay arrears of tax, ask for a copy of the Taxpayers Charter and the relevant Code of Practice as this sets out standards. For example, there is a Code Of Practice on Mistakes. You can then make reference to these in a letter to strengthen your case, asking for compensation if needed. If your complaint is about a tax district write to the District Inspector, if it is a collection office write to the Collector in Charge, if its to do with National Insurance contact the **National Insurance Contributions Office (NICO)** you have been dealing with. Head your letter 'Taxpayers Charter' as this will help you get a speedy response! See sample letter 42. Take advice, or contact an **Inland Revenue Enquiry Centre** in your area.

If you are still unhappy, write to ask the **Controller** for your area to review your case – your local office will give you contact details. If you do not like the response write to the **Revenue Adjudicator.** In dire circumstances you can go to the Adjudicator direct, for example where any delay could cause irreparable damage. As an alternative to this you could complain via your MP to the **Parliamentary Ombudsman** (see *Public services*).

If you think you are being asked to pay too much tax

Before disputing your tax liability:

- If you are an employee, check the correct amount of tax is being deducted from your earnings in accordance with your tax code. The employer could have made a mistake, if so see *Employment.*

- Check to see if any mistakes have been made by the Inland Revenue in calculating your tax, and whether you have claimed all the allowances and reliefs applicable to your circumstances – you can go back six years.

If you cannot resolve the matter informally with the tax office (or NICO) staff you can make a formal appeal to that office. A separate officer of the Inland Revenue will look at your case again.

Then, if you still disagree, appeal to the independent tribunal known as the **Commissioners** (see sample letter 43). This must be done in writing within 30 days of you receiving notification of the decision, except where you disagree with a PAYE coding which may be made any time in the tax year. A late appeal may be accepted but if it is not, you can appeal against the refusal. In your letter also apply for the collection of all or some of the tax to be postponed. If you do not do this, the Revenue may keep pursuing you for the tax even though you are appealing.

Your case will then be considered by the **General Commissioners** (lay people) but where a complex legal point is at issue you can ask for the case to be heard by the **Special Commissioners** (tax lawyers) instead. A formal hearing will take place. If you wish to appeal against the Commissioners decision you may be able to go to the **High Court**. Take advice on preparing your case and, if necessary, finding someone to represent you.

Arrears of tax arising due to an Inland Revenue mistake

If the Inland Revenue say you owe them money for a particular tax year, you may be able to get these arrears waived or appeal if this request is refused. This will be possible if (a) they had all the information they needed to make a decision and (b) by the time they let you know more than 12 months had gone by since the end of that tax year (exceptionally they may waive if its less than 12 months), or (c) you reasonably believed your tax affairs were in order. You can also get arrears waived if the tax office paid you too much tax rebate, then tried to reclaim it after the end of the tax year. When you claim say you are doing it under Extra Statutory Concession A.

Complaining about tax credits

To complain about the administration of tax credits first contact the person or office you have been dealing with. If necessary, then complain further to the Customer Service Manager of the relevant **Tax Credit Office (TCO)**. Then complain to the Director of the TCO. This complaints procedure is explained in the leaflet IR120 '*Tax Credit Office – You and the Inland Revenue*', available from Inland Revenue Enquiry Centres and the TCO helpline. You may be able to claim compensation. Take advice or contact the above Helpline. If you are not satisfied with the response of the Director of the TCO, complain to the **Independent Adjudicator** as above.

Sample letter 42: Complaint to a Tax District about services

1, Any Street
Anytown
Anyshire
AN1 2YZ

25th June, 2003

District Inspector
Tax Officer

Dear Sirs,

Re: Tax Reference Number *75985 2505 – Bristol* Tax District Office

I am writing to complain of what I regard as most unfair treatment at the hands of officers of your Tax District, treatment that in my view directly contravenes the Taxpayers Charter.

The circumstances are as follows: *I have tax payment arrears in the amount of £3,000 which I was informed in a letter from the Bristol Tax Office (see attached letter dated 12th August, 2002) was not due to be paid in full until April 2004. I have now received, on 1st June, a letter from the same office contradicting their previous statement, informing me that all amounts outstanding must be paid by April 2004. In my present financial situation, this will be an almost impossible task.*

Please investigate urgently and let me know what action you propose to take. If the matter is not dealt with to my satisfaction I will not hesitate to take the matter to the Controller for this area, and then to the Revenue Adjudicator, since I believe, as I hope you do, that the Taxpayers Charter should be enforced at all times.

Please keep me informed of your progress.

Yours faithfully,

David Chambers

David Chambers

Enc.

Sample letter 43: Notice of Appeal

1, Any Street
Anytown
Anyshire
AN1 2YZ

25th June, 2003

District Inspector
Tax Officer

Dear Sir,

Re: Tax Number *9437 55421*

Please regard this letter as a formal appeal for submission to the Commissioners. The reason for my appeal is *that I disagree with the Notice of Assessment issued to me on 31st April, 2003 for the tax year 2003/04.*

My grounds for appeal are:

1. *This Notice of Assessment says that I have underpaid in the tax year 2000/2001. You say that I wrongly received the married couple's allowance because my ex-wife, from whom I was separated, divorced and remarried.*
2. *Although I can now see that I should not have continued to receive the allowance after she remarried on 12th August, 2001, I did in fact advise you of this event and you did nothng until now.*

I am still attempting to negotiate a settlement with the District Office but I am submitting this appeal now in order to remain within the 30-day time limit. I would also like to apply for a postponement of *£630* of the amount of tax you say is due under the assessment, this being the amount I dispute liability for.

I enclose information to support my argument that the Notice of Assessment is incorrect – *a copy of my letter to you informing you of my ex-wife's remarriage.*

I look forward to being told of the date of the hearing, unless the matter is resolved in the meantime.

Yours faithfully,

David Chambers
David Chambers

Enc.

Insurance services

If the insurance company is the problem you could go to the broker or intermediary first (if you used one) and they may attempt to resolve things or arrange a settlement. Otherwise, complain directly to the company (see sample letters 44 and 45), as they will have their own complaints or disputes procedure. If in doubt, speak to their customer services people. If your policy was underwritten at Lloyds contact their complaints department and they will supply a complaints form. If it was with a friendly society you can ask for an internal arbitration to be arranged if your complaint is not resolved. You may have a complaint about an intermediary who sold you insurance but works for another service – see also *Solicitors' practices, Banking services* or *Investments and financial advice* if this applies.

If the complaint is about not meeting your claim you will need to check your policy closely, maybe, for example, you are underinsured or the item or incident you are claiming for may not be covered, or a 'wear and tear" figure may have been deducted. Take advice.

Other bodies you can go to

Next, there are ranges of bodies you can complain to. In the case of a broker the next step will be to write to the **Insurance Brokers Registration Council (IBRC)** – all except Lloyds brokers must be registered with them and they can revoke registration in serious cases. If you are complaining about insurance intermediaries who are not a broker, write to the **Corporation of Insurance and Financial Advisers** if they are a member.

Check if your insurance company is a member of the **Association of British Insurers (ABI)** or the **General Insurance Standards Council (GISC)**. They would then support you, particularly if your complaint shows that the company has contravened codes of practice. The GISC may mediate on your behalf. Otherwise these organisations may take action for you depending again if the company is a member: the **Financial Ombudsman Service**, the **Personal Investment Authority (PIA)**, the **Ombudsman Bureau** and the **Personal Insurance Arbitration Service (PIAS)**. For the PIA you should complain within six months of the final decision of the insurance company. They will give the company the chance to resolve the problem otherwise they will investigate. They can make a binding recommendation that the insurance provider changes its policies, and can order the provider to pay compensation. If you complain to the PIAS they will arbitrate if the insurance provider agree and the decision will be binding on the company.

Legal action

You could consider taking legal action against the company; they may, for example, be in breach of their policy – take advice. If you do take legal proceedings you cannot then also use the Financial Ombudsman Service, PIA or the PIAS, but you could do this later if you do not accept the decisions of these bodies. If you sue a broker and they do not pay up, you can then ask the IBRC to make a payment instead so long as you do this within six months.

- If you used a loss adjuster to help you with a claim and you were unhappy about their work, use internal complaints procedures. If these get you nowhere take the matter up with the **Institute of Public Loss Assessors**.

- If you fail to pay your premium on time, your insurance policy will lapse so this may cause any claim you make to fail. However, try appealing to the company if it is only a few days late. If you are a longstanding customer they may agree

to consider your claim, or they may allow a short 'period of grace' in the policy. This does not apply to motor insurance.

- Your complaint may be that the final premium you have to pay is different from the quote you originally had. The quote should stand if the insurance provider had the full facts at the time. If you used a broker or intermediary and they passed a quote on to you incorrectly, then you may be able to argue that they should meet the difference. If the insurance company had given inaccurate or out of date information to you or the broker, then they should take the blame and accept the quote. Otherwise you could refuse to take out the policy but you would have to pay for the period you were covered (at the quoted rate). Take advice.

- If your insurance company cannot afford to meet your claim you can ask for it to be met by the **Policyholders Protection Board** but at a rate of 90% with many policies. Lloyds' policies have their own protection so contact **Lloyds of London**. If your insurance broker cannot pay money owed to you, go to the IBRC, or the CIFA in the case of other intermediaries.

Useful addresses

Association of British Insurers (ABI)
51 Gresham Street
London EC2V 7HQ
Tel: 020 7600 3333
Fax: 020 7696 8999
Email: info@abi.org.uk
Website: www.abi.org.uk

Corporation of Insurance and Financial Advisers
174 High Street
Guildford
Surrey GU1 3HW
Tel: 01483 539 121

Financial Ombudsman Service
South Quay Plaza
183 Marsh Wall
London E14 9SR

Tel: 020 7964 1000
Helpline: 0845 080 1800
Fax: 020 7964 1001
Email: complaint.info@financial-ombudsman.org.uk
Website: www.financial-ombudsman.org.uk

General Insurance Standards Council (GISC)

GISC Dispute Resolution Facility
110 Cannon Street
London EC4N 6EU
Tel: 0845 601 2857
Fax: 020 7648 7808
Email: complaints@gisc.co.uk
Website: www.gisc.co.uk

Institute of Public Loss Assessors

14 Red Lion Street
Chesham
Bucks. HP5 1HB
Tel: 01494 782 342
Fax: 01494 774 928

Insurance Brokers Registration Council (IBRC)

The Registrar
Higham Business Centre
Midland Road, Higham Ferrers
Northants NN10 8DQ
Tel: 01933 359 083
Fax: 01933 359 077

Lloyds of London

1 Lime Street
London EC3M 7HA
Tel: 020 7327 5693/6950
Email: complaints@lloyds.com
Website: www.lloyds.com

Personal Investment Authority (PIA)
South Quay Plaza
183 Marsh Wall
London E14 9SR
Tel: 020 7216 0066

Personal Insurance Arbitration Service (PIAS)
Chartered Institute of Arbitrators
12 Bloomsbury Square
London WC1A 2LP
Tel: 020 7421 7444
Fax: 020 7404 4023
Email: info@arbitrators.org
Website: www.arbitrators.org

Sample letter 44: Disputing a decision by an insurance company not to proceed with your claim

1, Any Street
Anytown
Anyshire
AN1 2YZ

25th June, 2003

Insurance Company

Dear Sirs,

Re: Reference Number *24324 – Storm Damage*

I have received your letter dated *16th June* in which you denied liability for my claim of £400 on the above referenced policy.

I reassert the validity of my claim based on the terms of the policy, which states that *a claim can be made for any damage caused by 'an unpreventable accident.'*

Enclosed are photographs *depicting the destruction caused by the storm*, quotations from a loss assessor, and a report written by the repairer detailing the damage *to a previously sound structure.*

Furthermore, I am providing a *report from the Meteorological Office referencing the storm that hit the area on the date the damage occurred.*

I have shown clear and conclusive evidence that the damage was in no way preventable or a result of neglect on my part as your previous correspondence implies.

Please reconsider this claim. I look forward to receiving notice of settlement in a timely fashion. Otherwise I shall have no choice but to refer this matter to the appropriate Insurance Ombudsman without further notice.

Yours faithfully,

David Chambers

David Chambers

Sample letter 45: Disputing a decision by an insurance company to pay you too low an amount

1, Any Street
Anytown
Anyshire
AN1 2YZ

25th June, 2003

Insurance Company

Dear Sirs,

Re: Reference Number *110 – Stolen Necklace*

I am in receipt of your letter dated *12th June, 2003* and consider your offer of £*299* for replacing *my stolen necklace* to be unacceptably low.

The certified quotation I have enclosed shows this item had been valued in the amount of £*500* by *Braithwaite Jewellers* on *1st March, 2003*. I urge you to adjust your offer accordingly.

Please send me your response within 14 days. Otherwise, I shall have no choice but to refer this case to the Insurance Ombudsman Bureau (*or other body if the company is a member*).

Yours faithfully,

David Chambers

David Chambers

Enc.

Investments and financial advice

You would not normally have grounds for complaint if your investment failed to live up to expectations – that is a risk you take. However, you may have grounds if you were badly advised, or you received poor service or you were overcharged.

Tied versus independent financial advisers

You may have had financial advice from a tied adviser or an independent financial adviser, unless they were a solicitor, accountant or insurance broker advising you as part of other work they were doing for you – if so see *Solicitors' practices*, or *Insurance services*. If your complaint is about financial advice or poor service involving a deposit or savings account with a bank or building society see *Banking services* or with the Post Office, see *Post Office and mail delivery*. For complaints about loans including mortgages see *Credit*.

With tied advisers you have grounds for complaint if they fail to identify the company or group of companies that they represent, or if they fail to advise you of the most suitable for you within this portfolio. With independent financial advisers the grounds of complaint will be if they fail to advise you of the range of products on which they are qualified to advise. With both types other grounds for complaint might be poor service quality, or failure to disclose what commission they will receive before they sell the product to you.

Complaining about financial advice and investment companies

To complain about financial advice or investment companies first find out the complaints procedure for the company concerned – see sample letter 47 and 47. Some details may appear in the Terms of Business letter the adviser should have given you at the outset. If you are still dissatisfied you can complain to the appropriate self-regulatory body. These are:

- **The Personal Investment Authority (PIA)** – they will investigate independent financial advisers who are members. See sample letter 48.

- **The Investment Management Regulatory Organisation (IMRO)** – they will investigate complaints against the people who actually manage your investments.

- **The Securities and Futures Authority (SFA)** regulates advisers and dealers in stock and shares, government securities ('gilts'), futures and options.

As an alternative you can complain to a Recognised Professional Body such as **The Law Society** (if a solicitor advised you) the **Institute of Chartered Accountants** or the **Association of Chartered Certified Accountants** (if an accountant advised you). If an insurance company gave the advice you can complain to the **Financial Ombudsman Service** or the **Personal Insurance Arbitration Service**. If representative of a building society or a bank gave the advice you may also have redress via the **Banking Ombudsman** or the **Building Society Ombudsman**. Most of these bodies have an arbitrator or ombudsman who will investigate, and the regulatory bodies are able to award compensation.

Lost money at the hands of the investment company?

If through negligence or fraud you lose money at the hands of an investment company, you may be able to claim compensation from the **Financial Services Compensation Scheme (FSCS)**.

Pensions

For complaints about advice on employer pension schemes and personal pension providers the regulatory body is the **Pensions Advisory Service (OPAS)** and then the **Pensions Ombudsman**.

Mortgage products

If your complaint is to do with products linked to your mortgage, as well as the above, you can use the complaints procedures for banks and building societies (see *Banking services*), culminating in the **Banking Ombudsman** or the **Building Society Ombudsman**. However if the lender or intermediary was not a bank or building society, you can go to the **Mortgage Code Arbitration Scheme**.

The overseers

If you are dissatisfied with any of the complaints procedures operated by the above bodies complain to the **Financial Services Authority (FSA)**. They have overall responsibility for the function of the Regulators, as well as a watchdog role. You should go direct to them if your have general concerns about a company's policy or you feel changes in practice are needed.

Useful addresses

Association of Chartered Certified Accountants
64 Finnieston Square
Glasgow G3 8DT
Tel: 0141 582 2000
Fax: 0141 582 2222
Email: info@accaglobal.com
Website: www.acca.co.uk

The Banking Ombudsman Scheme
Financial Ombudsman Service
South Quay Plaza
183 Marsh Wall
London E14 9SR
Tel: 020 7964 1000
Helpline: 0845 080 1800
Fax: 020 7964 1001
Email: complaint.info@financial-ombudsman.org.uk
Website: www.obo.org.uk

The Building Society Ombudsman
South Quay Plaza
183 Marsh Wall
London E14 9SR
Tel: 020 7964 1000
Helpline: 0845 080 1800
Fax: 020 7964 1001
Email: complaint.info@financial-ombudsman.org.uk
Website: www.financial-ombudsman.org.uk

Financial Services Authority (FSA)
25 The North Colonnade
Canary Wharf
London E14 5HS
Tel: 020 7066 1000
Helpline: 0845 606 1234
Fax: 020 7676 1099
Email: consumerhelp@fsa.gov.uk
Website: www.fsa.gov.uk

The Financial Services Compensation Scheme (FSCS)
7th Floor, Lloyds Chambers
Portsoken Street
London E1 8BN
Tel: 020 7892 7300
Fax: 020 7892 7301
Email: enquiries@fscs.org.uk
Website: www.fscs.org.uk

Institute of Chartered Accountants in England and Wales
Chartered Accountants' Hall
PO Box 433
London EC2P 2BJ
Tel: 020 7920 8100
Fax: 020 7920 0547
Website: www.icaew.co.uk

Institute of Chartered Accountants in Scotland
CA House
21, Haymarket Yards
Edinburgh EH12 5BH
Tel: 0131 347 0100
Fax: 0131 347 0105
Website: www.icas.org.uk

The Investment Management Regulatory Organisation (IMRO)
25 The North Colonnade
Canary Wharf
London E14 5HS

Tel: 020 7676 1000
Helpline: 0845 606 1234
Fax: 020 7676 1009
Website: www.fsa.gov.uk

Law Society
The Law Society's Hall
113 Chancery Lane
London WC2A 1PL
Tel: 020 7242 1222
Email: info.services@lawsociety.org.uk
Website: www.lawsociety.org.uk

The Mortgage Code Arbitration Scheme
Chartered Institute of Arbitrators
12 Bloomsbury Square
London WC1A 2LP
Tel: 020 7421 7444
Fax: 020 7404 4023
Email: info@arbitrators.org
Website: www.arbitrators.org

Occupational Pensions Advisory Service (OPAS)
11 Belgrave Road
London SW1V 1RB
Tel: 020 7233 8080
Fax: 020 7233 8016
Email: opas@iclwebkit.co.uk
Website: www.opas.org.uk

The Pensions Ombudsman
11 Belgrave Road
London SW1V 1RB
Tel: 0845 601 2923
Fax: 020 7233 8016
Email: enquiries@opas.org.uk
Website: www.pensions-ombudsman.org.uk

Personal Insurance Arbitration Service (PIAS)

Chartered Institute of Arbitrators
12 Bloomsbury Square
London WC1A 2LP
Tel: 020 7421 7444
Fax: 020 7404 4023
Email: info@arbitrators.org
Website: www.arbitrators.org

Personal Investment Authority (PIA)

South Quay Plaza
183 Marsh Wall
London E14 9SR
Tel: 020 7216 0066

The Securities and Futures Authority (SFA)

25 The North Colonnade
Canary Wharf
London E14 5HS
Tel: 020 7676 1000
Fax: 020 7676 1099

Sample letter 46: Complaint about poor financial advice

1, Any Street
Anytown
Anyshire
AN1 2YZ

25th June, 2003

Financial Advisers

Dear Sirs,

Re: '*60-100*' Pension Plan

I am writing to express my dissatisfaction with the pension plan you recommended to me.

Following your advice, I switched my pension from the plan offered at work entitled '*Savers*' to a personal scheme referenced above. However, upon receiving my statement on *20th June, 2003,* which reflects the period from *1st April to 1st June,* I was dismayed to find that the plan was in fact inappropriate.

The Financial Services Act 1986 requires you to offer consumers your 'best advice,' taking into account their personal circumstances. You have clearly failed to do so as evidenced by the performance of the above account.

Consequently, I demand you compensate me in the amount of £150. This represents the difference between the monies I will receive from the pension you recommended and what I would have received from an appropriate arrangement, plus your service fee.

I remind you that according to the above Act, you may not ignore this complaint but are required by law to deal with it. You have *14* days in which to respond. Failure to do so will leave me with no choice but to refer this case to the office of the Pensions Ombudsman.

Yours faithfully,

David Chambers

David Chambers

Sample letter 47: Complaint about inappropriate sale of an investment

1, Any Street
Anytown
Anyshire
AN1 2YZ

25th June, 2003

Financial adviser

Dear Sirs,

Re: *ISA* – Reference Number *5454*

On *5th January* this year, I spoke to you about my desire to purchase an investment product that would meet the needs and objectives I clearly outlined to you. The above product was suggested as being appropriate to my circumstances. However, upon receiving my statement on *20th June*, which reflects the period from *20th January* to *20th June, 2003*, I was dismayed to find the investment was in fact, inappropriate.

Again, the following were and still are my investment requirements:

For the amount of £10,000 to be placed in an account were I can receive the minimum of 10% interest.

The Financial Services Act 1986 requires you to offer consumers your 'best advice,' taking into account their personal circumstances. You have clearly failed to do so as evidenced by the performance of the above investment product.

Consequently, I demand you compensate me in the amount of £200. This represents the difference between monies I will receive from your product and what I would have received from an appropriate product.

I remind you that according to the above referenced Act, you may not ignore this complaint, but are in fact required to deal with it. You have *14* days in which to respond. Should I not a receive satisfactory response from you, I am prepared to refer this matter to the Personal Investment Authority Ombudsman Bureau.

Yours faithfully,

David Chambers

David Chambers

Sample letter 48: Complaint to PIA Ombudsman

1, Any Street
Anytown
Anyshire
AN1 2YZ

25th June, 2003

PIA Ombudsman
South Quay Plaza
183 Marsh Wall
London E14 9SR

Dear Sirs,

Re: *Pension People*

I have been in conflict with the above named firm, which I believe is one of your members, for *three months* now and I'm afraid the matter is still yet to be resolved.

Consequently, I am now referring the matter to you. In summary my complaint is as follows:

Pension People advised me to invest in the '60-100' Plan which is extremely inappropriate and contradictory to my requirements, resulting in the loss of £150 when I transferred from my employer's 'Savers' plan.

I would appreciate it if you could review the enclosed correspondence regarding my dispute.

I anticipate your expedient and decisive response.

Yours faithfully,

David Chambers

David Chambers

Enc.

Landlords of long leaseholders

This chapter is for you if you own property leasehold. In complaining refer to the relevant terms in your lease. Sometimes terms may be couched in difficult to understand legalese, if this is the case take advice. Also, not all your rights may be written in the lease so you may find it helpful to consult the Codes of Practice approved by the **Office of the Deputy Prime Minister** as these state the law and good practice. You could also consult the **Leasehold Advisory Service (LEASE)**.

If you live in a block of flats or converted house you may find your dispute is best handled by joining together with the other tenants. Indeed tenants have the right to seek formal recognition for a tenants association if they set one up. Such a body has more rights to information than you have as an individual tenant, for example, the right to be consulted about the employment of an agent. Take advice.

Service charges

Complain if the landlord is not adhering to the lease in setting service charges or if you think they are unreasonably high. Ask for a summary of the costs on which the service charge is calculated (see sample letter 49), and if you are still dissatisfied ask to see the accounts and receipts (see sample letter 50). You have this right. If they ask you to pay charges more than 18 months after they incurred the expense, you may be within your rights to refuse to pay them – take advice.

If major works (costing more than £1,000 or £50 per house/flat, whichever is the greater) are being planned you have the right to be consulted. You can challenge proposed costs if you think they are unreasonable, or complain if you think of works or services will not be carried out to a sufficient standard. If the works are urgent the landlord can go ahead without consulting but you can apply to the **County court** if you think the landlord is acting too hastily.

If you cannot reach agreement with the landlord you can take the matter to a **Leasehold Valuation Tribunal (LVT)** which will consider all the facts and adjudicate. The fee involved would depend on the work required, but the maximum possible is currently £500 and you could apply jointly with other tenants and share the costs.

Dealing with other concerns

- You have a right to have sight of information about insurance cover, and if your lease fails to provide adequate cover, or if the premiums are excessive, complain. If the landlord does not resolve things and you are the one paying the insurance premiums take the matter to a County court or the LVT for a ruling. Take advice.

- If you have concerns about the landlord's management practices, in some cases, for a fee, you can arrange a management audit by an independent accountant or surveyor (or both) to get evidence of bad management. If this does not bring about changes, refer the matter to a County court or LVT. They will make regard to the Codes of Practice in making their rulings. In some cases you can ask the court or LVT to appoint a managing agent where there is not one, or you can even request a compulsory acquisition to transfer the interest in the property to the leaseholders. You will have to get the majority of leaseholders in the same building to apply. Take advice.

- There is another option – in many cases you have the right to purchase your freehold (collectively with other tenants if you live in flats). Take advice.

- If it is not possible to negotiate changes to the lease you may be able to apply to the County court to have changes made if the lease does not make proper provision for insurance, and, in the case of flats, repairs and maintenance and the amount of the service charge – take advice.

Useful addresses

The Leasehold Advisory Service (LEASE)
70-74 City Road
London EC1Y 2BJ
Tel: 0845 345 1993
Fax: 020 7253 2043
Email: info@lease-advice.org
Website: www.lease-advice.org

Leasehold Valuation Tribunal (LVT)
70-74 City Road
London EC1V 2BJ
Tel: 0845 345 1993
Fax: 020 7253 2043
Email: info@lease-advice.org
Website: www.lease-advice.org

The Office of the Deputy Prime Minister
26 Whitehall
London SW1A 2WH
Tel: 020 7944 4400
Fax: 0207 944 6589
Email: leasehold.reform@odpm.gsi.gov.uk
Website: www.odpm.gov.uk

Sample letter 49: Requesting a summary of accounts on which service charge is based

1, Any Street
Anytown
Anyshire
AN1 2YZ

25th June, 2003

Landlord (or Managing Agent)

Dear Sir,

Re: *1, Golden Apartments, Parish Road, Richmond*

I am resident in one of the flats in the above property. I am writing under the authority of Section 21 of the Landlord and Tenant Act 1987 to ask you for a summary of the accounts relating to the service charge for the property for the period *December 2002* to *June 2003*.

I look forward to hearing from you within seven working days. Please note that should you refuse to supply me with this summary I can apply to the Leasehold Valuation Tribunal for the appointment of a manager to run the block.

Yours faithfully,

David Chambers

David Chambers

Sample letter 50: Requesting documents supporting summary of accounts on which service charge is based

1, Any Street
Anytown
Anyshire
AN1 2YZ

25th June, 2003

Landlord (or Managing Agent)

Dear Sir,

Re: *1, Golden Apartments, Parish Road, Richmond*

Thank you for providing me with a summary of the accounts relating to the service charge of the above property for the period *December 2002* to *June 2003*.

I am now exercising my right under Section 22 of the Landlord and Tenant Act 1987 and wish to inspect the documents supporting the summary, i.e. bills, receipts, etc., and to take copies of them. Please afford me reasonable facilities for this inspection, as you are legally bound to do. I look forward to hearing from you within seven working days.

Yours faithfully,

David Chambers

David Chambers

Landlords and tenants

This chapter applies to tenants of private landlords, local authorities and Registered Social Landlords (RSLs) – that is, tenants of housing associations, trusts and other non-profit making companies. It can also be used if you are a landlord yourself. You will have a stronger case in complaining if the tenancy agreement has been breached in some way, as this is the contract between you and the landlord. If you do not have anything in writing there will still be an agreement – it will be whatever arrangements you and the landlord made at the time you took on the tenancy. But also you have legal rights – some of which are set out below. Some such rights vary depending on the kind of tenancy you have. Take advice.

If you are a council or housing association (or other RSL) tenant your landlord will probably have published a handbook or guide, which sets out your rights, the landlord's standards of service, and how to complain. The Council Tenants Charter also sets out the position for all council tenants and this mostly covers housing association tenants as well. As a council tenant you could ask your local councillor to help pursue a complaint.

How to complain

Firstly, try to talk to the landlord or the agent if there is one, or if you are a council or housing association tenant, contact the local housing office. If this does not work, check to see if there is a complaints procedure and follow this – agents, larger landlords, housing associations and the council will have one. Otherwise, put your concern in writing to the manager responsible if there is one, or to the landlord direct. If you are a council tenant see also *Local authorities*. If you are unhappy with the way your complaint is dealt with you can go to the **Local Government Ombudsman**. If you are a tenant of a social landlord such as a housing association in a similar situation you can go to the **Independent Housing Ombudsman**. On issues of wider concern you could contact the regulatory body for the **Housing Corporation**.

Challenging eviction

Complain if you are threatened with eviction but unless you can convince the landlord to see things your way, your chances of success will depend on your legal position so take advice. You can, in most cases, refuse to leave, in which case the landlord has to serve a possession summons on you, and the County court will call a hearing to consider whether the landlord has followed the correct legal procedures and has grounds in law to evict you. If they rule that the landlord is correct you may be ordered to pay his/her costs in going to court. There are exceptions. For example, with some tenancies a landlord can get the court to make a speedy decision without a hearing called 'expedited proceedings', and if you share living accommodation with the landlord, eviction may be possible without recourse to court. Take advice.

Harassment and illegal eviction

What if your landlord ignores these procedures and tries to harass you into leaving? Harassment could be anything from actually throwing you or your possessions out, disconnecting your fuel supply or sitting back while another of her/his tenants makes your life hell. In this case complain immediately to your local authority as they can intervene and if necessary prosecute. The staff responsible may be in the housing department or the legal department and sometimes they are referred to as the tenancy relations officer. If the council offices are closed, go to the police. If the landlord evicts you illegally you may also be able to claim damages against him or her, for example, for the distress and inconvenience, damage to goods or the cost of finding alternative accommodation at short notice. If you wish you could also seek an injunction from a court to return to the tenancy. Take advice.

Objecting to rent levels

For most private tenancies if the landlord tries to put your rent up you can refuse to pay unless this was allowed for in the agreement (see sample letter 51). However, you will have to pay if you have a tenancy that is not fixed term (or the fixed term has expired) but only if the landlord has followed legal procedures in proposing an increase. If you do not agree to the increase you can then appeal to a **Rent Assessment Committee**. Apply on their special form – they must receive it before the new rent becomes due. The Committee will decide what the rent should be bearing in mind the current market and they could increase it further! This will then be your rent and the landlord cannot charge you more, though in a year's time s/he could propose a new increase (and you could appeal again!).

This appeal process is also open to you if you have just begun a fixed term tenancy and you think the rent is too high compared to comparable tenancies.

In some cases different rules apply. For example, if you have been a private tenant in the same accommodation since prior to 15 January 1989 you will be a regulated tenant so take advice. If you are a council or housing association tenant, you have no right of appeal on rent levels.

Varying the terms of a tenancy

In some cases if you are a private tenant and unhappy with your existing terms of your tenancy, say if you want to be allowed a pet, or you want less rooms, you may propose new terms. To do this, a form is available from the **Rent Assessment Committee**. If the landlord does not accept the proposals you can appeal to the Committee on another form. Your landlord can also propose new terms in this way, and if you object you can use this appeal process.

Repairs and maintenance

With repair and maintenance problems complain as above, allowing the landlord 7-14 days to put things right unless it is an emergency.

In most cases your landlords will be legally responsible for keeping the structure, fixtures and fittings, and exterior of your home in good repair, for example, the roof, drains, toilets and basins, central heating, electrical wiring, gutters, door and windows (usually if your tenancy agreement says you are responsible this is wrong, except in the case of long leaseholders). The landlord is also obliged to keep furniture and appliances such as cookers and heaters in good repair where they were provided by him/her in the first place.

In addition to this, if you are a council tenant (or in some cases a housing association tenant) some additional minor repairs are covered under the free 'right to repair' scheme, which includes blocked sinks, leaking roofs and blocked flues. There are timescales the council must adhere to otherwise you can complain, (see *Local authorities*) and ask them to appoint another contractor to do the job (see sample letter 52).

Next, for problems and defects which constitute a health hazard, or if the property is in very poor condition, contact the local authority **Environmental Health Department** (even if you are a council tenant). They will investigate and if necessary see the landlord. If you have a private landlord they may serve a Notice on the landlord to carry out the work. If the landlord ignores this they can get a court order to get the repairs carried out by a certain date or, alternatively, they may carry out the repairs themselves and reclaim the cost from the landlord. If the repair cannot be carried out at a reasonable expense and the accommodation is in a dire state it may be held to be unfit for human habitation, or even ordered to be demolished. In such cases the council may re-house you if the landlord has no suitable alternative accommodation.

Legal action

If the Environmental Health Officer is unwilling to take up the case, you could consider taking legal proceedings in the **County court** for the repairs to be carried out and for damages to be awarded to you for inconvenience, damage to property, and so on. See *Taking things further.* You may also have to consider this if you are a council tenant, as the Environmental Health Officer will not prosecute the council. You could also bring a private prosecution in the **Magistrates' Court** under the Public Health Act if the Environmental Health Officer is unwilling to do this. Take advice.

Doing repairs yourself

If you are getting nowhere with your landlord there are schemes where you can get small repairs done at your own expense and deduct the cost from the rent

If you are a private tenant the repairs must cost less than the equivalent of two months rent. Wait about four weeks after your first letter requesting the repairs. Send another letter saying you will do the work unless it is done by a certain date. Enclose two or three estimates and ask the landlord to let you know within 48 hours whether s/he intends to carry out the repairs. If the repairs are not carried out get the work done and write to the landlord requesting payment. If you are denied compensation, state that you will deduct the precise amount from the rent, saying that you are recovering a debt, not refusing to pay the rent.

If you are a council housing association tenant, the repairs must cost between £20 and £200 at the time of writing. This is the 'right to repair' scheme – the landlord will advise you of the exact procedure.

Have your say on policy

If you are a council tenant, you should be encouraged to have your say on the council's housing services as the council should have a Tenancy Participation Compact with the tenants. A tenants group may have also been formed in your area. Take advice or contact the Tenants Participation Advisory Service (TPAS). If you are denied this sort of input complain (see *Local authorities*). Whatever kind of tenant you are you could consider joining with other tenants of the same landlord and forming a tenant association.

Useful addresses

Housing Corporation
Contact your local office, or head office at:
Maple House
149 Tottenham Court Road
London W1T 7BN
Tel: 020 7393 2000
Fax: 020 7393 2111
Email: enquiries@housingcorp.gsx.gov.uk
Website: www.housingcorp.gov.uk

Independent Housing Ombudsman
Norman House
105-109 Strand
London WC2R 0AA
Tel: 020 7836 3630
Helpline: 0845 7125 973
Fax: 020 7836 3900
Email: ombudsman@ihos-org.uk
Website: www.ihos.org.uk

Rent Assessment Panels

Eastern
For Bedfordshire, Berkshire, Buckinghamshire, Cambridgeshire, Hertfordshire, Oxfordshire, Suffolk, Norfolk, Northamptonshire, Luton, Milton Keynes, Peterborough, Southend-on-Sea, Thurrock & Essex
Great Eastern House
Tenison Road
Cambridge CB1 2TR
Tel: 01223 505 112
Fax: 01223 505 116
Email: rap.eastern@odpm.gsi.gov.uk

London
For all London Boroughs
10 Alfred Place
London WC1E 7LR
Tel: 020 7446 7700
Fax: 020 7637 1250
Email: rap.london@odpm.gsi.gov.uk

Midlands
For Staffordshire, Shropshire, Herefordshire, Worcesterhire, West Midlands, Warwickshire, Leicestershire, Derbyshire, Nottinghamshire, Rutland, Stoke-on-Trent & The Wrekin
2nd Floor, East Wing
Ladywood House
45-46 Stephenson Street
Birmingham B2 4DH
Tel: 0121 643 8336
Fax: 0121 643 7605
Email: rap.midlands@odpm.gsi.gov.uk

Northern
For Blackburn, Blackpool, Cheshire, Cumbria, Darlington, Durham, East Riding of Yorkshire, Greater Manchester, Halton, Hartlepool, Kingston-upon-Hull, Lancashire, Lincolnshire, Merseyside, Middlesborough, North East Lincolnshire, North Lincolnshire, North Yorkshire, Northumberland, Redcar and Cleveland, South Yorkshire, Stockton-on-Tees, Tyne and Wear, Warrington, West Yorkshire & York
20th Floor, Sunley Tower
Piccadilly Plaza
Manchester M1 4BE
Tel: 0161 237 9491
Fax: 0161 237 3656
Email: rap.northwestern@odpm.gsi.gov.uk

Southern
For Hampshire, East and West Sussex, Surrey, Kent, Isle of Wight, The Medway Towns, Portsmouth, Southampton, Brighton and Hove, Wiltshire, Dorset, Devon, Bath, Somerset, Bournemouth, City of Bristol, Cornwall, Isle of Scilly & Gloucester
1st Floor, Midland House
1 Market Avenue
Chichester PO19 1JU

Tel: 01243 779 394
Fax: 01243 779 389
Email: rap.southern@odpm.gsi.gov.uk

Wales
1st Floor, West Wing
Southgate House
Wood Street
Cardiff CF10 1EW
Tel: 029 2023 1687
Fax: 029 2023 6146

Sample letter 51: Resisting landlord's rent increase

1, Any Street
Anytown
Anyshire
AN1 2YZ

25th June, 2003

Landlord or Agent

Dear Sir,

Re: *1, Courts Place*

You have advised me that you wish to increase my rent from *£350* per calendar month to *£420* as from next week (*1st July, 2003*).

Please regard this letter as notice that I do not accept the increase.

You will be aware that I have an Assured Shorthold Tenancy Agreement under the Housing Act 1988 which is for one year fixed term. I have to advise you that during this fixed term, which still has *seven* months to run, you have no means in law of increasing the rent without my agreement since there is no provision in the Tenancy Agreement, which allows you to increase the rent.

I will therefore continue to pay my rent as initially agreed for the duration of the fixed term.

Yours faithfully,

David Chambers

David Chambers

Sample letter 52: 'Right to Repair' Notice for council and housing association tenants

1, Any Street
Anytown
Anyshire
AN1 2YZ

25th June, 2003

The Council

Dear Sirs,

Re: *22, South Street, Newcastle-upon-Tyne*

I *visited* your office and spoke to *Mr Matthews* requesting that my leaking roof be repaired urgently. I had taken advice and had been told that *a leaking roof* is a 'qualifying repair' under the statutory ' Right to Repair' scheme. Your colleague agreed with me and said that the work would be done within the seven-day minimum set under this scheme for this type of repair.

Unfortunately 12 days have now elapsed and still this work has not even been started. I was reminded of this fact when *last nights downpour completely saturated the bed and carpet in my spare room.*

In accordance with the 'Right to Repair' scheme I am requesting that you get another contractor in to do the work as a matter of great urgency. If this contractor fails to get the work done on time I am entitled to claim up to £50 compensation under the scheme.

In addition to this I hold the Council responsible for the state of *my spare bedroom*, so please take note that I am seeking quotations for repair or renewal of the damaged items, and once I have these I will require the Council to meet these costs as well. Otherwise, I will not hesitate to issue a claim against the Council in the County court.

Moreover, should this issue not be resolved to my satisfaction I will follow the Council's complaints procedures with determination.

Yours faithfully,

David Chambers

David Chambers

Local authorities

The structure of local government will vary depending on where you live. In some parts of the country there are three separate organisations that have different responsibilities, i.e. County Council, District Council and Parish Council. In other areas there may be only one major organisation (a unitary authority). Most local authorities have their own websites – see **www.ukonline.gov.uk** for an index and links.

Local authorities have responsibilities for services such as libraries, museums, schools, planning control, public roads and pavements, street lighting, public leisure and amenities, traffic control, refuse collection, trading standards, environmental health, social services, council housing, building regulation, administration of housing benefit, council tax collection. But beyond that they have a wider brief to foster the development and well being of the community within their boundaries, where appropriate in partnership with other organisations. This brief is interpreted widely so the additional services this entails will vary from area to area.

Some services may be contracted out to outside bodies, but the council complaint procedures should still apply, though each individual body may well also have its own you can pursue. Some services are separate from the council, though council members will serve on their governing bodies. This includes fire authorities, national park authorities, police authorities and joint boards. The procedures below will apply.

How to complain

First you will need to establish which department of the council is responsible and what the complaints procedure is for that department. The procedure may come with a charter setting out the standards you should expect. With a smaller organisation there will probably be one procedure for everything. Otherwise write to the most senior manager of the department. You could copy your letter to your local councillor at the same time, or you could only involve the councillor if you get no joy from the department – what you do here will depend on the severity of your complaint.

Next, write to the **Chief Executive of the Council,** who may lean more heavily on the department – see sample letter 53. There may be a particular councillor who chairs the committee that oversees that department who you could write to also, but consult with your local councillor first.

Claiming damages

If as a result of council action or inaction you suffer a loss, such as loss of income, personal injury or damage to your property you may be able to take legal action for damages – take advice. If you feel you have been the victim of discrimination on grounds of sex, race or disability, or there has been a breach of your human rights, take advice and see *Taking things further.*

Policies

You could use the above procedures to complain about wider policy issues. Alternatively, you may find it more appropriate to write letters to the local press, or join with other like-minded people and plan some lobbying. You could join one of the political parties that are represented on the Council and try to influence change from within. You could even get to stand for election. Alternatively some councils consult with the community on a regular basis via public meetings or the media or the internet, so maybe you could take advantage of this.

Complaining further – the Local Government Ombudsman

Are you still dissatisfied? Do you still feel the council were too slow to act, or failed to follow their procedures, or indeed acted illegally? Or do you feel the council treated you unfairly or gave you incorrect information? In such cases you can now go to the **Local Government Ombudsman,** an independent body who can assist you with all local government matters with the exception of parish councils. (In Northern Ireland, go to the Northern Ireland Ombudsman – see *Public services*). You have to show you have been caused injustice as a result of misadministration, such as financial loss, distress or upset, or not getting the service you were entitled to. Write in with your complaint or preferably use the form that comes with the Ombudsman's leaflet or on their website. You could ask a councillor to complain for you.

If they decide the complaint falls within their remit they will investigate. While this is going on the council may offer to put things right and if the Ombudsman's office thinks this is fair they will stop the investigation.

They may produce a report and if they find in your favour this will include recommendations on how the council should put things right. This may well include general policy recommendations to improve services for others in your situation. The council will then decide whether to implement and how. You cannot appeal against an Ombudsman's report. But the Ombudsman will review a decision on your complaint made by letter (i.e. where a report has been issued) if you send in new information, or if you think the decision on your complaint was wrong or unfair.

Useful addresses

Local Government Ombudsman for England
Advice line number: 0845 602 1983
Website: www.lgo.org.uk

For London boroughs north of the river Thames (including Richmond but not including Harrow or Tower Hamlets), Essex, Kent, Surrey, Suffolk, East and West Sussex, Berkshire, Buckinghamshire, Hertfordshire & the City of Coventry
Millbank Tower
Millbank
London SW1P 4QP
Tel: 020 7217 4620
Fax: 020 7217 4621

For London Borough of Tower Hamlets, City of Birmingham, Cheshire, Derbyshire, Nottinghamshire, Lincolnshire and the north of England (except the Cities of York and Lancaster)
Beverly House
17, Shipton Road
York YO30 5FZ
Tel: 01904 380 200
Fax: 01904 380 269

For London boroughs south of the river Thames (except Richmond) and Harrow; the Cities of York and Lancaster; and the rest of England, not included in the above-mentioned areas
The Oaks No. 2
Westwood Way
Westwood Business Park
Coventry CV4 8JB
Tel: 024 7682 0000
Fax: 024 7682 0001

Local Government Ombudsman for Wales
Derwen House
Court Road
Bridgend CF31 1BN
Tel: 01656 661 325
Fax: 01656 673 279
Email: enquiries@ombudsman-wales.org
Website: www.ombudsman-wales.org

Scottish Public Services Ombudsman
23, Walker Street
Edinburgh EH3 7HX
Tel: 0870 011 5378
Fax: 0870 011 5379
Email: enquiries@scottishombudsman.org.uk
Website: www.scottishombudsman.org.uk

Sample letter 53: Letter of general complaint

1, Any Street
Anytown
Anyshire
AN1 2YZ

25th June, 2003

Chief Executive – Local Authority

Dear Sir,

Re: *Grass Cutting* - Reference Number *2145*

I am writing to express my dissatisfaction with the way my complaint has been dealt with by your Council.

My original complaint was that your Council have neglected to mow the grass outside my house for three months now and are suggesting that the land is my responsibility despite the fact that they have been mowing it for the past three years.

I enclose all correspondence in respect of the complaint, including my record of phone conversations taken place. You will see I first complained informally in person at *the Council Buildings in Maltravers Street* on *12th May, 2003*. Since then there have been two letters from the Department concerned (enclosed) but they have both been very dismissive in tone, making it appear I was wasting their time. *This suspicion was confirmed when I visited Mr Small in that he started yawning in front of me, then told me to 'get a life'.* This I regard as an appalling breach of your Councils customer service charter.

I am most disappointed by the Council's response so far so I am writing to you to ask you to investigate both my original complaint and the way in which it has been handled and let me know the outcome.

If you do not deal with this to my satisfaction within 14 days I will refer the matter to the Local Government Ombudsman.

Yours faithfully,

David Chambers

David Chambers

The media

Complaints about the Media usually fall under the headings of either (a) inaccurate or unfair treatment or (b) harassment or invasion of privacy.

The press and other printed media

If your complaint is about unfair or inaccurate treatment in a national newspaper, write to the editor or the newspaper's ombudsman, or the readers' representative. For local newspapers, magazine or other periodicals write to the editor, and send a copy to the owner or publisher. The **Press Complaints Commission** telephone helpline can give you contact details of the editor if you cannot obtain them. Before writing, however, consider the following:

- Have you been libelled or slandered?
  This is where the media outlet (or indeed any individual) has published or broadcast accusations about you which are untrue and you feel damage your character, reputation or credit worthiness. See *Taking things further.*

- Has there been a breach of the Code of Practice?
  All printed publications in the UK should conform to a Code of Practice, which is monitored by the **Press Complaints Commission**. In essence the Code says that all material published must not be inaccurate or misleading. If it is, a prominent correction should be published, with an apology if necessary and the chance for the wronged person to reply.

If you think that either of the above has occurred say so in your letter, see sample letter 54. This will grab the recipient's attention more quickly. If you think you have been libelled or slandered you could say you want the publication to 'make amends as under Section 2 of the Defamation Act 1996.' The amends could be an offer to make a correction to the statement complained of; an offer to make an apology to you; or an offer to pay you compensation and costs as agreed. Take advice.

It is helpful to work out what you want done about your complaint, and to put this in your letter. For example, either an apology, an acceptance that they will do better next time, compensation, a published retraction, or a further article that corrects things in passing saying, 'New sources reveal...' Alternatively you may be able to get a letter published to put your side of the story. You may need to negotiate with the editor.

Press Complaints Commission

If you feel your complaint was not satisfactorily dealt with you may be able to go on to complain to the Press Complaints Commission (PCC) itself, or bypass the earlier stages and go straight to them. You could ring the helpline first for initial advice. If the PCC decides to take up the complaint they will investigate and have their decision printed in the publication concerned.

Legal action?

In serious cases of defamation you may want to consider legal action rather than follow complaints procedures, for example you could seek an injunction (say if the accusation is likely to be repeated) or claim damages, or both. If your privacy was breached you may also be able to sue under Article 8 of the Convention on Human Rights, which is covered by the Human Rights Act 1998. Take advice.

The internet

To complain about content on the internet there are two options. You could contact the creator or owner of the website through details on the website itself, quite often they invite feedback but you will need to word your complaint to try to ensure you get a reply. Alternatively, the **Internet Watch Foundation** could be contacted; they will take action on any complaints about content which is potentially illegal, for example to do with privacy, national or economic security, protection of minors. See above if you feel you have been libelled or slandered.

Radio and television – including cable and satellite

For the broadcast media you can try making an immediate protest by telephoning or emailing the presenter or producer – a TV listings magazine will tell you who they are.

- For the BBC national radio or TV, write to the **BBC Programme Complaints Unit** (see sample letter 55) or use their website. There are separate areas for feedback, for individual programmes and for making a more serious complaint. Alternatively, you can phone the BBC duty officer and ask for your complaint to go into the daily log. If the complaint is about local services, contact the local radio or TV stations direct.

- For programmes on ITV, Channel 4, (S4C in Wales) or a commercial radio station, phone the TV channel or radio station's **duty officer** and ask for the complaint to be recorded in the log. Alternatively, you could write to the information office of the television or radio station, or use their websites as for BBC.

- For a complaint about a programme on satellite, cable or digital TV, phone or write directly to the television company or channel, or use their website.

Again if you feel you have been libelled or slandered act as for the printed media above.

Complaining further

For national and local commercial radio and restricted services, including special event, hospital and student radio write to the **Radio Authority**. They will not investigate any complaint that is the subject of legal proceedings. If your complaint is upheld the Radio Authority can ask them to broadcast an apology and can impose a range of penalties including warnings, fines or, ultimately, revoke a station's licence.

For all non-BBC television services: ITV, Channel 4, Cable and Satellite you can contact the **Independent Television Commission (ITC)**. To complain about programmes on S4C in Wales write to the Welsh 4th Channel Authority.

For all complaints about fairness or standards you can complain to the **Broadcasting Standards Commission (BSC)**. Fairness includes unjust treatment or unwarranted infringement of privacy. Standards are usually to do with the depiction of sex, violence, bad language or insensitivity. The BSC cannot deal with complaints that are (or could be) the subject of legal proceedings and you must complain within set time limits (take advice). You can use the BSC's standard complaints form.

The BSC could do a number of things including demanding the broadcaster to take internal action or publish a summary of its decision on air or in a newspaper or magazine.

Other angles

Complain as above or take legal action if information or pictures are obtained, or attempted, through intimidation, invasion of your privacy or harassment. Unless the enquiries are in the public interest, journalists should not photograph you on private property without your consent, or phone or question you after being asked to stop, nor remain on your property after they have been asked to leave, nor follow you.

If you feel anything in the media is sexist or racist, or presents certain other people unfairly complain as above but also enlist the aid of bodies that tackle discrimination, for example the **Equal Opportunities Commission** or the **Commission for Racial Equality** or a local **Race Equality Council** (see *Taking things further*). If the issue is mental health consult the **National Association for Mental Health (MIND)** or the **Scottish Association for Mental Health** (see *National Health Services*).

You may also wish to complain about a particular journalist. You can do this via their editor, but if the journalist is member of a union such as the National Union of Journalists (NUJ) you have another avenue. Most of the unions have a Code of Conduct or Ethics, and this may have been breached by their behaviour in gathering information. If the union agrees that the journalist has breached its Code they may be reprimanded, fined, suspended or banned from union membership. See if the media outlet will advise you what union the journalist is in.

If you think something published or broadcast is obscene, report it to the police who will decide whether to prosecute under the Obscene Publications Act.

Useful addresses

BBC Information
PO Box 1922
Glasgow G2 3WT
Tel: 0870 010 0222
Website: www.bbc.co.uk/info

Broadcasting Standards Commission (BSC)
7 The Sanctuary
London SW1P 3JS
Tel: 020 7808 1000
Fax: 020 7233 0397
Email: bsc@bsc.org.uk
Website: www.bsc.org.uk

Channel 4
124 Horseferry Road
London SW1P 2TX
Tel: 020 7306 8333
Duty officer: 020 7306 8333
Fax: 020 7306 8347
Email: viewerenquiries@channel4.co.uk
Website: www.channel4.com

Independent Television Commission (ITC)
ITC Viewer Relations Unit
33 Foley Street
London W1W 7TL

Tel: 0845 601 3608
Website: www.itc.org.uk

Internet Watch Foundation
5 Coles Lane
Oakington
Cambridgeshire CB4 5BA
Tel: 01223 237 700
Fax: 01223 235 921
Email: admin@iwf.org.uk
Website: www.iwf.org.uk

ITV
200 Gray's Inn Road
London WC1X 8HF
Tel: 020 7843 8215/8320/8321
Fax: 020 7843 8158
Website: www.itv.co.uk

Press Complaints Commission (PCC)
1 Salisbury Square
London EC4Y 8JB
Tel: 020 7353 1248
Helpline 020 7353 8355
Scottish helpline: 0131 220 6652
Welsh helpline: 029 2039 5570
Email: pcc@pcc.org.uk
Website: www.pcc.org.uk

The Radio Authority
Holbrook House
14 Great Queen Street
Holborn
London WC2B 5DG
Tel: 020 7430 2724
Fax: 020 7405 7062
Email: reception@radioauthority.org.uk
Website: www.radioauthority.org.uk

Sample letter 54: Letter to the editor of a publication (newspaper, magazine etc) complaining about an article

1, Any Street
Anytown
Anyshire
AN1 2YZ

25th June, 2003

Daily News

Dear Editor,

Re: *Daily News,* article entitled *'Nepotism,'* published on *1st June, 2003*

I am writing to complain about an article that appeared in the above publication and enclose a copy of the piece in question, for your information. In this you stated that *the only reason I had gained my current position at the Bank of London was due to my father giving me the job.*

The content of this article contains accusations, which are untrue, and I feel damage my reputation and character. I would like you to make amends as under section 2 of the Defamation Act 1996. I would like those amends to be an apology and a correction to appear prominently in your publication.

Also I feel that your publication has contravened the Code Of Practice monitored by the Press Complaints Commission in that the material published was inaccurate and misleading. Consequently, I will not hesitate to complain to the Commission if this matter is not resolved to my satisfaction.

I look forward to hearing from you shortly.

Yours faithfully,

David Chambers

David Chambers

Enc.

NB *If you would like to claim compensation you could say so in this letter but you may wish to take advice first on how much to reasonably ask for.*

Sample letter 55: Complaint to the BBC Governors' Programme Complaints Unit (PCU) about a programme broadcast by the BBC

1, Any Street
Anytown
Anyshire
AN1 2YZ

25th June, 2003

BBC

Dear Sirs,

Re: *Soap Opera*

I am writing to complain about the above programme, which was broadcast at *8pm* on *1st June, 2003.*

My complaint is *that I consider the programme to be incredibly derogatory to women and should never have been produced.*

I regard this matter as a specific and serious breach in programme standards (as set out in BBC Producers' Guidelines). I would ask you to carry out an investigation and to put things right.

I look forward to hearing the outcome of your investigation.

Yours faithfully,

David Chambers

David Chambers

National Health Services

This chapter deals with complaints about all providers of NHS services. This includes NHS hospitals, GPs and health centres, dentists, pharmacists, midwives, health visitors, opticians, physiotherapists where they work for the NHS and other agencies working under contract for the NHS. Your rights of NHS patients are set out in charters. Before complaining it is a good idea to check the relevant one as this will set out the standards of service to be expected. Ask the provider in question, or failing that, the **Health Authority** or **NHS Direct**.

There are a wide range of bodies providing support to people with different illnesses, disabilities and conditions. Some may act for you or campaign on behalf of people in your situation – take advice. On pregnancy issues contact the **British Pregnancy Advisory Service**. If your complaint is about private medical services see *Buying services*. You could also get help from a **Community Health Council (CMC)** – these are independent patients watchdogs – the nearest to you will be found in your phone book.

NHS complaints procedure

The NHS complaints procedure is best used if you want an apology, or to highlight what you see as bad practice to get a change of policy. All NHS service providers, as well as independent organisations who provide NHS services under contract, must have a complaint procedure, so first you will need to find out from the provider what this is. It will vary slightly from one hospital to another, from one health centre to another, but certain minimum standards must be adhered to.

Complain to the provider within six months of the incident (see sample letter 56), though there are some exceptions to this – say if you were too ill or traumatised, or you did not know you had anything to complain about till after the six months. Put your case in full writing to the provider, giving details such as dates, names of any offending parties, witnesses etc. You may be wary of complaining direct to the provider because of what has happened. In this case approach the **Health Authority** for your area. They may investigate the complaint themselves or appoint a lay conciliator to do so.

Local resolution

At first the NHS provider will attempt what is referred to as a Local Resolution – that is they will appoint someone who will carry out an investigation, interviewing you, the accused practitioner(s) and any others involved. You will receive the outcome of your complaint in writing and you will be advised how to request an independent review if you are still dissatisfied. See sample letter 57.

Independent review

You will be asked to explain in writing why you wish to continue your complaint. A convener, a non-executive director of the **Health Authority**, will decide whether your complaint should proceed, and if so whether to refer the matter back to the provider to look at again, or arrange for you and the provider to attend a conciliation, or set up an independent review panel to investigate further. A panel will appoint independent clinical assessors if your compliant is about a clinical decision.

If you are not happy with the decision of the convener or the outcome of the panel investigation – or if you thought you were dealt with unreasonably – you can go to the **Health Service Ombudsman**.

Health Service Ombudsman

There is a separate ombudsman for England, Wales and Scotland. They are completely independent of the NHS. You must write to them within a year of the incident, or when you first realised it to be a problem (exceptionally this time limit may be extended). The Ombudsman can provide a special form to do this if you wish. The ombudsman can investigate most complaints, but they do not deal with NHS disciplinary issues or matters you could take to a court or tribunal, say to claim damages. In Northern Ireland, use the Northern Ireland Ombudsman (see *Public services*).

If an investigation is to be carried out you will be notified and all relevant papers, including possibly your medical records, will be requested and you will be interviewed, as will other people where thought necessary. The investigation may take several months, and at the end you and the NHS provider concerned will be sent a report on the outcome. If your complaint is upheld the Ombudsman will either seek an apology, exert pressure to get a decision or a policy changed, or get costs you incurred refunded. Damages will not be recommended.

Personal and professional misconduct

In cases where a medical practitioner has acted improperly you may be able to complain of 'professional misconduct.' To do this contact the relevant professional body for details of their complaints procedures, see below or take advice if it is not listed here. For alternative medicine you could contact the **Health Professions Council**. They should investigate and if they think your complaint is justified they may discipline the practitioner – in severe cases they can strike the person off their register, barring them from practising.

Taking legal action to claim damages

If you think you have suffered ill health or loss owing to a medical practitioner's negligence (failure to exercise professional standards of skill or care) for example by wrongly diagnosing or treating your illness you will need to take legal action – take advice or consult **Action for Victims of Medical Accidents (AVMA)**. Legal

proceedings must be started in court within three years of you becoming aware of the injury or damage, but be warned they are usually complex and can take a long time to resolve. Starting legal proceedings does not prevent you from pursuing the NHS complaint service, indeed you may be advised to do this first, but you will not be able to go to the Ombudsman.

Take advice to see if you have any chance of claiming financial compensation from your **Health Authority,** the **Department of Health** and/or the manufacturers if prescribed drugs or medicines have damaged your health. If a number of other people have made similar complaints this would help. An individual pharmacist who supplies you with medicine that is unfit for consumption could be prosecuted and you should refer the matter to the **Pharmaceutical Society of Great Britain.**

The Vaccine Damage Payment Scheme offers compensation (currently £100,000) to those who have suffered severe damage as a result of vaccination against certain diseases. Write to the **Vaccine Damage Payment Unit, Department of Social Security** and take advice.

Specific complaints

- You may be able to complain of assault if a medical practitioner treated you without your consent (except in certain emergency or mental illness situations). This means you could report the matter to the police and take legal action. Consent may be oral or in writing, but for it to be valid you must have been given sufficient information and not coerced or unreasonably influenced by trauma drugs etc. Prescribing you drugs on an experimental basis could also constitute an assault if you did not give your consent.

- You can complain about services and treatment in a psychiatric hospital as above but you could first check the Department of Health's Code of Practice on the Mental Health Act 1983 to see whether this is being followed. You can also report any concerns to the **Mental Health Act Commission** who will investigate. Take advice or contact the **National Association for Mental Health (MIND)** or the **Scottish Association for Mental Health.**

- If you are a formal patient in a psychiatric hospital you can apply to a **Mental Health Review Tribunal** to challenge your detention. Take advice as above. You do this within 14 days of admission (except if you are admitted for an emergency assessment). You can apply again once in the first six months and once during each subsequent year in hospital. If the Tribunal decide in your favour they could order your discharge or transfer, or grant you home leave.

- If your child has to go into hospital and you have concerns about their care during their stay you could get in touch with **Action for Sick Children** for advice on what to expect. Then you will know if you have grounds for complaint using the procedures in this chapter.

- There are maximum waiting list times in the NHS Charter both for inpatient treatment and first appointments as an outpatient – take advice. Complain as above if you feel your wait is unreasonably long. It is worth contacting the hospital appointments department or the consultant's secretary every so often to establish when you are likely to be seen. If your medical condition worsens ask your GP to consider recommending you to be given greater priority on the list.

- Failing this your **GP** could consider trying to transfer to a hospital elsewhere with a shorter waiting list. Your **Health Authority** could give you or your GP information on local waiting lists. **The College of Health** publish a Guide to Hospital Waiting Lists and a run a Waiting List Helpline, **NHS Direct** will also advise. In Scotland there is a free NHS helpline that advises on waiting lists. In Northern Ireland you could contact the relevant Board helpline.

- You can ask your GP to arrange a second opinion either from a specialist or another GP, but your GP is not obliged to do this. With certain medical problems you may be to see a doctor elsewhere, for example at a **Family Planning Clinic** or **Well Woman Clinic**. Alternatively, you could change your GP. This can be done at any time, simply take your medical card to register with a new GP. However a new GP will not have to accept you. Your Health Authority will find you one if necessary. The only other option left to you will be to see a specialist privately.

- If you are not satisfied with the arrangements for your discharge from hospital, ask for this decision to be reviewed (or a relative, carer or other representative could do this on your behalf) – see sample letter 58. The hospital should advise you. You might do this if you felt you needed further treatment as an inpatient, or you are not satisfied with the community care services arranged for you when you leave, or you do not want to be sent to a residential care or nursing home. While the review is in progress you should remain in hospital or other care funded by the NHS. If you are not satisfied with the outcome of the review, or if you are refused a review use the **NHS Complaints Procedure.**

• With opticians, if you are dissatisfied with NHS services complain as above. If your concern is about their private services see *Buying services* and if the glasses or contact lenses are not suitable see *Buying goods.* If you think they are not optically suitable complain to the prescribing optician. You could get a second opinion from another optician. If the prescription is wrong you may be able to claim compensation from the optician for any expenses you have incurred as well as getting a refund.

• If you think your dentist has overcharged you take the matter up with the practice first. For NHS treatment there are statutory charges. If you have been charged as a private patient yet you thought you were an NHS patient, you only have grounds for complaint if you made it clear at the beginning that you wanted to be treated as an NHS patient, or you had signed the NHS dental treatment form.

Useful addresses

Action for Sick Children
c/o National Children's Bureau
8 Wakley Street
London EC1V 7QE
Tel: 020 7843 6444
Website: www.actionforsickchildren.org

Action for the Victims of Medical Accidents
44 High Street
Croydon CR0 1YB
Tel: 020 8686 8333
Fax: 020 8667 9065
Email: admin@avma.org.uk
Website: www.avma.org.uk

British Pregnancy Advisory Service
Austy Manor
Wooton Wawen
Solihull
West Midlands B95 6BX

Tel: 0845 730 4030
Fax: 01564 794 935
Website: www.bpas.org

College of Health
St Margaret's House
21 Old Ford Road
London E2 9PL
Tel: 020 8983 1225
Fax: 020 8983 1553
Email: info@collegeofhealth.org.uk
Website: www.collegeofhealth.org.uk

General Dental Council
37 Wimpole Street
London W1G 8DQ
Tel: 020 7887 3800
Fax: 020 7224 3294
Email: Complaints@gdc-uk.org
Website: www.gdc-uk.org

General Medical Council
178 Great Portland Street
London W1W 5JE
Tel: 020 7580 7642
Fax: 020 7915 3641
Email: gmc@gmc-uk.org
Website: www.gmc-uk.org

General Optical Council
41 Harley Street
London W1G 8DJ
Tel: 020 7580 3898
Website: www.optical.org

The Health Professions Council
Park House
184 Kennington Park Road
London SE11 4BU
Tel: 020 7582 0866

Fax: 020 7820 9684
Website: www.hpc-uk.org

Health Service Ombudsman
Website: www.health.ombudsman.org.uk

England
Millbank Tower
Millbank
London SW1P 4QP
Tel: 020 7217 4051
Fax: 020 7217 4000
Email: OHSC.Enquiries@ombudsman.gsi.gov.uk

Scotland
23 Walker Street
Edinburgh EH3 7HX
Tel: 0870 011 5378
Fax: 0870 011 5379
Email: enquiries@scottishombudsman.org.uk

Wales
5th Floor, Capital Tower House
Greyfriars Road
Cardiff CF10 3AG
Tel: 029 2039 4621
Email: WHSC.Enquiries@ombudsman.gsi.gov.uk

Mental Health Act Commission
Maid Marian House
56 Hounds Gate
Nottingham NG1 6BG
Tel: 0115 943 7100
Fax: 0115 943 7101
Email: ChiefExec@mhac.trent.nhs.uk
Website: www.mhac.trent.nhs.uk

National Association for Mental Health (MIND)
15-19 Broadway
London E15 4BQ

Tel: 020 8519 2122
Helpline: 0845 766 0163
Fax: 020 8522 1725
Email: contact@mind.org.uk
Website: www.mind.org.uk

NHS Education for Scotland (NES)
22 Queen Street
Edinburgh EH2 1NT
Tel: 031 226 7371
Fax: 0131 225 9970
Website: www.nes.scot.nhs.uk

NHS Direct
Helpline: 0845 46 47
Website: www.nhsdirect.nhs.uk

NHS Helpline for Scotland
Tel: 0845 4 24 24 24

Pharmaceutical Society of Great Britain
1 Lambeth High Street
London SE1 7JN
Tel: 020 7735 9141
Fax: 020 7735 7629
Email: enquiries@rpsgb.org.uk
Website: www.rpsgb.org.uk

Scottish Association for Mental Health
Cumbrae House
15 Carlton Court
Glasgow G5 9JP
Tel: 0141 568 7000
Fax: 0141 568 7001
Email: enquire@samh.org.uk
Website: www.samh.org.uk

Vaccine Damage Payment Unit, Department of Social Security
Palatine House

Lancaster Road
Preston PR1 1HB
Tel: 01772 899 693

Welsh National Board for Nursing, Midwifery and Health Visiting (WNB)
 2nd Floor, Golate House
101 St Mary Street
Cardiff CF10 1DX
Tel: 029 2026 1400
Fax: 029 2026 1499
Email: info@wnb.org.uk
Website: www.wnb.org.uk

Sample letter 56: Complaint about an NHS provider

1, Any Street
Anytown
Anyshire
AN1 2YZ

25th June, 2003

NHS Provider

Dear Sirs,

Re: Complaint about your service

I am writing to complain because I am dissatisfied with the service provided by *Briers Surgery* in *Epsom.*

The details of my complaint are as follows: *I found Dr. Stephens to be very abrupt, did not listen to what I had to say and seemed to rush me out of the door without hardly discussing my symptoms. I understand that GPs are under enormous pressure but I do believe in getting a high standard of patient care.*

Please investigate this matter and let me know the outcome. If I am still dissatisfied I serve notice that I will consider making a request for an independent review.

Yours faithfully,

David Chambers

David Chambers

Sample letter 57: Requesting an Independent Review

1, Any Street
Anytown
Anyshire
AN1 2YZ

25th June, 2003

Convenor
Health Authority

Dear Sirs,

Re: Complaint against *Briers Surgery, Epsom*

I am writing to say that I am not satisfied with the response of the above NHS provider to my complaint - please see my letter attached and their reply.

I understand you have been appointed as convenor in this case. I would greatly appreciate it if you would consider having an independent review of my complaint carried out. My reasons for making this request are:

1. I do not consider that I received adequate patient care.
2. I am still suffering from terrible symptoms not addressed by Dr. Stephens.

As you can see I regard the matter as being very serious. I look forward to hearing the outcome of your decision.

Yours sincerely,

David Chambers

David Chambers

Enc.

Sample letter 58: Seeking review of Community Care Needs Assessment prior to discharge from hospital

1, Any Street
Anytown
Anyshire
AN1 2YZ

25th June, 2003

Social Work Department
Hospital

Dear Sirs,

Re: *Miss Peters, Bluebird Ward, Kew Hospital*

As you know, *Miss Peters* has carried out a *Community Care Needs Assessment prior to my discharge from hospital.* I am confirming formally that I am not happy with the outcome of the assessment. After much thought, I have decided that *I do not wish to leave my home and go into residential care, although I might consider sheltered housing.*

Therefore, I would be pleased if you would review the assessment that has been made.

I understand that until the review process is completed I should not be discharged from NHS care.

If you do not accede to this request I will exercise my right to use the NHS complaints procedure for this hospital.

Yours faithfully,

David Chambers

David Chambers

The neighbourhood and the environment

If you have a complaint about a neighbour, first discuss the problem with them or write to them (see sample letter 59). Failing this, there are three ways forward – mediation, getting other authorities to take action, or taking legal or other action yourself. The neighbour may be another family living next door, but it could equally be a local factory, shop or nightclub. With other environmental problems, there are specific bodies you can complain to.

Mediation

A neighbourhood mediation service may help resolve problems in some cases without taking legal action. An independent third party will listen to your views and those of the other party and help you reach an agreement. Take advice or contact **Mediation UK** to see if there is such a service in your area.

Getting other authorities to take action

You can complain to your local authorities **Environmental Health Department** – see sample letter 61. They have wide ranging powers to tackle problems, and in addition many councils have bylaws to cover specific problems such as fireworks and loud music.

If the problem is serious enough to be classed as a statutory nuisance, for example noise, an officer will contact those responsible. If this fails, providing there is enough evidence of the problem, the next step will be for the department to issue a formal notice on them so that the complaint may be resolved. If this notice is ignored, the department could do a range of things including prosecuting the offenders or seeking an injunction. In some cases, for example noise, they could seize the offending noise-making equipment. Note that you will probably be less likely to succeed if the problem is caused by a local business as they may convince a court that they are doing all they can to minimise the noise.

In order to improve your chances of getting something done try to get others in your neighbourhood to complain at the same time, or at least be prepared to act as witnesses to support your complaint. If you feel the Environmental Health Department failed in its duties, see *Local authorities*.

You could also contact the police if the problem is urgent, for example if an all night party disturbs you, or if you feel the violence could arise.

Taking legal action

As an alternative in some circumstances such as noise problems you could take your own legal action in the form of a complaint to the **Magistrates Court** or, in Scotland, the Sheriffs Court under Section 82 of the Environmental Protection Act 1990. This is a private prosecution. You will have to first give the person you are accusing 3 days notice in writing of your intentions. The court may hear the case in the presence of yourself and the accused. If they decide in your favour they will order them to abate the noise nuisance and say how this should be done. If they disregard this you may have to go through the process again – the accused may be then be fined. Take advice.

As an alternative you could start legal proceedings in the **County court** to seek an injunction to get the person or persons responsible to restrict the noise and possibly claim compensation for inconvenience or distress or damage to health. Take advice.

- To complain and to ask about claiming compensation with regard to noise from civil aircraft contact the local airport or the aircraft operators. If you live near Heathrow Airport, Gatwick Airport or Stansted Airport, use their freephone services. For general information on policy contact the **Department for Transport – Aviation Division**.

- On noise from military aircraft complain to any **RAF station, RAF Regional Community Relations Office**, or military flying unit if there is one known in your area. Alternatively you can write direct to the **Ministry of Defence, Secretariat (Air Staff)**. If you are claiming compensation write to the **Ministry of Defence Claims Branch**. If the noise is from a military aerodrome write to the **Ministry of Defence, Directorate of Safety**.

- If you are suffering from traffic noise because a new road has been built passing near your home you may be able to claim compensation or have insulation paid for. In the first instance contact **The Highways Agency (England)**,

the **Scottish Office Development Department** or the **National Assembly for Wales Highways Directorate**.

- Similarly for new rail routes, contact the **Department for Transport**.

- If you or your neighbourhood are the victim of anti-social behaviour, or if you are racially harassed, complain as above or to the local council housing office if the offender is a council tenant (see sample letter 62). The former two may prosecute, and if the offender is a council tenant they may face eviction. In the case of racism you could also get the support of the **Race Equality Council** (see *Taking things further*).

- If you are disturbed by the noise or smell created by a neighbour's domestic pets, complain as above. If you suspect that the problem arises because of ill treatment, contact your local branch of the **RSPCA** or, in Scotland, the **Scottish Society for the Prevention of Cruelty to Animals (SSPCA)**.

- If a neighbour's vegetation overhangs your garden, you are legally entitled to lop all foliage or branches overhanging up to boundary level, though you must get the consent of the local council in the case of a tree if there is a preservation order on it or if you are in a conservation area. You may prefer to write to the neighbour first (see sample letter 59). Return the branches and any fruit on their side, to the neighbour's garden being careful not to cause damage to them (otherwise the neighbour may try to claim compensation from you).

- If your neighbour's bonfire is dangerous, you could phone the Fire Brigade or enter the neighbour's garden yourself to control it. If the bonfire is causing a hazard to road users, the police could be contacted. The neighbour may also be contravening local bylaws so check with the **Environmental Health Department.**

- Noisy children are not classified as a 'nuisance' in law, so there is little you can do about them apart from talk to their parents. However if children are causing annoyance by playing football in the street an offence is being committed, so contact the police.

- If a child damages your property there is no point in suing them unless they are old enough to know what they have done. Nor is it worthwhile if the child has no money to pay up. You may, however, be able to sue the parents for damages on the grounds of negligence if they have trusted the child with something, which is beyond their capacity to use responsibly (for example, an air gun).

- To complain about proposed developments (for example industrial units you think will be an eyesore) find out from the local authority **Planning Department** whether the proposals require planning permission and whether this has been applied for. If planning permission is not required, or if it has already been granted, there is little you can do, but if you were not asked for your views you could complain (see *Local authorities*). If permission is required, and work has gone ahead without it, the planning department may order the work to cease. If permission has been applied for, put your objections in writing to the Planning Department within 8 weeks. See sample letter 63.

- If you have concerns about environmental issues in your area such as air quality, conservation, risks to wildlife, fisheries, flood defences, flood warning systems, navigation, land quality, pollution, illegal dumping of hazardous wastes, waste control or river quality, report these to the **Environment Agency** as they have the statutory responsibility for these issues. There are also a wide range of environmental campaign and support organisations that may assist, for example **Friends of the Earth**.

- If you are dissatisfied with the Environment Agency's response contact their local office and the General Manager for the region. Failing that, write to the relevant Directorate at Regional level or the Head Office. You then have recourse to the **Local Government Ombudsman** (see *Local authorities*) if your complaint is about flood defence or land drainage matters; or the **Parliamentary Ombudsman** on all other work (see *Public services*). In some circumstances, for example, refusal of a licence or permission, you could also complain to the **Department for the Environment, Food and Rural Affairs**.

- If street lighting is not sufficient complain to your local authority; if you have a parish council they may be responsible.

- If construction or repair work being undertaken causes you to have an accident, causes your health to suffer or results in damage to any of your possessions you may have a claim for compensation from the body responsible. Take advice.

- If you are disturbed so much by this work you have to temporarily move home, you may be able to claim some of the expenses for doing this. Contact the council **Planning Department** and take advice.

- If your home is compulsorily purchased and you dispute the amount of compensation you are offered complain (see *Local authorities*) whether you are a tenant or owner-occupier. If the dispute concerns the value of your home, you could appeal to the **Lands Tribunal**.

- If your property is reduced in value by the new development you may be able to get compensation from the local authority. Contact your local council **Planning Department** and ask for a 'Blight Notice.' If the amount you claim is disputed, the District Surveyor will inspect your property. If you disagree with their estimate appeal to the **Lands Tribunal**, or if you are unhappy about how your application was handled complain as above (see *Local authorities*).

Useful addresses

Department for the Environment, Food and Rural Affairs
Nobel House
17 Smith Square
London SW1P 3JR
Tel: 020 7238 6000
Fax: 020 7238 6609
Email: helpline@defra.gsi.gov.uk
Website: www.defra.gov.uk

Department for Transport
Great Minster House
76 Marsham Street
London SW1P 4DR
Tel: 020 7944 8300
Fax: 020 7944 6589
Website: www.dft.gov.uk

Department for Transport – Aviation
Great Minster House
76 Marsham Street
London SW1P 4DR
Tel: 020 7944 8300
Fax: 020 7944 6589
Email: aed@dft.gsi.gov.uk
Website: www.aviation.dft.gov.uk

Environment Agency
Flood warning line: 0845 988 1188
General enquiry line: 0845 933 3111 – to be put through to local office
Emergencies: 0800 807 060
Email: enquiries@environment-agency.gov.uk
Website: www.environment-agency.gov.uk

Friends of the Earth
26-28 Underwood Street
London N1 7JQ
Tel: 020 7490 1555
Fax 020 7490 0881
Website: www.foe.org.uk

Friends of the Earth Scotland
Information Department
72 Newhaven Road
Edinburgh EH6 5QG
Tel: 0131 554 9977
Fax: 0131 554 8656
Website: www.foe-scotland.org.uk

Gatwick Airport
Flight Evaluation Unit
Room 757, South Office Block
Gatwick Airport
West Sussex RH6 0NP
Tel: 0800 393 070
Email: lgwnoise_line@baa.com
Website: www.baa.co.uk

Heathrow Airport
Flight Evaluation Team
BAA Heathrow
2nd Floor, Building 820
Heathrow Airport, Hayes
Middlesex UB3 5AP
Tel: 0800 344 844
Email: lgwnoise_line@baa.com
Website: www.baa.co.uk

The Highways Agency – Traffic, Safety and Environment Division
Room 13/16, St Christopher House
Southwark Street
London SE1 OTE
Tel: 0845 750 4030
Email: noise@highways.gsi.gov.uk
Website: www.highways.gov.uk

Lands Tribunal

England & Wales
48/49 Chancery Lane
London WC2A 1JR

Tel: 020 7947 7200
Fax: 020 7947 7215
Email: lands@courtservice.gsi.gov.uk
Website: www.courtservice.gov.uk/tribunals/lands/lands_home.htm

Scotland
1 Grosvenor Crescent
Edinburgh EH12 5ER
Tel: 0131 225 7996
Fax: 0131 226 4812
Email: mailbox@lands-tribunal-scotland.org.uk

Mediation UK
Alexander House
Telephone Avenue
Bristol BS1 4BS
Tel: 0117 904 6661
Fax: 0117 904 3331
Email: enquiry@mediationuk.org.uk
Website: www.mediationuk.org.uk

Ministry of Defence
Ministry of Defence Secretariat (Air Staff) 2B
Room 8249, Main Building
Whitehall
London SW1A 2HB
Website: www.mod.uk

Ministry of Defence – Claims Branch
Directorate of Claims and Legal (Finance and Secretariat)
Claims 2, Room 616
St Giles Court, 1-13 St Giles High Street
London WC2H 8LD
Tel: 020 7807 0061
Website: www.mod.uk

National Assembly for Wales
National Assembly for Wales
Cardiff Bay
Cardiff CF99 1NA

Tel: 029 20 825111
Website: www.wales.gov.uk

Royal Society for the Prevention of Cruelty to Animals (RSPCA)
Enquiries Service
Wilberforce Way, Southwater
Horsham, RH13 9RS
Helpline: 0870 555 5999
Fax: 0870 753 0284
Website: www.rspca.org.uk

Scottish Society for the Prevention of Cruelty to Animals (SSPCA)
Braehead Mains
603 Queensferry Road
Edinburgh EH4 6EA
Tel: 0131 339 0222
Fax: 0131 339 4777
Email: enquiries@scottishspca.org
Website: www.scottishspca.org

Scottish Environmental Protection Agency
Erskine Court, Castle Business Park
Stirling FK9 4TR
Tel: 01786 457 700
Fax: 01786 446 885
Emergency Hotline: 0800 807 060
Website: www.sepa.org.uk

The Scottish Office Development Department
National Roads Directorate
Victoria Quay
Edinburgh EH6 6QQ
Tel: 0131 556 8400
Fax:0131 244 8240
Email: ceu@scotland.gov.uk
Website: www.scotland.gov.uk

Stansted Airport
Noise Management Unit
Enterprise House

Stansted Airport
Essex CM24 1QW
Tel: 0800 243 788
Email: stanstednoiseline@baa.com
Website: www.baa.co.uk

Sample letter 59: Overhanging tree notice

1, Any Street
Anytown
Anyshire
AN1 2YZ

25th June, 2003

Dear *Mr Hughes,*

I am writing to let you know that I intend to cut the branches of the oak tree, which overhangs my property from yours. My reasons for doing so are as follows:

They are blocking out the sun from half of my garden and are causing my grass to die.

I am legally entitled to do this at the point where the branches cross the boundary between our two properties, unless a Preservation Order protects this tree. I should be grateful if you would confirm whether such an order exists.

As we do not live in a conservation area I am not intending to ask the local council before cutting the tree.

Please let me know whether you would like to cut the branches, to which you are legally entitled.

I look forward to hearing from you shortly.

Yours sincerely,

David Chambers

David Chambers

Sample letter 60: Complaint about noise from building site

1, Any Street
Anytown
Anyshire
AN1 2YZ

25th June, 2003

Building Company

Dear Sirs,

I am writing to complain about the intolerable level of noise coming from your firm's building site at the following address:

31, Vicarage Lane, Southsea, West Sussex

I have repeatedly asked your site manager, Mr *Peters,* to reduce the noise but there has been no reduction in it whatsoever. As you are aware, Section 60 of the 1974 Control of Pollution Act gives local authorities extensive powers of control not only over the hours at which building work can be carried out and the type of machinery used, but also over the level of noise permitted.

If the noise levels are not reduced in the next few days I will have no alternative but to complain to the local environmental health officer.

Yours faithfully,

David Chambers

David Chambers

Sample letter 61: Complaint to Environmental Health Department about excessive noise from neighbours

1, Any Street
Anytown
Anyshire
AN1 2YZ

25th June, 2003

The Environmental Health Officer
Local Authority

Dear Sirs,

Re: *Mr & Mrs Curtis, 24 Sea Road, Brighton*

I am writing to ask that you help to resolve my complaint with my neighbours *Mr & Mrs Curtis* of *24 Sea Road, Brighton*.

My complaint is that they produce excessive and therefore unreasonable noise, interfering with my enjoyment of the property to the extent that I find it intolerable. I have politely asked my neighbours to stop making so much noise, but to no effect. I have also obtained written statements from other affected neighbours to support my complaint, copies of which I am enclosing.

I understand that the Noise Act 1996 gives the council immediate powers to deal with high levels of noise from residential properties between the hours of 11pm and 7am Considering it is often during the night that noise is excessive, I trust that you will be able to act quickly and decisively to put it to an end.

I look forward to hearing what course of action you will take.

Yours faithfully,

David Chambers

David Chambers

Sample letter 62: Complaint to environmental health department about anti-social council tenants

1, Any Street
Anytown
Anyshire
AN1 2YZ

25th June, 2003

The Housing Department
Local Authority

Dear Sirs,

Re: *Mr & Mrs Brown - 3, High Street, SE21*

I understand that under the Housing Act 1996 councils can opt to use new, swift powers of eviction to deal with troublesome local authority housing tenants.

I should be grateful if you would confirm whether or not you have opted to use these powers and, if so, whether you can act to deal with tenants who occupy the following property: *3, High Street, SE21.*

I speak both for myself and on behalf of neighbours when I say that these council tenants are consistently anti-social and are a nuisance for the following reasons:

1. *They have parties every Friday and Saturday night until 4am creating incredible noise.*
2. *Beer bottles from the party are thrown onto my front lawn.*
3. *They refuse to turn the music down and are incredibly uncooperative.*

I look forward to hearing what course of action you will take.

Yours faithfully,

David Chambers

David Chambers

Sample letter 63: Notice objecting to planning permission

1, Any Street
Anytown
Anyshire
AN1 2YZ

25th June, 2003

Planning Department – Local Authority

Dear Sirs,

Re: Development of *19, Lyndhurst Avenue, Durham* – Reference Number *6396*

We understand that *Collins Entertainments Ltd.* have sought planning permission from yourselves to redevelop the former bank at the above address, and convert it into a nightclub. We are residents of *Lyndhurst Avenue* and you will see from the enclosed map that we live just 50 metres from this building.

Please regard this letter as our Notice objecting to the proposed development. Our objections are on several grounds:

- Noise disturbance at night: This is a quiet residential area. The noise decibels that will emanate from a nightclub would be to our detriment in that it would cause a great deal of stress and interruption of sleep. Even if the club itself manages to insulate noise coming from their building they would not be able to deal with the inevitably noisy crowds of young people who will be walking past our house well into the small hours.
- Increased traffic: The roads will become much busier than they are now, causing us concern about noise, road safety, and parking. We are not convinced that there will be sufficient parking made available so we expect a lot of vehicles to park in the streets around here, causing widespread inconvenience and a further deterioration to our environment.
- Crime: We have a fear that the crime rate may increase with so many night clubbers descending on the area. Many will be under the influence of alcohol and this could lead to all sorts of disturbances.

In essence we do not object to nightclubs in principle, but we feel strongly that this is the wrong area for one to be sited.

If planning permission were granted this would radically change the nature of our area and greatly damage the quality of our lives, not to mention others who live in this neighbourhood. Because of this a local residents action committee has been set up to campaign against the proposals and if the development does proceed, we will use every legal remedy open to us to complain, for example, the Noise Act 1996 and the Environmental Protection Act 1990. The campaign group will hold their first press conference this week.

I look forward to knowing your decision on this matter.

Yours faithfully,

David Chambers

David Chambers

The Police

The police complaints procedure

If you want to complain about an incident you could go to your local police station – your complaint will be logged. Otherwise you could write to the Chief Constable of the force, or, in London, the Commissioner of the Metropolitan Police – see sample letter 64. Alternatively, you could write directly to the **Police Complaints Authority** and they will forward your letter.

Your correspondence should contain brief facts of the incident(s) and if possible the identities of the officers involved. For uniformed officers an identity number is visible on their uniform. If the complaint is serious you could also send a copy to the Police Authority as they have responsibility for overseeing the police force in your area and have a duty to monitor complaints. Local authority councillors serve on this so the local authority will advise you further. In London you do not have this option but some London boroughs have police committees to watch over police activity so you could copy your letter there.

A police officer will deal with your complaint and they will interview you at a venue of your choice. You are allowed to have someone with you. A written statement will then be prepared for your signature, but it is better to have one already prepared – you can always add to it before you sign. The investigation will establish if the officer(s) were in breach of the Police and Criminal Evidence (PACE) Act Codes of Practice or the Police Code of Conduct. Take advice if you want details of these Codes.

Informal resolution or formal investigation?

If your complaint is relatively minor, you can agree to informal resolution, but you can insist on a formal investigation if you wish (see sample letter 65). Informal resolution would usually result in you being offered an apology or an explanation.

A different police officer will look into your complaint and you and any witnesses may be interviewed again. If the complaint is regarded as serious a report will be made to the Police Complaints Authority. They will consider whether to supervise the investigation, as an independent body. If the complaint is about a senior officer

(Assistant Chief Constable or above) the matter will be referred to the **Police Authority** for your area or the **Police Commissioner for the Metropolitan Police,** for investigation. If you feel unhappy about the way things are proceeding, you could try writing to the PCA direct.

If your complaint is upheld you will receive an apology and /or an explanation. The police officer(s) concerned may have to face disciplinary action and may also be referred to the **Crown Prosecution Service** for criminal proceedings, depending on the nature and severity of the offence. The PCA will receive a record of the investigation whether or not they supervised it, and they could challenge or overrule these proceedings if they thought necessary. At any proceedings you may be called as a witness – if so take advice.

Legal challenges

If you get no joy from the complaints procedure it may be worth seeing if you have a case under the Human Rights Act – take advice. If you feel you have been wrongly convicted of an offence you will need to appeal to a higher court. It is also possible to ask the Home Secretary to consider referring your case to a **Court of Appeal** or to grant a free pardon.

Other issues

- If you have sustained injuries as a result of an alleged assault by the police (or indeed anyone) you can claim compensation from the **Criminal Injuries Compensation Authority**. Of course, it would help if you had made a successful complaint to the police but this is not essential. Take advice before accepting an award as you have a right of appeal.

- You could take legal action for compensation from the police for such things as arrest and detention without good cause, financial loss as a result of police action and assault. Take advice. You must bring proceedings within three years of the incident, though there are some exceptions.

- If your complaint is that the police are holding on to some property belonging to you, you should write to the Chief constable for the force concerned. If the property is still not returned, or if you have not received a satisfactory explanation for this, you can apply to your local **Magistrates Court** for an Order releasing the property – take advice.

• If you are concerned about the policies of the police force in your area, for example if you think there are not enough constables on the beat or if you disagree with the police handling of a demonstration, contact the councillors on the Police Authority as above, or write to the Police Authority direct. For London you have to write to the **Home Office** but if there is a police committee run by your borough, they may assist. Also you could attend one of the community consultation meetings the Police are obliged to organise. **Liberty** runs a Legal Helpline that may be able to offer advice and assistance.

Useful addresses

Criminal Injuries Compensation Authority
Morley House, 26-30 Holborn Viaduct
London EC1A 2JG
Tel: 020 7842 6800
Fax: 020 7436 0804
Email: enquiries.cica@gtnet.gov.uk
Website: www.cica.gov.uk

Home Office
7th Floor, 50 Queen Anne's Gate
London SW1H 9AT
Tel: 0870 000 1585
Fax: 020 7273 2065
Email: public.enquiries@homeoffice.gsi.gov.uk
Website: www.homeoffice.gov.uk

Liberty
21 Tabard Street
London SE1 4LA
Tel: 020 7403 3888
Fax: 020 7407 5354
Email: info@liberty-human-rights.org.uk
Website: www.liberty-human-rights.org.uk

Police Complaints Authority
10 Great George Street
London SW1P 3AE
Tel: 020 7273 6450
Email: info@pca.gov.uk
Website: www.pca.gov.uk

Sample letter 64: Complaint to local police service

1, Any Street
Anytown
Anyshire
AN1 2YZ

25th June, 2003

Chief Constable

Dear *Det. Insp. Hughes,*

Re: Complaint

Please regard this as a letter of complaint. On *12th May, 2003* at *11.17pm* I was stopped in the street, at the *High Street, London Bridge, SE1* and searched by Police Constable *Hurst (Number 2142).*

I wish to complain about this incident. *I was walking home minding my own business when he pounced on me out of the blue and began to pick on me in an insulting and aggressive manner. I felt humiliated and very scared.*

I do not feel that the police should conduct themselves in this way, so I would like to bring this incident to your attention in the hope that you will investigate and do something to prevent a recurrence. I need your intervention to restore my shattered confidence in the local police force.

In addition, I believe that the PC did not follow the Police and Criminal Evidence Act 1984 Codes of Practice - in this case in particular *Code A - in that he did not treat me with courtesy and consideration, and indeed he had no reasonable grounds for stopping and searching me in the first place.*

I look forward to hearing from the Police Officer you appoint to investigate this complaint. Please note I would prefer to be interviewed in my own home rather than at a police station.

I am sending a copy of this letter to the Police Complaints Authority for their information.

Yours sincerely,

David Chambers

David Chambers

Sample letter 65: Requesting a formal investigation of a complaint

1, Any Street
Anytown
Anyshire
AN1 2YZ

25th June, 2003

Chief Constable

Dear Sir,

Re: *Harassment complaint* – Reference Number *546*

I am writing about the above complaint made by myself.

I am advised that the investigating officer has taken the view that my complaint is suitable for an informal resolution. However, I disagree as I feel strongly that the incidents I am complaining about warrant a formal investigation due to the seriousness of the matter. My reasons are as follows:

1. *PCs Stephenson and Lawrie came round to my house at least three times a week and stopped me on my motorbike twice a week without proper reason.*
2. *They interviewed my family unnecessarily in an abrupt and forceful manner.*
3. *They searched my property without gaining proper authorisation first.*

I look forward to a new investigator being appointed to deal with this complaint. Please keep me informed of the progress of this case.

I have sent a copy of this letter to the Police Complaints Authority for their information.

Yours faithfully,

David Chambers

David Chambers

Post Office and mail delivery

At the time of writing just one company is licensed to provide a universal postal service – **Consignia**. Consignia runs three main services, all separately managed: **The Royal Mail, Post Office Network Unit** and **Parcelforce Worldwide**.

First you will need to establish which of the services has caused the problem. Each have their own contact details for complaints but it may initially be worth attempting to resolve the matter informally, for example with the Post Office manager, the local Royal Mail sorting office or the Parcelforce depot. With some complaints it may be useful to refer to any failure of the postal service to adhere to the performance standards agreed with the regulator of the **Postal Services Commission (Postcomm)**. Take advice from the watchdog organisation for mail services **Postwatch**. If your complaint is about financial or banking services provided from Post Offices see *Banking services*, for social security payments see *Social security*.

There are of course other mail delivery services you may have a complaint about, for example courier and parcel services. These are licensed by Postcomm so you could contact Postwatch after exhausting their internal procedures. Also see *Buying services.*

Should you still be dissatisfied write to **Postwatch** (or use their online complaints form). After investigation, they may intervene to try to get agreement with the company on remedying your concern. If the company does not act, they could refer the matter to the Postcomm to request enforcement action.

Specific issues

- If you live in a rural community and you are concerned about losing your local Post Office, or it has already disappeared, you could help form a local campaign group. Alternatively, you could consult Postwatch, the **Countryside Agency,** or the Rural Community Council or the Parish Council for your area.

- If your mail is lost, damaged or misdelivered complain to Royal Mail as above – see sample letter 66. You can claim compensation if you are the sender but the amount will usually depend on the level of service you had chosen. At the time of writing you can claim up to £27 for loss of normal first or second-class post, but you will be asked to produce a Certificate of Posting (you can only get that from a Post Office when you ask them to send the mail). In any event you cannot usually claim for damage to ceramics or glassware, or loss of cash or tokens.

Useful addresses

Consignia
Website: www.consignia.com

Countryside Agency
John Dower House
Crescent Place
Cheltenham GL50 3RA
Tel: 01242 521 381
Fax: 01242 584 270
Email: info@countryside.gov.uk
Website: www.countryside.gov.uk

Parcelforce Worldwide *or contact your local depot, or*
Helpline: 0800 224 466
Website: www.parcelforce.com

Postal services Commission (Postcomm)
Hercules House, Hercules Road
London SE1 7DB
Tel: 020 7593 2100
Fax: 020 7593 2142
Email: info@psc.gov.uk
Website: www.psc.gov.uk

Post Office Network Unit Customer Services *or contact your local Post Office, or*
Helpline: 0845 722 3344
Website: www.postoffice.co.uk

Postwatch
Consumer Services
28 Grosvenor Gardens
London SW1W 0TT
Tel: 0845 601 3265
Email: info@postwatch.co.uk
Website: www.postwatch.co.uk

Royal Mail Customer Service
Freepost
Colnebank House, 30 St Peter's Street
Colchester CO1 1HY
Helpline: 0845 774 0740
Website: www.royalmail.com

Sample letter 66: Complaint regarding delayed and damaged mail

1, Any Street
Anytown
Anyshire
AN1 2YZ

25th June, 2003

Complaints Manager
Royal Mail

Dear Sir,

Re: *First class mail* – Complaint about *delay and damage*

I am writing to complain about the poor service on the part of Royal Mail. I posted a letter to *my sister* enclosing some *photographs of my recent wedding* and the letter was handed in for posting at *Littlehampton* Post Office on *10th June.* I obtained a Certificate of Posting and enclose a copy of this as evidence of my purchase. The letter failed to arrive at *my sister's home* until *14th June,* that is, *four* working days later. This is despite the fact that your standards of service state that nine out of 10 first class letters are delivered the following working day after posting.

I feel *four* working days is disgracefully slow, *especially as I posted the letter in the morning and neither I nor my sister live in a remote rural area.*

However, even more irritatingly, my sister tells me on receiving the mail she found it half torn open and two photographs were missing. I enclose Form P58 in order to claim my compensation, but I would also like to receive an explanation and an apology for this very poor service.

Unless I hear from you within the next seven days I will refer the matter to Postwatch, as I know they are concerned about the standards of your mail delivery services.

Yours faithfully,

David Chambers

David Chambers

Public services – central government

This chapter broadly covers all services provided by government departments or agencies. In other chapters there is more detail about particular services, for example see *Inland Revenue, Social security*. For local government see *Local authorities*.

Find out the procedure

If you have any concerns first find out from a member of staff if the organisation has:

- A complaints procedure.
- A charter or statement of service standards of some kind.

Put your complaint in writing (use any complaint procedures if they exist) – see sample letter 67. If there is a charter it may help to refer to this where you think the standards have not been applied. You may be able to find out more from the **Cabinet Office** or the organisation's own website or leaflets. Alternatively, take advice. There is a universal website that has an a link to all government bodies at **www.ukonline.gov.uk**.

What if nothing seems available, or maybe you would just like to get the matter resolved quickly? Then ask to see, or write, to the person who deals with complaints. If you cannot get this information you will need to speak to a more senior person.

If things are not resolved ask if there is an Ombudsman or Adjudicator to take your complaint to. Take advice or find out from the Cabinet Office or the government body direct as above. You could also consult the **British and Irish Ombudsman Association** and they will tell you which ombudsman does what.

The Parliamentary Ombudsman

In any event there is a universal ombudsman you can complain to if you feel you have suffered due to poor administration or refusal by the government body to provide you with information. This is the **Office of the Parliamentary Commission** for **Administration (OPCA)**, commonly referred to as the Parliamentary Ombudsman. There are equivalents for Scotland, Wales and Northern Ireland. To complain, complete their form, available on their website or in their leaflet, and ask a Member of Parliament to send it on to them. Usually this would be your constituency MP. The Ombudsman will investigate if it falls within their remit. If they agree with your complaint they will recommend that the government body remedies things for you or changes policies to avoid the problem recurring.

If your complaint is about the Scottish Executive, the parliament corporation or public authorities dealing with devolved Scottish matters there is a related but separate ombudsman called the **Scottish Public Services Ombudsman**. The procedure is the same as above but complain via your constituency Member of the Scottish Parliament or one of your regional MSPs. There is also a **Welsh Administration Ombudsman** to complain about the administrative actions of the National Assembly for Wales and public authorities dealing with devolved Welsh matters. Here you can complain direct.

Useful addresses

British and Irish Ombudsman Association
Secretary
24 Paget Gardens
Chislehurst
Kent BR7 5RX
Tel/Fax: 020 8467 7455
Email: bioa@btinternet.com
Website: www.bioa.org.uk

Cabinet Office
Admiralty Arch
London SW1A 2WH
Tel: 020 7270 1234
Website: www.cabinet-office.gov.uk

Northern Ireland Ombudsman
Progressive House, 33 Wellington Place
Belfast BT1 6HN
Tel: 028 9023 3821/0800 343 424
Fax: 028 9023 4912

Email: ombudsman@ni-ombudsman.org.uk
Website: www.ni-ombudsman.org.uk

Office of the Parliamentary Commissioner for Administration (OPCA)
(Parliamentary Ombudsman)
Millbank Tower, Millbank
London SW1P 4QP
Enquiries: 0845 015 4033
Tel: 020 7217 4163
Fax: 020 7217 4160
E mail: OPCA.Enquiries@ombudsman.gsi.gov.uk
Website: www.ombudsman.org.uk

Scottish Public Services Ombudsman
23 Walker Street
Edinburgh EH3 7HX
Tel: 0870 011 5378
Fax: 0870 011 5379
Email: enquiries@scottishombudsman.org.uk
Website: www.scottishombudsman.org.uk

Welsh Administration Ombudsman
5th Floor, Capital Tower
Greyfriars Road
Cardiff CF10 3AG
Tel: 029 2039 4621
Helpline: 0845 601 0987
Email: WAO.Enquiries@ombudsman.gsi.gov.uk
Website: www.ombudsman.org.uk/pca/wales

Sample letter 67: Initial letter of complaint

A1, Any Street
Anytown
Anyshire
AN1 2YZ

25th June, 2003

River Quality Department, Environment Agency

Dear Sirs,

Re: A complaint about your service -- Reference Number *4824718*

I have been advised by a member of staff working in this department (*or your published complaints procedures*) that you are the person I should write to in respect of my complaint.

My complaint is as follows: *The river that runs at the back of my property is being continually polluted by toxic waste from the local 'Borough' factory. I understand that your agency was informed of this some time ago and the local residents were hopeful that action would take place, but up to now nothing has been done.*

For your information, I enclose evidence in the way of *photographs and newspaper articles* discussing this matter and I am happy to discuss this issue with you informally. As redress, I would like *an explanation as to why our countryside is being destroyed and information on when the pollution will be terminated.*

I would be grateful if you would attend to this matter within seven days (*or in the period specified by the complaints procedure if known*). If you fail to do so I will not hesitate to obtain and follow the complaints procedure for the DEFRA as suggested by the Cabinet Office. As you are no doubt well aware this will lead to a full investigation of your departments/sections activities, a situation that I am sure you would prefer to avoid.

I look forward to your reply.

Yours faithfully,

David Chambers

David Chambers

Enc.

Pubs and wine bars

Complaining informally is the usual thing to do, but if you want to go further it depends on the ownership of the bar.

If it is a managed or tenanted house, write to the company that owns it. They may well have a complaints procedure. If it is a managed house it is directly under the control of the owning company, so the company can deal with your complaint more effectively. A tenanted house is only under the control of the owning company inasmuch as the company lease the establishment to the tenant (the licensee). However, if they have received a number of complaints they may decide against renewing the tenant's lease when the time is due.

If the establishment is a free house, owned by the landlord, there may be nobody else 'in house' to complain to.

- If you are served short measure complain as above. Cider, beer and spirits have to be served in standard measures. There is no standard measure for wine but

if the wine bar specifies the amount they serve in a glass and you get less, you have grounds for complaint. If your complaint is not heeded, contact the **Trading Standards Service** who may intervene and could prosecute.

- If you have complaints about quality of food or drink, or poor service, see *Restaurants and cafés*. All the rules about buying goods services apply (see *Buying goods, Buying services*).

- Complain to the police if the pub or wine bar attracts unruly behaviour or if it is very noisy. You could also object when its licence comes up for renewal. This happens every year at the local magistrates court, but take advice. You would need to have good reasons and the backing of other people and businesses in the area, as well as the police, to have a good chance of success.

- If you have been treated unfairly because of your race or because you are disabled, you may be able to claim compensation, if necessary, by taking legal action – see sample letter 68 and *Taking things further.*

Sample letter 68: Complaint about disability discrimination in a pub

1, Any Street
Anytown
Anyshire
AN1 2YZ

25th June, 2003

General Manager/Licensee

Dear Sir,

Re: *Smith's Pub*, visited on *24th June* at *12:45pm*

I am writing to complain in the strongest possible terms because I have suffered a humiliating and distressing experience on visiting the above pub, which, I understand, is owned by your company. I am registered blind. I decided to go there for a drink and pub lunch yesterday while I was in town for an afternoon meeting. It is not a pub I had visited before but I went there feeling confident that I would receive a friendly and considerate service.

How misguided I was. The woman at the bar refused to serve me, saying the pub was far too busy and she didn't have time to help me out if I couldn't cope. She said it would be best if I came back later, or maybe tried the local blind club. I'm sure the implication was that I would spill food and drink all over the place.

First, I am not completely blind, just partially sighted. Secondly, even if I had been totally without sight there is no way I should have suffered that kind of treatment. I am a frequent pub visitor in my home town and have never faced such humiliation. (Yes I can drink a pint and eat a meal without spilling anything!) I hold your company to be in breach of the Disability Discrimination Act 1995 in that it has unlawfully discriminated against me, treating me 'less favourably' because of my disability by making it 'impossible or difficult to access the service'.

In recognition of this I require two outcomes. Firstly, I would like some compensation for injury to feelings. Secondly, I would like you to ensure a change of your policies and staff training procedures to ensure that this kind of discrimination does not take place again. It would also help if you could have your menus available in Braille as this would greatly aid some people with sight difficulties.

If you fail to take the above action I will not hesitate to bring a claim to the County court for compensation and to seek an injunction to prevent further discrimination of this nature.

I look forward to your reply.

Yours faithfully,

David Chambers

David Chambers

231

Rail services

Underground trains

For underground services outside London, first write to the service operator – their name and address must be displayed and at the station. For London underground services, complain first to the Manager of the tube line in question – this information will be on display at the station.

Give the details of the complaint, date and time of journey, and the route and direction of the service in question. The operator should have a compensation policy. For example, in London if you have been delayed for more than 15 minutes London Underground Ltd is to blame so it is worth completing a refund form (you can get one from any underground station). If they agree with your complaint you will receive a voucher for the value of the journey.

Your next step outside London is to write to the appropriate **Passenger Transport Executive** (see *Buses and coaches*). Finally, you have recourse to the **Rail Passengers Committee** for your area. In London you can complain to **London Underground Ltd Customer Services** and then to the **London Transport Users Committee (LTUC)** – see *Buses and coaches*.

Overland rail services

For complaints about overland rail services first write to the train operators customer services office. You can get a complaints form from the station or phone your complaint in – the information or booking service at the station will give you further details, failing that there will be notices at the station and on trains telling you what to do. It may help your complaint if you can refer directly to their passengers' charter (all operators must have one) as this sets out their standards as well as complaints procedures.

For complaints about services out of London, contact the **Rail Passengers Committee (RPC)** in your area. The **Rail Passengers Council** will advise you if you are not clear who this is. If it is a London service you go to the **London Transport Users Committee (LTUC)** (see *Buses and coaches*). These bodies may decide to refer your complaint to the **Office of the Rail Regulator (ORR)** – the regulatory

body – or, if your concern is to do with the granting of a franchise to a particular company, or stations facilities for the disabled, or penalty fares, the **Strategic Rail Authority (SRA)** may exert some pressure to bear.

Delays and cancellations – compensation

These are the minimum refunds the companies have to pay (if the problem is their fault). However, some companies may be more generous! For day tickets, if as a result of the delay or cancellation you cannot travel on your intended train you can claim a full refund. If you can travel but arrive more than one hour late at your destination station you will be able to claim at least a ten per cent refund. Usually you will get vouchers not cash. Refunds can be claimed either at the station, by writing to the train operating company or by using one of their complaints forms. You will need to produce the ticket as evidence. Also claim other expenses such as a taxi fare to complete your journey, enclosing receipts. See sample letter 69.

If you were using a season ticket and the company misses its punctuality or reliability targets over a twelve-month period, you can ask them to give you a discount on your next season ticket purchase (the minimum is five per cent, though its ten per cent if both targets are missed). There should be posters displaying these targets at stations.

Various issues

- You should have the opportunity to complain about withdrawals and restrictions of services, as these have to be publicised in advance. If not, complain anyway as above. There may be a transport campaign group in your area, or you could contact **Transport 2000** (see *Buses and coaches*).

- For complaints about a rail service at a station find out who runs the station and complain to them – this could be the train operating company, or **Network Rail**. There will be notices up to make this clear. Whoever it is write to their customer relations' people.

- You can appeal against a penalty fare imposed on you by London Underground (see *Buses and coaches*). If it is a rail operator you can appeal to the **Revenue Protection Support Office** – the address is on the penalty fare notice or receipt.

- If you are given wrong information for example on fares or timetables that has caused you inconvenience or ended up in you paying more than you needed complain to the provider – it may be the train operator, or the **National Rail Enquiry Service (NRES)**. Give the time and date you made the call and your telephone code so that the call centre can be identified. If you get nowhere complain as above.

- Complaints about catering on trains should be made to the train operator, for catering at stations contact the company. For food served at stations complain to the Catering Manager of the station or the individual shop or restaurant (see *Restaurants and cafés and Buying goods*). With possible health hazards complain also to the **Environmental Health Department** in the local authority area at the beginning or end of the journey or where the station is located.

- If you suffer injury or damage to property at the hands of a rail operator complain to the operator or **Miller Rail Claims** with full details of your loss. When it comes to personal injuries claims unless they are minor take advice.

- If you are concerned with the disabled access arrangements ask for the operators disabled persons protection policy and draw on this to complain. If this fails complain as above. If they were breaching the policy, the **Office of the Strategic Rail Authority** would be interested. All new rail carriages coming into service from 31 December 1998 have to comply with a number of access requirements.

Useful addresses

General Consumer Council for Northern Ireland
Elizabeth House, 116 Holywood Road
Belfast BT4 1NY
Tel: 028 9067 2488
Helpline: 0845 601 6022
Fax: 028 9065 7701
Email: info@gccni.org.uk
Website: www.gccni.org.uk

London Transport Users Committee (LTUC)
6 Middle Street
London EC1A 7JA
Tel: 020 7505 9000
Fax: 020 7505 9003
Email: enquiries@ltuc.org.uk
Website: www.ltuc.org.uk

London Underground Ltd
Customer Service Centre
55 Broadway
London SW1H 0BD
Tel: 0845 330 9880
Fax: 020 7918 4093
Email: customerservices@thetube.com
Website: www.thetube.com

Miller Rail Claims
Room A201, Macmillan House
London W2 1FT
Tel: 020 7922 6571
Fax: 020 7922 6578

Network Rail

40 Melton Street
London NW1 2EE
Tel: 020 7557 8000
Helpline: 0845 711 4141
Fax: 020 7557 9000
Website: www.networkrail.co.uk

Office of the Rail Regulator (ORR)

1 Waterhouse Square, 138-142 Holborn
London EC1N 2TQ
Tel: 020 7282 2000
Fax: 020 7282 2045
Email: contact.cct@orr.gsi.gov.uk
Website: www.rail-reg.gov.uk

Rail Passengers Committees (RPCs)

Website: www.railpassengers.org.uk

Eastern England
3rd Floor, Zone 4
Stuart House, City Road
Peterborough PE1 1QF
Tel: 01733 312 188
Fax: 01733 891 286

Midlands
6th Floor, Mclaren Building
35 Dale End
Birmingham B4 7LN
Tel: 0121 212 2133
Fax: 0121 236 6945

North Eastern England
Ground Floor, Unit 2
Holgate Court, Holgate Park
Poppleton Road
York YO26 4GB
Tel: 01904 787 711
Fax: 01904 795 689

North Western England
9th Floor, Rail House
Store Street
Manchester M1 2RP
Tel: 0161 244 5982
Fax: 0161 244 5981

Scotland
5th Floor, Corunna House
29 Cadogan Street
Glasgow G2 7AB
Tel: 0141 221 7760
Fax: 0141 221 3393

Southern England
3rd Floor, Centric House
390/391 Strand
London WC2R 0LT
Tel: 020 7240 5308
Fax: 020 7240 8923

Wales
St David s House, Wood Street
Cardiff CF10 1ES
Tel: 029 2022 7247
Fax: 029 2022 3992

Western England
10th Floor, Tower House
Fairfax Street
Bristol BS1 3BN
Tel: 0117 926 5703
Fax: 0117 929 4140
Website: www.west-railusers.com

Rail Passengers Council
Whittles House
14 Pentonville Road
London N1 9HF

Tel: 020 7713 2700
Fax: 020 7713 2729
Website: www.railpassengers.org.uk

Strategic Rail Authority (SRA)
Parliamentary and Public Communications
55 Victoria Street
London SW1H 0EU
Tel: 020 7654 6000
Fax: 020 7654 6010
Website: www.sra.gov.uk

Sample letter 69: Complaint about a rail company

1, Any Street
Anytown
Anyshire
AN1 2YZ

25th June, 2003

Rail Company

Dear Sirs,

Re: Complaint about your Company's Rail Service

I am writing to complain about your company's rail service. The rail journey in question was on *30th May at 7:30am from London to Peterborough*. I enclose a copy of my rail ticket as proof of my trip.

My complaint is that *the train in question arrived 90 minutes late at the destination and this caused me considerable inconvenience.*

I believe that what occurred is in breach of your company's rail passenger's charter and I would like a full explanation, together with an apology and compensation. I understand that I am entitled to claim at least a 10% refund in these circumstances.
(NB This is the minimum. If the company is more generous in its charter, claim the amount specified).

If I do not get a satisfactory response I will refer the matter to the Rail Passengers Committee *(or London Transport Users Committee for London)* and either they in turn may inform the Office of the Rail Regulator or the Strategic Rail Authority. Alternatively, I will do this myself.

I look forward to your reply.

Yours faithfully,

David Chambers

David Chambers

Enc.

Residential care and nursing homes

In all cases, first speak informally to a senior member of staff if possible. If you are not sure if you have grounds for complaint take advice. Many organisations may provide support and advice, such as **Age Concern** (you could contact your local office), **Counsel and Care** and **Elderly Accommodation Counsel**. If you are eligible your fees will be met in part by the Benefits Agency and in part by Social Services. Should a problem with payment arrangements arise or you wish to challenge a decision (i.e. not meeting the full cost of your care) see *Social security* or *Social services*.

Residential care home

In deciding whether to complain further obtain the Code of Practice called 'Home Life' from the registration authority (part of your local authority Social Services Department). This is regarded as good practice. How you complain depends on which of three situations applies:

- If you are in a home that the local authority owns and manages itself use the 'in house' procedure for the home. To take things further see *Social services*.

- If you arranged the stay in the home yourself use the home's procedures – see sample letter 70.

- If you are in an independent care home but you have been placed there by the local authority you can use both procedures.

Your next step is to write to the registration authority. They register all independent homes and have to inspect local authority homes, so they will investigate your complaint and may order action to be taken. If you are not happy with the way the registration authority handled your complaint you could go to the **Local Government Ombudsman** (see *Local authorities*).

Nursing home

Similarly how you complain about a nursing home depends on your situation. Find out if there is a complaints procedure, otherwise write to the most senior manager.

- If you were placed there by a local authority you should complain to them – see *Social services.* Your concern will be passed on to the **Health Authority** but the Social Services Department will continue to be involved.

- If you were placed in the home by the Health Authority (i.e. by hospital staff) use the **NHS complaints procedure**. See *National Health Services.* You could also complain to the Health Authority registration officer if the issue is about standards of care (see sample letter 71). In both cases in Northern Ireland you can contact the Board's Registration and Inspection Unit.

- If you or a relative arranged to go in the home independently you have recourse to the **Health Authority registration officer** as above.

Ill-treatment

If your complaint is about ill-treatment or misuse of your money you could report the matter to the police. The people you complain to may do this on your behalf. You or a relative could contact **Action on Elder Abuse** for advice.

Useful addresses

Action on Elder Abuse
Astral House, 1268 London Road
London SW16 4ER
Tel: 020 8765 7000
Fax: 020 8679 4074
Email: aea@ace.org.uk
Website: www.elderabuse.org.uk

Age Concern
Astral House, 1268 London Road
London SW16 4ER
Tel: 0800 009966
Website: www.ageconcern.org.uk

Counsel and Care
Twyman House
16 Bonny Street
London NW1 9PG

Tel: 020 7485 1566
Helpline: 0845 300 7585
Website: www.charitynet.org/~counsel+care

Elderly Accommodation Counsel

3rd Floor, 89 Albert Embankment
London SE1 7PT
Tel: 0207820 1343
Fax: 020 7820 3970
Email: enquiries@e-a-c.demon.co.uk
Website: www.housingcare.org

Sample letter 70: Complaint about an independent residential care home

> *1, Any Street*
> *Anytown*
> *Anyshire*
> *AN1 2YZ*
>
> 25th June, 2003
>
> General Manager
> Residential Care Home
>
> Dear Sir,
>
> Re: *Maryville Nursing Home*
>
> I am writing to make a formal complaint about the way I and several of my fellow residents are treated at the above home, which I understand is one of the homes owned by your company.
>
> I have already raised my concerns informally with *Mrs Walker*, the manager of the home, but so far no action has been taken despite her assurance that she will 'look into it'.
>
> My complaint is with regard to *the rude and insensitive way in which I am treated by two of the staff at the home - Mrs Richards and Miss Dean.* The details are as follows:
>
> *Their manner is always abrasive and on the verge of spiteful, they are continually unhelpful and confiscate gifts we receive, such as chocolate and other food, that have been sent to us by our families.*
>
> At the moment the other residents affected do not wish to have their names revealed to you - quite frankly they fear the consequences if the two staff got to hear that they had complained. However, if you were seen to be taking decisive action I know they will be prepared to talk to you.
>
> I look forward to receiving your response. Should this complaint not be dealt with to my satisfaction I will refer the matter to the Registration and Inspection Authority for this area to establish whether there has been a breach of the Registered Homes Act 1984 and/or the Code of Practice for care homes - 'Home Life'.
>
> Yours faithfully,
>
> *David Chambers*
>
> David Chambers

Sample letter 71: Complaint about a nursing home

1, Any Street
Anytown
Anyshire
AN1 2YZ

25th June, 2003

Nursing Homes Registration Officer - Health Authority

Dear Sirs,

Re: *Jane Peters - Washington Nursing Home*

I am writing on behalf of *my mother* (the above named lady) to make a formal complaint about the standard of care she receives at the above nursing home where she is resident. I have discussed my concerns on several occasions with senior staff at the home, and latterly the general manager himself, but it is clear to me that no real action has been taken to improve things.

My mother was placed in the home by the *Chichester* Hospital so I understand I can avail myself of the National Health Service Complaints procedure. However, as my complaint is about the standard of care she has a right to expect under the Registered Homes Act 1984, I felt it appropriate to contact your office directly.

The detail of my complaint is as follows: *The home appears to be very unclean and seems to have a degrading policy in place of washing the resident's clothes all together and then dressing them in anyone's garments rather than their own. I understand some of the patients have senile dementia and are unaware of this fact but I do believe that they should be able to keep their dignity and have their belongings respected.*

Due to these concerns, I am seriously considering arranging for her to be moved to another home, but I am reluctant to do this because she is very ill and the change may further damage her health. Therefore I would ask you to carry out an investigation urgently.

Please let me know when you wish to see my mother at the home, as I will need to be in attendance also due to her state of health. Please keep me informed of the progress of the investigation.

Yours faithfully,

David Chambers

David Chambers

Restaurants and cafés

There may be complaints procedures, for example if the restaurant or café is part of a chain or a retail store – see *Buying services*. Otherwise you may need to deal with the manager or owner direct.

Paying less than the price

If you think the food, drink or service is unsatisfactory, make your complaint while you are at your table. Of course to some extent standards will vary depending on the type of establishment and the prices but you have a statutory right to expect 'reasonable care and skill' within a 'reasonable time.' If the complaint is a minor one, for example that your wine is insufficiently chilled, tell the appropriate member of the waiting staff. If it is a more serious complaint ask to see the head waiter or the manager or send the items back.

If your complaint does not improve things you could negotiate to pay what you regard as reasonable, or even simply deduct from the bill an amount as compensation. A rule of thumb is to deduct 10 per cent to register your disgust, 50 per cent if things are dreadful, and 90 per cent if they were diabolical! (Source – *Consumer Association Good Food Guide*). If the service was poor, deduct a

reasonable amount from the service charge. If the waiting staff were rude or kept you waiting too long, deduct the entire service charge.

This is perfectly legal and is known as 'set off', but only do it after you have reported your complaint to the manager. Leave your name and address and show some proof of identity if possible. Explain your actions to the head waiter or manager. All this is important so it does not look as if you are trying to defraud the restaurant. The restaurant may call the police, they may even turn up, but they will not take any action unless you intended to leave without paying for no genuine reason or if you caused a violent scene over your bill.

If the restaurant sues you, you can dispute liability in court. As an alternative you can pay the bill but put it in writing that you do this 'under protest' 'without prejudice to any legal action you may wish to take,' then request money back later and compensation for your losses. If this fails, take legal action (see sample letter 72).

Specific issues

- If you have your meal and then you are overcharged compared to the prices in the menu – complain! You are only obliged to pay the prices and any extra charges listed. Prices must include VAT and any service charges must be specified otherwise you do not have to pay them. Complain to **Trading Standards**. They will investigate and warn or prosecute the restaurant if necessary.

- The restaurant service must be as described. You would have grounds for complaint if, for example, the 'fresh Dover sole' came out of the deep freeze or the 'four course lunch for £5.99 advertised on a sign outside turned out to be a two course lunch for £8.50. Again **Trading Standards** will investigate.

- If you think food or drink you are served is unfit complain as above and also to the local authority **Environmental Health Department**. Under the Food Safety Act 1990 it is a criminal offence to supply food which is not of the nature, substance or quality demanded.

- You can write to claim damages because you became ill after eating or drinking at a restaurant (see sample letter 73) but in order to take legal action, you would need to provide a specimen of what you consumed to help the Environmental Health Department's analysts with their investigation, together with medical evidence from your doctor if possible.

Sample letter 72: Complaint about quality of food served

1, Any Street
Anytown
Anyshire
AN1 2YZ

25th June, 2003

Restaurant

Dear Sirs,

Re: *Meal* on *11th June, 2003* at *7.30pm*

We came for dinner at your restaurant on *11th June* and I was disappointed to find that upon tasting my *chicken pie with vegetables*, which had been ordered, it was not satisfactory for the following reason:

The chicken was undercooked and the vegetables burnt.

I expressed my disappointment immediately and requested that the price of the dish be deducted from the bill. However, upon receiving the bill for £41.30, I discovered nothing had been done to adjust for the uneaten dish. I was given no alternative but to pay the bill in full, which I did under protest, making it clear that I would seek proper compensation from your establishment at a later date.

As you must know, the Food Safety Act 1990 makes it a criminal offence to supply food, which is not of the 'nature, substance or quality demanded'. As the dish you served was not of reasonable quality I hold you in breach of contract and wish to exercise my right to compensation.

I shall expect to receive a cheque for £20 within 10 days. Otherwise, I shall have no alternative but to issue you a County court claim for recovery of the amount owed to me without further notice.

Yours faithfully,

David Chambers

David Chambers

Sample letter 73: Claiming compensation for food poisoning

1, Any Street
Anytown
Anyshire
AN1 2YZ

25th June, 2003

Restaurant

Dear Sirs,

Re: *Meal* on *31st May, 2003* at *8.00pm*

On *31st May* my party of *six* came to have dinner at your restaurant. Shortly after our visit, *five* members of the group came down with food poisoning.

My GP has concluded that our illnesses were directly caused by the consumption of food served at your restaurant. I am also considering reporting the matter to the Council's Environmental Health Department. As I am sure you are aware, under the Food Safety Act 1990 it is a criminal offence to sell food, which is damaging to health. I therefore hold you responsible and in breach of contract.

Each of us is entitled to compensation for the suffering we have endured, time off work and other expenses. The figure I have arrived at as reasonable compensation for each of us is £35.

I look forward to receiving your payment.

Yours faithfully,

David Chambers

David Chambers

Schools

Are you the parent, or guardian, of a pupil at the school? Or perhaps you are a pupil or student yourself? Many day-to-day problems can be resolved by informal discussion with the form teacher or other teacher concerned, though concerns about school policy may be best informally raised with the head of department or school head.

Sometimes it may be worth having sight of a school policy before taking things further. The starting point is to check the schools prospectus, and also the Home School Agreement – an agreed document setting out what should be expected of the parents, pupils and the school in providing education. These should contain information on the school ethos, policies on attendance, discipline, behaviour, homework, standards of education and the complaints procedure. Draw on these to complain to the School Head (see sample letter 73).

Next steps

Follow this complaints procedure. Alternatively you could raise the matter in writing with the school governor responsible, failing that the chairperson or one of the parent governors. Possibly you may be invited to a formal meeting or an internal appeals procedure. If your concern is shared with other parents or pupils perhaps you could consider a joint approach. The schools Parent Teacher Association may assist. Support may also be available from the **Advisory Centre for Education** or the **Campaign for State Education**.

Complaining further

If the school is maintained the next step is to complain or appeal to the **Local Education Authority (LEA)**, which is part of your Local Authority – see sample letter 74. There are different procedures for different types of complaint, as below. If you are critical about the way the LEA dealt with your complaint you may be able to go the **Local Government Ombudsman** (see *Local authorities*). In the case of voluntary schools, such as church schools, you should take up your complaint at whatever level of the organisation controls the school, for example the local Diocesan Board.

If you get no joy from the school (voluntary aided or maintained) or the LEA, another option you have is to complain to the **Department for Education and Skills** (or the equivalent Government Department in Scotland, Wales or Northern Ireland). They can (under Sections 96 and 497 of the Education Act 1996) direct the school to carry out its duties properly (see sample letter 75).

Other Issues

- The school's uniform policy must be sensitive to race, culture, disability or gender otherwise you could complain that it is discriminatory (see *Taking things further*). A school may specify a particular make of clothing for a uniform, but if you get something that is not quite the same but looks similar, maybe cheaper, you would have good grounds for complaint if the school objected.

- The school should have a policy on dealing with bullying or harassment that includes ways to tackle racially motivated bullying. If the pupil is going to stay away from school while the issue is being tackled it is better to get medical evidence from the GP detailing the stress or anxiety. If there is racism involved, seek the support of the local **Race Equality Council** (see *Taking things further*). You could also consider taking legal action against the school and the LEA – take advice – and you could see the police if the offender is over ten-years-old. In addition, contact the **Anti-bullying Campaign** or the **Anti-Bullying Network**.

- In the event of an accident, take advice. Legal action for negligence against the school or the LEA may be appropriate if it was something they could have avoided happening. Although schools do not usually have insurance to cover accidents to pupils, some of the activity centres schools use have to be licensed by the **Adventure Activities Licensing Authority (AALA)** so here could be another route for your complaint.

- Complaints about school assessments or the marking of internal examinations should be made to the school. With Key Stage test results you could ask the school to request a review by an external marking agency. For external exams such as GCSEs, AS or A levels you can ask the school Head to consider requesting the examining board to make an enquiry. If you are still dissatisfied with the results you can ask the Head to appeal to the **Examinations Appeal**

Board (EAB). Any review or appeal could lead to your grade being decreased rather than increased!

• Grounds for complaint about detention would include not having at least 24 hours written notice, a teacher not present to supervise, unreasonable punishment in the circumstances or no arrangements for travel home.

• The law outlaws any physical contact by a school staff member against a pupil that is intended to cause pain, injury or humiliation. Therefore in some cases you may have an option of complaining to the police and/or considering taking legal action against the teacher, school or LEA. Take advice.

• Complain to the school head and then the chairperson of the governing body if you think a pupil's exclusion from school is unreasonable or for too long a time. Next step is to make representations to the LEA. If the decision goes against you, you can appeal. Subsequently, a hearing will be held but be warned, if the decision is in your favour the school also have the right to appeal. If all else fails see if legal action might succeed, for example, the **Human Rights Act.** Complain if the school fails to arrange for the pupil to receive schoolwork at home and to have it marked. If the pupil ends up being permanently excluded the LEA must arrange suitable alternative education.

- If you are unhappy about a Connexions service at the school (providing advice and guidance to pupils) direct your complaint to whichever organisation in your area is coordinating the service. Ask the school or take advice.

- Free transport is available to some pupils provided it is to a school the LEA regard as suitable. You will have grounds for complaint if the pupil cannot walk far for health or disability reasons, the transport does not cover the whole journey, or it is either too far or not safe enough to walk (usually the distance is two miles for a pupil under eight-years-old and three miles for pupils between the age of eight and sixteen). If your dispute is about distance an independent assessment from a local surveyor or the **Ordnance Survey** may help your case.

- If the school fails to resolve a complaint about school meals contact the LEA's school meals organiser where the LEA has provided the meals. If a private company provides the meals you could still approach the LEA as they set the contracts for the companies (also see *Restaurants and cafés*). Check with the LEA that the national nutritional standards are being kept to.

- If a pupil has been denied first choice of school, firstly informally explain your objections either to the school head, chairperson of the school governing body or LEA. This may resolve the issue. If this fails you have a right to appeal to a local appeals committee. Take advice. This is independent of the LEA and school, but the LEA will provide you with the details. If you are not happy with the way the appeal process is handled go to the **Local Government Ombudsman** (see *Local authorities*).

- There are set procedures a school must follow, together with a Code of Practice, if a pupil is thought to have special educational needs. If you feel the procedures are not being followed, or insufficient support is available, complain as above. If you disagree with an LEA decision not to arrange a formal assessment you can appeal to a **Special Educational Needs & Disability Tribunal**. You can also complain to the **Secretary of State** if you disagree with the need for such an assessment. Take advice – there are many organisations working in this field such as **Network 81**.

Useful addresses

Adventure Activities Licensing Authority (AALA)
17 Lambourne Crescent
Cardiff Business Park
Llanishen
Cardiff CF14 5GF
Tel: 029 2075 5715
Website: www.aala.org

Advisory Centre for Education (ACE)
1C Aberdeen Studios, 22 Highbury Grove
London N5 2DQ
Tel: 0808 800 5793
Fax: 020 7354 9069
Email: ace-ed@easynet.org.uk
Website: www.ace-ed.org.uk

Anti-Bullying Campaign
185 Tower Bridge Road
London SE1 2UF
Tel: 020 7378 1466
Fax: 020 7378 8374

Anti-Bullying Network
Moray House School of Education
University of Edinburgh
Holyrood Road
Edinburgh EH8 8AQ
Tel: 0131 651 6100
Email: abn@mhie.ac.uk
Website: www.antibullying.net

Campaign for State Education (CASE)
158 Durham Road
London SW20 0DG
Tel/Fax: 020 8944 8206
Email: tulloch-case@mcrl.poptel.org.uk
Website: www.casenet.org.uk

Department for Education and Skills
Sanctuary Buildings, Great Smith Street
London SW1P 3BT
Tel: 0870 000 2288
Fax: 01928 79 4248
Email: info@dfes.gsi.gov.uk
Website: www.dfes.gov.uk

The Examination Appeals Board (EAB)
83 Piccadilly
London W1J 8QA
Tel: 0207 509 5995
Website: www.theeab.org.uk

Network 81
1-7 Woodfield Terrace
Stansted
Essex CM24 8AJ
Tel: 0870 770 3262
Fax: 0870 770 3263
Email: Network81@tesco.net
Website: www.network81.co.uk

Ordnance Survey
Customer Service Centre
Romsey Road
Southampton SO16 4GU
Tel: 0845 605 0505
Fax: 023 8079 2615
Email: customerservices@ordsvy.gov.uk
Website: www.ordsvy.gov.uk

Special Educational Needs & Disability Tribunal (SENDIST)
7th Floor, Windsor House
50 Victoria Street
London SW1H 0NW
Helpline: 01325 392 555
Fax: 020 7925 6926
Website: www.sendist.gov.uk

Sample letter 73: Complaint to the School Head

1, Any Street
Anytown
Anyshire
AN1 2YZ

25th June, 2003

The Headteacher

Dear *Mr Phillips*,

Re: *James Chambers – Year 10*
     Class Teacher: Mrs Jones

I am writing to make a complaint, and to ask you to investigate. I have already discussed the matter with Mrs Jones but I do not feel the matter has been adequately resolved. Furthermore, I feel that there has been a breach of the Home School Agreement because it states, *'any child should be protected and safe whilst in school grounds'* and your school's policy on *bullying* seems not to have been applied.

My complaint is as follows: *My son has been repeatedly bullied for three months now, including physical beatings, by his fellow classmate Andrew Butler. This has resulted in him missing three weeks of school through stress and illness as the enclosed GP medical certificate shows. I have spoken to Mrs Jones about the situation but nothing has been resolved.*

I do hope that you find my complaint worthy of further investigation and I will be pleased to provide further information if needed. In addition, I will be happy to meet with you to discuss the matter in greater detail.

I look forward to your comments by *9th July.* If I am still dissatisfied I will write to the Chairperson of the School Governors and the LEA.

Yours sincerely,

David Chambers

Enc.

Sample letter 74: Complaint to the Local Education Authority

1, Any Street
Anytown
Anyshire
AN1 2YZ

25th June, 2003

Chief Education Officer – Local Education Authority

Dear *Mr Thomas,*

Re: *James Chambers – Year 10, Class Teacher: Mrs Jones, St. Peter's School*

I am writing to you because I am very concerned about a matter that has arisen at the above school. I have made a complaint to the School Head, and subsequently the Chairperson of the School Governors but to date I do not feel that my complaint has been adequately dealt with. I would be pleased if you would investigate and let me know the outcome by *19th July, 2003.* I enclose copies of my correspondence including the replies I have received.

My original complaint is as follows: *My son has been repeatedly bullied for three months now, including physical beatings, by his fellow classmate Andrew Butler. This has resulted in him missing three weeks of school through stress and illness. I have spoken to Mrs Jones about the situation but nothing has been resolved.*

I am concerned about the way the complaint has been dealt with because *I do not feel that the school has done enough to protect my son or has disciplined the alleged bully in an effective away as my son still feels incredibly threatened.*

I will be pleased to provide further information if needed, and I will be happy to meet with you to discuss the matter further.

I look forward to your reply. If I am still dissatisfied I will write to ask the Secretary of State to intervene under Sections 496 and 497 of the Education Act 1996.

Yours sincerely,

David Chambers

David Chambers

Enc.

Sample letter 75: Complaint to the Secretary of State

1, Any Street
Anytown
Anyshire
AN1 2YZ

25th June, 2003

Secretary of State, Department for Education and Skills

Dear *Mr Collins,*

Re: *James Chambers, Yr 10, Class Teacher: Mrs Jones, St. Peter's School, West Sussex LEA*

I am writing to make a formal complaint to you because I am very concerned about a matter that has arisen at the above school. Despite writing to the School Head, the Chairperson of the School Governors and finally to the LEA, to date I still do not feel that my complaint has been adequately dealt with.

I enclose copies of all my correspondence, including the replies I have received, for your information and am requesting that, in response to my complaint, you invoke the powers you have under Sections 496 and 497 of the Education Act 1996 to direct the LEA and/or the School Governors to carry out its duties properly.

My original complaint is as follows: *My son has been repeatedly bullied for three months now, including physical beatings, by his fellow classmate Andrew Butler. This has resulted in him missing three weeks of school through stress and illness. I have spoken to Mrs Jones about the situation but nothing has been resolved.*

I am concerned about the way the complaint has been dealt with because *I do not feel that the school or the LEA has done enough to protect my son or has disciplined the alleged bully in an effective away as my son still feels incredibly threatened.*

I will be pleased to provide further information if needed. I have copied this letter and enclosures to my local MP *Paul Rolf.* Looking forward to hearing from you.

Yours sincerely,

David Chambers

David Chambers

Enc.   Cc: *Paul Rolf MP*
          (NB It would be best to send a brief covering letter to the MP enclosing the above.)

Shopping from home

This is about goods or services you may buy from home via mail order, internet, digital TV, email, fax or telephone.

Know your rights

You have just the same rights as when you buy goods or services in shops, but also you have extra rights, so you can complain as for *Buying goods* and *Buying services* – see sample letter 76. Before complaining, first check the agreement you made when the item was purchased and the information made available before purchase. By law there should have been clarity in writing on such points as delivery dates, any guarantees and after sales service, suppliers full contact details and your right to cancel. You have grounds for complaint if there has been a breach of that agreement.

In many cases (under the Distance Selling Regulations 2000) you have the right to cancel for any reason, provided you inform the seller in writing (fax, letter or e

mail) within seven working days of receiving the goods (see sample letter 77). Depending on the agreement you may have to pay for their return. This also applies to services but here you must cancel within seven working days of agreeing to have the service. There are exceptions. For example, personalised goods, perishable goods, financial services – take advice. You also have a right to a refund if you do not get a delivery within 30 days.

If you were mislead by the advertising itself, see *Advertising*. If the supplier is a member of the **Mail Order Traders Association (MOTA)** you have another place to complain to as they have a code of practice and an arbitration scheme which may help. This is mostly catalogue companies. Many companies that advertise direct in the media or on posters are members of the **Direct Marketing Association (DMA)** and they too have a code of practice and arbitration scheme.

Buying over the internet: UK traders

Though you have the above rights when buying goods over the internet, there is sometimes the additional protection of an online code of practice. Check if your trader subscribes to one – they set out standards you can expect, including your rights to return goods, delivery times and prices. The code will include complaints procedures you can use if the standards are not being kept to, for example, not being able to get a refund, misuse of your credit card, or if you need to assert your statutory rights. An example is the Which? Web Trader Code set up by the **Consumer Association**. Some codes of practice have been accredited by Trust UK which means they display an 'e-hallmark' on their websites which guarantees certain minimum standards apply, so you can complain to them – this may have an impact if you are getting nowhere with the trader.

Other issues

- If the supplier is outside of the UK, see *Buying goods*.

- If you pay in advance then hear no more from the supplier here are some options. If you bought on credit for more than £100 you may be able to complain to the credit card company and get your money back – see *Credit*. If you bought from a newspaper or magazine (except a classified ad) they may be members of a scheme that will repay you. The publication may well advertise this fact and tell you how to complain, usually there will be a time limit. Otherwise for details contact the **National Newspapers' Mail Order**

Protection Scheme (NNMOPS) (for national daily newspapers), the **Newspaper Society** (regional and local papers) or the **Periodical Publishers Association** (magazines).

• Disappearing traders should be reported to **Trading Standards** or the police. They may help track them down, and prosecute if any criminal offence has been committed, though this will be unlikely to get you your money back. You may be covered under your house contents insurance for losses.

• If you are sent goods you did not order, complain to the supplier. If the goods are an unsolicited gift, you are under no obligation to send them back or pay for them. The supplier may be committing a criminal offence if they demand payment – complain to **Trading Standards**.

• If you want to stop or restrict the amount of unsolicited junk mail you receive, use the following services:

  • **Mail** – Mailing Preference Service (MPS) – which will not cover unaddressed leaflets, inserts in magazines and bills, and local mailings.

  • **Telephone Marketing** – Telephone Preference Service (TPS)

  • **Faxes** – Fax Preference Service

  • **Emails** – Email Preference Service (E-MPS)

If once you have registered the problem has not gone away complain to the appropriate organisation as above. They will investigate and report to the **Office of the Information Commissioner** who has powers to fine companies who break the rules.

Useful addresses

Direct Marketing Association (DMA)
DMA House, 70 Margaret Street
London W1W 8SS
Tel: 020 7291 3300
Fax: 020 7323 4165
Email: dma@dma.org.uk
Website: ww.dma.org.uk

Email Preference Service (E-MPS)

Website: www.e-mps.org

Fax Preference Service (FPS)

DMA House, 70 Margaret Street
London W1W 8SS
Tel: 020 7291 3330
Fax: 020 7323 4226
Email: fps@dma.org.uk
Website: www.fps-online.org.uk

Mailing Preference Service (MPS)

DMA House, 70 Margaret Street
London W1W 8SS
Tel: 020 7291 3310
Fax: 020 7323 4226
Email: mps@dma.org.uk
Website: www.mps-online.org.uk

Mail Order Traders Association (MOTA)

Drury House, 19 Water Street
Liverpool L2 0RP
Tel: 0151 227 9456
Fax: 0151 227 9678

The National Newspapers' Mail Order Protection Scheme (NNMOPS)

18A King Street
Maidenhead SL6 1EF
Tel: 01628 641930
Fax: 01628 637112
Email: enquiries@mops.org.uk
Website: www.mops.org.uk

The Newspaper Society

Bloomsbury House
74-77 Great Russell Street
London WC1B 3DA
Tel: 020 7636 7014

Fax: 020 7631 5119
Website: www.newspapersoc.org.uk

Office of the Information Commissioner
Wycliffe House
Water Lane
Wilmslow
Cheshire SK9 5AF
Tel: 01625 545 745
Fax: 01625 524 510
Email: data@dataprotection.gov.uk
Website: www.dataprotection.gov.uk

Periodical Publishers Association
Queens House
28 Kingsway
London WC2B 6JR
Tel: 020 7404 4166
Fax: 020 7404 4167
Email: info1@ppa.co.uk
Website: www.ppa.co.uk

Telephone Preference Service (TPS)
DMA House, 70 Margaret Street
London W1W 8SS
Tel: 020 7291 3320
Fax: 020 7323 4226
Email: tps@dma.org.uk
Web: www.tpsonline.org.uk

Sample letter 76: Mail order goods rejection

1, Any Street
Anytown
Anyshire
AN1 2YZ

25th June, 2003

Trader

Dear Sirs,

Re: Reference Number *213* – Purchase of *T-shirt and Man's Shirt* on *12th June, 2003*

On *12th June* I ordered the following items listed in your mail order catalogue:

1. *Female blue T-shirt with pineapple logo (ref 210)*
2. *Man's white shirt (ref 310)*

I received these goods on *18th June*. However, I am not happy with these items for the following reasons:

The goods are not of satisfactory quality, because of the following serious defects:
There were black ink marks on the white shirt.

The goods do not match their description in the catalogue, because:
The T-shirt that arrived was pink instead of blue.

The goods are not reasonably fit for their purpose, because:
The T-shirt is also the wrong size in that it is small when I asked for medium.

Under the Sale of Goods Act 1979 as amended by the Sale and Supply of Goods Act 1994 you are in breach of contract and I am legally entitled to a full refund of the purchase price, plus the cost of postage and packing. Please send me a cheque for *£59.99* within 10 days and advise me what you would like me to do with the goods. If you do not reimburse me I will have no alternative but to issue a County court claim without further notice.

Yours faithfully,

David Chambers

David Chambers

Sample letter 77: Cancelling contract for a purchase made at home

1, Any Street
Anytown
Anyshire
AN1 2YZ

25th June, 2003

Sales Company

Dear Sirs,

Re: *Vacuum Ceaner* purchased on *20th June, 2003* – Reference Number *2423*

I am requesting the cancellation of the contract referenced above. This contract was the result of an unsolicited visit by one of your sales associates, signed on *20th June, 2003*. I felt I had no choice during this visit but to sign the contract for *£499*, but I no longer wish to make this purchase. Please cancel this contract and refund my deposit of *£99.50*.

Under the Distance Selling Regulations 2000, I have the right, as a consumer, to cancel the contract from this unsolicited visit. I am requesting this within the seven-day cooling-off period allowed by these Regulations, and therefore am entitled to a full refund of my deposit.

Thank you for your timely resolution of this matter.

Yours faithfully,

David Chambers

David Chambers

Social security

There are two main routes for complaining about social security. One route applies if you are unhappy with the service you received, for example delays, inefficiency, mistakes, unsatisfactory advice or information, staff attitudes. A different route has to be used if you wish to challenge a decision that has been made about your social security entitlement. If your complaint overlaps into both areas you may have to use both routes at once.

Complaints about services

If your complaint is about the handling of your Tax Credits (such as Working Families Tax Credit) see *Inland Revenue*, if it is about Child Support see *The Child Support Agency*.

Benefits Agency

If your complaint is about any benefit administered by the Benefits Agency (or Social Security Agency in Northern Ireland) initially contact the office concerned and try to speak to the person who dealt with your case, or their supervisor. With some complaints you may be able to claim compensation.

The whereabouts of the office depends on the benefit you were claiming. For example, income support, incapacity benefit and retirement pension are all administered by your local Benefits Agency office (except Northern Ireland), other benefits are dealt with by the Benefits Agency centrally or regionally.

If you get no joy here contact the customer services manager in writing. Alternatively, from any office you can get a leaflet about complaining which contains a special form. The next stage is to ask for an 'independent review' of your complaint (see sample letter 78) and an independent panel will look at the matter again. If you are still discontented send a letter for the personal attention of the Chief Executive of the Benefits Agency at the **Department for Work and Pensions**.

Other bodies dealing with social security

If your complaint is about housing or council tax benefit contact the local authority responsible (or Housing Executive in Northern Ireland) see *Local authorities*. Again it may help to look at their customer charter or equivalent but also take advice about statutory requirements, for example you must be paid within 14 days of the local authority receiving your completed application or else a payment on account should be made to you. Complaints about war pensions should be made to the **Veterans Agency**.

For complaints about jobseeker's allowance two offices are responsible – the Benefits Agency for the benefit itself and the Employment Service for ensuring you meet the conditions for claiming, such as being available for work. The Jobseeker's Charter will set the service you should expect. If in doubt contact the **Employment Service** at the job centre and your complaint will be passed on to the Benefits Agency if it affects them.

Going to the ombudsmen

Your next step would be to complain to the **Local Government Ombudsman** (for housing and council tax benefit) (see *Local authorities*) or via your MP to the Parliamentary Ombudsman (or the Northern Ireland Ombudsman – see *Public services*) for all other benefits. In some circumstances you may be able to jump direct to this stage, for example if the internal complaints procedure for the office was impractical for you – take advice.

Challenging a decision that has been made about your social security entitlement

The following applies to most social security benefits except Housing and Council Tax Benefits. You can dispute their decision or you can appeal to an independent body – a Unified Appeal Tribunal. If you have a right of appeal on the decision you can choose to go straight to appeal or dispute first then go to appeal. This will depend on the nature of your case – take advice.

You should have received a letter setting out what benefit (if any) it has been decided you are entitled to, how much and for what period. There should be information on why the decision has been made and you will be advised whether you can ask for a written statement of reasons. If you have been given this option you must receive the reasons within 14 days provided you made the request within a month of the decision. This may help you work out your grounds for challenging the decision.

Disputing the decision

To dispute a decision apply in writing to the office that dealt with your benefit, setting out your reasons including any facts you feel the office failed to consider – take advice. In most cases there is a time limit of one month. This time limit can be extended by 14 days where you have asked for written reasons as above. If the decision is revised it will normally take effect from the date of the original decision so you may then be entitled to backdated benefit. If you are dissatisfied you may be able to appeal, or, if you have new information, apply to dispute this decision – take advice.

There is an alternative course of action open to the office – they could supersede the original decision. This means the original decision will still stand for the time it was made but a new decision has been made to take into account a new situation (for example, your circumstances may have changed). In this case you may not be due any backdated benefit.

Appeals

For most social security, you can appeal to a **Unified Appeal Tribunal**. Within one month of the decision send in one of their appeal forms, otherwise write, stating why you think the decision is wrong, and if anyone is representing you. A 14-day extension applies as for disputes where you ask for written reasons. Late appeals may be allowed only exceptionally – take advice.

When they receive your appeal the office will check to see if the original decision should be revised. If they do make changes you will need to decide whether you still have grounds to carry on with your appeal. If so you will have another month to make any alterations. If the appeal goes ahead the office submit their reasons for making the decision with all the facts and relevant legislation and send this on a Pre-Hearing Enquiry Form to you. On this form set out the evidence to support your case and return it within 14 days – take advice.

The tribunal may consider your case at an oral hearing – you can request one if you wish. They consider the arguments put by you and by the Benefits Agency, and then make their decision.

Appealing further

In some circumstances you can have a tribunal decision set aside for a technical reason, such as the appeal papers were not sent to your representative or you were not able to attend the hearing. Then a new tribunal would have to consider your case. Take advice.

You may be able to appeal to the **Social Security and Child Support Commissioners**, but only if it is thought the tribunal made an error in law. Take advice. You have to apply for permission to appeal from the tribunal chairperson usually within one month of you being sent written reasons for their decision. If you are turned down you have another month to apply to the Commissioners permission to appeal.

There could be some delay for your case to be heard but it may be possible to get things speeded up if you are in dire need by writing to the Commissioners.

Useful addresses

Chief Executive Benefits Agency
The Department for Work and Pensions
Correspondence Unit
Room 540, The Adelphi
1-11 John Adam Street
London WC2N 6HT
Tel: 020 7712 2171
Fax: 020 7712 2386
Website: www.dwp.gov.uk

Office of Social Security and Child Support Commissioners
5th Floor, Newspaper House
8–16 Great New Street
London EC4A 3NN
Tel: 0207 353 5145
Fax: 0202 936 2171

Veterans Agency
Norcross, Blackpool
Lancs. FY5 3WP
Tel: 0800 169 2277
Fax: 01253 330 561
Email: help@veteransagency.mod.uk
Website: www.veteransagency.mod.uk

Sample letter 78: Asking for a complaint about Benefits Agency services to be referred to an Independent Review Panel

1, Any Street
Anytown
Anyshire
AN1 2YZ

25th June, 2003

Customer Services Section
Benefits Agency

Dear Sirs,

Re: Reference Number 7678 – Income Support claim

I am writing about a complaint I have made with regard to the standard of the service I have received from this office. I discussed the issue informally with one of your staff, and because I did not feel the matter was resolved I wrote to you as the Customer Services Manager responsible for this office. I have your reply but I do not feel this addresses my principal concern, that your reception staff misadvised me as to my benefit entitlement.

This resulted in me not claiming the income support I was entitled to, though I did make a claim four weeks later after being advised by the local Citizens Advice Bureau. I am attempting to pursue a backdated claim for this benefit given your error, and I may have to take the claim to an appeal tribunal.

Meanwhile, however, I would like to refer my complaint about your service to an Independent Review Panel. I feel the panel should address the fact that The Benefits Agency Customer Charter has been breached – this says any advice given to me by agency staff must be 'accurate, clear, full and helpful'. This was patently not the case as far as my experience is concerned.

In the light of this I would ask the Benefit Agency to award me compensation for the loss of income I suffered.

I look forward to being kept informed of the progress of your investigation into this complaint.

Yours faithfully,

David Chambers

David Chambers

Social services

This chapter covers the work of the Social Services Department of a local authority, and includes any service they contract out. Your complaint may be that you disagree with your needs assessment or what help (if any) is provided as a result. Alternatively, it could be you are unhappy either with the standards of service, the behaviour of the social work staff or staff that provide services such as meals on wheels, home care, transport to day centres, respite facilities, day care and the like. See also *Residential care and nursing homes.*

All Social Services Departments and agencies they contract with must have a certain complaints procedure. In addition these agencies may have there own separate procedure, which you may also be able to use, for example **Age Concern,** **MENCAP** or **MIND**. Find out about the procedures and if your complaint is about your needs assessment take advice on how to argue your case. It will depend on your circumstances but if you have disabilities, ill health, family problems or you are a carer you are more likely to get help. It may also help to look at the local authorities Community Care Charter and Community Care Plan as these will set out their duties, resources, criteria for assessments, charges, standards and consultation processes. These will link to other policies that may also be relevant, for example the hospital discharge policy.

Informal and formal complaints

You can complain informally to any of the Department's staff. They are then obliged to try to deal with the problem or refer you to someone who can (see sample letter 79). Depending on the response you can then choose to carry on the complaint informally or make a formal complaint.

If you want to complain formally the department must advise you of the procedure including the name of the 'designated officer,' whom will most likely be someone working in the Department. Put the complaint in writing, and the matter has to be dealt with within 28 days, or else you should have good reason for the delay.

Review

If you are still dissatisfied you can request a review. You must do this in writing within 28 days of receiving the department's response. Both you and a representative of the social services department will have the opportunity to put your cases to a three-person review panel (the Chairperson at least must be independent). The panel must meet within 28 days. You have the right to make written representations in advance of the meeting, and to call witnesses to support your case. You could ask the designated officer for an advance copy of the department's written representations though s/he will not be obliged to let you have this. If they agree with you the panel will make recommendations to the Department.

An alternative

As an alternative to the above procedure, to get an issue resolved urgently find out who the monitoring officer is for the local authority – usually a senior manager is designated for this role. Complain to them and they will investigate.

Still dissatisfied?

If you are not happy with the way your complaint is dealt with write to the **Local Government Ombudsman** (see *Local authorities*). You could also consider taking legal action against the department to claim damages for negligence, in that they failed in their duty of care. Fighting such a case may not be easy. Take advice. You could also consider claiming for a breach of one or more of the human rights under the Human Rights Act 1998, for example if you have suffered what you consider to have been degrading treatment, or taking action on the grounds of race, sex or disability discrimination if appropriate. See *Taking things further.*

More general policy issues

To raise wider issues of concern around policy you should write to the **Director of Social Services** for the local authority in question. Also you could write to the chairperson of the council committee who has responsibility for the Department. Social Services Departments are obliged to consult the community in planning for the year ahead, you could find out when the next meetings are to be held and have your say then.

Sample letter 79: Requesting review of needs assessment

1, Any Street
Anytown
Anyshire
AN1 2YZ

Mrs H Golding
Team Leader
Social Services District 4
Social Services Department
Barford County Council

Dear *Mrs Golding,*

Re: *Mr Albert Chambers,* Assessed on *12th April and 30th May* – Reference Number 4562

I am writing to ask you to review a needs assessment carried out by one of your staff, Paul Masters. My father underwent the assessment on the above dates and it was concluded that he should receive meals on wheels and a twice-weekly visit from a home care assistant. It was also agreed that a stair lift and several handrails should be installed in his home to make getting about easier for him. However, he and I are disappointed that no arrangements were made for him to receive personal care on a daily basis. I fear for his safety if he is left alone for any period of time, given that he is very frail. I realise that he does not wish to go into a residential home but I do feel that he should receive more support to live at home.

This is particularly necessary because, as I explained when he was being assessed, I am not able to visit him as often as I would like due to working full time and having to bring up my own children.

Please can you consider the above and review *my father's* needs assessment. If you feel there are no grounds for review my father and I will have no alternative but to follow your complaints procedure and request the name of the designated officer to whom I should write.

I look forward to being advised of your decision within the next seven days.

Yours faithfully,

David Chambers

David Chambers

Solicitors' practices

First ask for an explanation from the solicitors practice – the most common reason for a dispute is a breakdown in communication (see sample letter 80). With some delays, for example, there could be factors at work outside the solicitor's control such as the complexity of your case or the behaviour of the third party. Some cases can run into years, particularly those involving personal injuries and probate. See also *Barristers*. Some solicitor's work from local authorities, advice services or commercial firms in which case you may have other avenues of complaint (see *Local authorities, Advice services, Buying services*) and where the solicitor is providing financial services see also *Investments and financial advice*.

How to begin

All practices have a written complaints procedure, which will tell you who handles complaints. Write to that person setting out details, giving examples and any dates (see sample letter 81), or you can use a special **Office for the Supervision of Solicitors (OSS)** form. This is an organisation set up by the **Law Society** to deal with complaints. Phone their helpline for advice.

Involving the Office for the Supervision of Solicitors

If you are still dissatisfied or you fail to get a response in a reasonable time, usually 14 days, your next step is to make a formal complaint to the OSS using another form obtainable from them. Say why you think the response was unsatisfactory and what outcome you are looking for. OSS are mainly concerned about poor professional service (for example delays, not keeping you informed, not following your instructions) or poor professional conduct (for example breaching your confidentiality, rudeness, overcharging).

The OSS will first refer the matter back to the practice to give them another chance to sort things out. If this fails they will formally investigate, studying paperwork and interviewing all parties. If they agree with your complaint they can use wide ranging powers, for example reduce the solicitors bill, order the solicitor to pay up to £5,000 in compensation, require the solicitor to correct mistakes at their own expense, set in motion disciplinary proceedings, advise you to take legal action against the solicitor for negligence.

Further steps

If the solicitors practice has been awarded a Community Legal Service **Quality Mark** for its services this will be indicated at the offices, on their notepaper, and on the Community Legal Service website. You could also complain to the awarding body called the **Legal Services Commission**, once you have exhausted the procedures within the practice. They will investigate and seek explanations, and a number of serious complaints may bring about the withdrawal of the Quality Mark.

Concerns about fees

If you think you have been overcharged first ask for the itemised bill (see sample letter 82), and try to work out from this what items to dispute. Then speak with the solicitor. Remember some costs are disbursements, expenses the solicitor has to meet on your behalf therefore not in their control. If this does not resolve things there are a number of possibilities depending on the type of work carried out.

Getting a remuneration certificate

If the bill did not include court work (non-contentious work), and you have not yet paid the bill, you could ask the solicitor to apply for a remuneration certificate from the OSS to determine whether it is fair and reasonable – see sample letter 83. Do this within one month of getting the bill. However, you cannot use this procedure if you had already agreed the fee in advance with the solicitor. You would normally first have to pay half the solicitors fee plus all the disbursements and VAT. You can also use this procedure if a court has ruled you have to pay the third party costs.

The bill will either be approved or reduced after you and the solicitor have been given a chance to comment. The solicitor's standard of work may be taken into account. Once an assessment is made, you or the solicitor will then have 28 days to appeal. Any appeal is looked at afresh by a **Law Society** committee.

Getting the bill assessed

You can apply to the court to have a bill assessed, whether or not you have paid the bill and whether or not the bill includes court work. Again, you can do this where you have been held liable in a court case to pay the third parties legal costs. You apply to the **High Court** unless the bill is for contentious work in the County court for less than £5,000 in which case apply to your local County court – take advice. If the bill is more than a month old the court could decide it is too late to assess, so be armed with an explanation. A court official will either approve the bill or reduce it after considering the solicitor's breakdown and your response to it. You could end up paying more because you will have to pay the costs of assessment unless the reduction is more than twenty per cent of the bill, in which case you will not have to pay any charges.

Disputing the bill in court

Another way of disputing the bill is to only pay a proportion you think appropriate, making clear why you are doing this, and wait for the solicitor to sue you in court for the balance. Then you have the opportunity to argue why you feel you should not pay the remainder, and the court will decide. The court may not decide in your favour if you could have used the other procedures above, and there is a risk of ending up with court and other costs – take advice. The solicitor cannot begin legal proceedings unless s/he has advised you in writing of your rights to dispute the bill.

Publicly funded legal services (was Legal Aid)

If you are refused publicly funded legal services, or you disagree with the financial contribution it is held you should make, appeal to your **Legal Services Commission** regional office. Write within 14 days or complete their form available from the solicitor. The appeal may be heard orally or by means of the paperwork only. If you lose you can re-apply but once you have been turned down three times you can appeal no more.

If as a result of using publicly funded legal services you win your case and gain financially you may be asked by the Commission to financially contribute to the costs of pursuing your case (the statutory charge). If you disagree with the amount ask the Commission to review the matter. If they find in your favour you will then have to take action in the County court. Take advice.

If you are refused legal aid for a criminal case because the Magistrates Court ruled that the case did not merit this, you can ask them for a review. Take advice.

If they think a solicitors charges are too high the Legal Services Commission may carry their own assessment. You have to be given the chance to comment and attend any hearing because it could lead to your financial contribution being reduced. The solicitor will inform you. Take advice.

Other points

- If you are dissatisfied you could **change your Solicitor**, but if you are getting publicly funded legal services you must have the permission of the Legal Services Commission to do so. If you are paying privately the solicitor will usually ask you to pay for the work he or she has done before releasing your papers to the new solicitor and there will of course be some delay and extra cost to enable the new solicitor to get to grips with your case.

- If you have suffered a loss at the hands of a practice and you are not compensated, you could take **legal action** against the firm, for example if the solicitor failed to exercise professional care or skill. Take advice. Contact the OSS, as they may refer you to a member of their negligence panel for up to one hour's free legal advice on whether you would be likely to have a case.

- You can apply to the **Solicitors Compensation Fund** if you have lost money as a result of the solicitor's negligence or dishonesty and there is no other way of recovering the money (e.g. the solicitor cannot be traced and is uninsured). You can obtain a Compensation Fund Information Pack from the OSS. Following their investigation the OSS may refer you to the Fund anyway if appropriate. Your legal costs in establishing your claim should be met by the Fund.

• If you have a complaint about a **Legal Executive or a Licensed Conveyancer** in a solicitors practice you would use the same complaints methods as for solicitors. However, there are professional bodies, the **Institute of Legal Executives** and the **Council for Licensed Conveyancers,** so if you have concerns about their professional conduct write to them. A licensed conveyancer may work elsewhere, for example, from their own business or an estate agency so see *Buying services* or *Estate agents.*

• If you are dissatisfied with the way OSS dealt with your complaint you can ask the **Legal Services Ombudsman (LSO)** to investigate the matter. This should in most cases be done within three months of the OSS informing you of your decision. If the LSO investigate and agree with your complaint they will make formal recommendations to the practice. This may resolve things for you, or it could give you grounds for taking legal action. Take advice.

Useful addresses

Community Legal Service
Website: www.justask.org.uk

Council for Licensed Conveyancers
I6 Glebe Road
Chelmsford
Essex CM1 1QG
Tel: 01245 349 599
Fax: 01245 341300
Website: www.conveyancer.org.uk

Institute of Legal Executives
Kempston Manor
Kempston
Bedford MK42 7AB
Tel: 01234 841 000
Fax: 01234 840 373
Email: info@ilex.org.uk
Website: www.ilex.org.uk

Law Society

The Law Society's Hall
113 Chancery Lane
London WC2A 1PL
Tel: 020 7242 1222
Email: info.services@lawsociety.org.uk
Website: www.lawsociety.org.uk

Legal Services Commission

Head Office
85 Grays Inn Road
London WC1 X 8TX
Tel: 020 7759 0000
Fax: 020 7759 0536
Website: www.legalservices.gov.uk

Legal Services Ombudsman (LSO)

England & Wales
3rd Floor, Sunlight House
Quay Street
Manchester M3 3JZ
Tel: 0845 601 0794
Fax: 0161 832 5446
Email: lso@olso.gsi.gov.uk
Website: www.olso.org

Scotland
17 Waterloo Place
Edinburgh EH1 3DL
Tel: 0131 556 9123
Fax: 0131 556 9292
Email: ombudsman@slso.org.uk
Website: www.slso.org.uk

The Office for the Supervision of Solicitors

Victoria Court
8 Dormer Place
Leamington Spa
Warwickshire CV32 5AE

Tel: 0845 6086565
Fax: 01926 431435
Email: enquiries@lawsociety.org.uk
Website: www.lawsociety.org.uk

Sample letter 80: Seeking information on progress

1, Any Street
Anytown
Anyshire
AN1 2YZ

25th June, 2003

Solicitor

Dear *Mr Collins,*

Re: Reference Number *324 – Purchase of 23, Footscrays Lane, Essex*

On *2nd March, 2003* I engaged you to undertake *the legal side of purchasing the above property* on my behalf. That was *nearly five* months ago. I cannot understand why it is taking you so long to complete the task. Therefore, in order to allay my increasing apprehension, please address the following concerns:

- What are my exact costs to date?
- What caused this delay?
- What remains to be done?
- How much longer do you estimate completion will take?

I anticipate your timely reply.

Yours sincerely,

David Chambers

David Chambers

Sample letter 81: Complaint about a solicitor

1, Any Street
Anytown
Anyshire
AN1 2YZ

25th June, 2003

Solicitor's Firm

Dear Sirs,

Re: Reference Number *324 – Purchase of 23, Footscrays Lane, Essex*

On *2nd March, 2003*, I instructed you to undertake the above case on my behalf.

I am unhappy about the professional service I have received from your firm and want to make a complaint for the following reasons:

1. *It has been five months since Mr Collins took on my case and we are still no nearer to completion.*
2. *I have received no information from your company on when this matter is likely to be finalised.*

I consequently request that you take the following action:

1. *Provide me with all information on what has been done so far.*
2. *Arrange completion within the next three weeks.*

Please note that I will not hesitate to refer this matter to the Office for the Supervision of Solicitors if my complaint does not receive a satisfactory response.

Yours faithfully,

David Chambers

David Chambers

Sample letter 82: Requesting an itemised account

1, Any Street
Anytown
Anyshire
AN1 2YZ

25th June, 2003

Solicitor

Dear *Mr Collins,*

Re: Reference Number *324 – Purchase of 23, Footscrays Lane, Essex*

I am in receipt of your bill dated *20th June* for the work on the above case but am unclear about the fees I have been charged.

To clarify the matter, please send me a detailed, itemised breakdown of the account of charges for the services you have performed, as I am legally entitled to under Section 64 of the Solicitors Act 1974. If you intend to charge me for this, please let me know before proceeding.

I look forward to hearing from you shortly.

Yours sincerely,

David Chambers

David Chambers

Sample letter 83: Requesting a Remuneration Certificate

1, Any Street
Anytown
Anyshire
AN1 2YZ

25th June, 2003

Solicitor's Firm

Dear Sirs,

Re: Reference Number *324 – Purchase of 23, Footscrays Lane, Essex*

I am in receipt of your letter dated *20th June, 2003* detailing the charges for the services you have provided up to *end of May*.

I feel these charges are unreasonably high and would be grateful if you could apply for a Remuneration Certificate from the Office for The Supervision of Solicitors on my behalf. As I am sure you are aware, I am entitled to such a Certificate stating what should be a reasonable and fair charge for the work you have done.

To avoid incurring interest on the amount of this outstanding bill I am enclosing a cheque for the full sum on the strict condition that it is subject to the Remuneration Certificate; and that I will be reimbursed should the Certificate state that your fees should have been lower.

Please confirm your acceptance of the above.

Yours faithfully,

David Chambers

David Chambers

Surveyors and valuers

To complain about a surveyor you raise the problem informally within the company, if not complain in writing to the principal (larger firms may have complaints procedures) – see sample letter 84. Where the company is an Estate Agent see *Estate agents* also. If you exhaust this process you could go to the **Royal Institution of Chartered Surveyors (RICS)**.

You could take legal action for damages if you relied on surveyors' advice, for example, in going ahead with a property purchase and then finding it was inaccurate or failed to identify a problem. However, take advice, as your success will depend on the kind of survey you contracted to have done and what was actually said in the survey report.

Much more is expected from a full structural survey than the basic 'house buyers' inspection that is to confirm the value of the property. If the value arrived at was wrong the surveyor would be liable. However, if you discover the roof felting needs replacing, but the surveyors said in the report that they could not get access to the roof, they would probably not be liable. The surveyors will not normally be able to hide behind any disclaimer they may have used in the report.

As for valuers, if s/he is a surveyor the above applies. If the valuer was a member of staff at an Estate Agency, see *Estate agents* to complain.

Useful addresses

Royal Institute Of Chartered Surveyors (RICS) – England & Wales
Surveyor Court, Westwood Way
Coventry CV4 8JE
Tel: 0870 333 1600
Email: contactrics@rics.org.uk
Website: www.rics.org.uk

Royal Institute Of Chartered Surveyors (RICS) – Scotland
9 Manor Place
Edinburgh EH3 7DN
Tel: 0131 225 7078
Website: www.rics-scotland.org.uk

Sample letter 84: Complaint about an unsatisfactory report on a property

1, Any Street
Anytown
Anyshire
AN1 2YZ

25th June, 2003

The Principal
Surveyor's Practice

Dear Sir,

Re: *11, Tower Road, Marlow*

I completed on the purchase of the above property on *1st May, 2003* and took possession on *12th May*. I did this on the basis of the House Buyers Report carried out by *Mr Bellows* of your practice.

Unfortunately, since moving in I have identified a severe penetrating damp problem in the back bedroom. I have sought the advice of two local builders on this and they say this is due to brickwork needing repainting and leaking gutters needing replacing. The cheaper of the two quotes I have obtained to put the matter right amounts to £650 including VAT.

I hold your Practice liable to meet this expense, as the *damp problem* was present when your surveyor inspected the house. He was under a legal duty to carry out his work using a reasonable amount of skill and care, and a reasonable level of competence. He failed to do so in that he should have discovered the problem and referred to it in his report. I am therefore legally entitled to seek this compensation.

I will give you 14 days in which to inspect the problem and to let me know whether you will meet my request. I will then arrange for the builder to carry out the repairs.

If you fail to reimburse my expense I will not hesitate to take legal action against you in the County court.

I look forward to your reply.

Yours faithfully,

David Chambers

David Chambers

Taxis and private minicabs

Taxis

Complain first to the driver, then to their firm – see sample letter 85. If you do not get anywhere complain in writing to the licensing authority, quoting the identification number, which should be inside and outside the vehicle. This is usually the local authority, but in London is the **Metropolitan Police Public Carriage Office**. If you live in an area where the taxis are not licensed then you could take the matter up with the local authority **Trading Standards Service** if the dispute is about charging.

Private minicabs

Complaints about minicab operators should be made to the driver or the firm. You can complain further, quoting the licence number, to the licensing authority – usually the local authority – if the minicab is licensed (they are only licensed in

some areas). Otherwise contact **Trading Standards** when the dispute is about charging.

You have grounds for complaint about overcharging only if the fare was quoted in advance and then exceeded. Most minicab firms will only give estimates, in which case you can only claim to have been overcharged if the fare is unreasonably higher than the estimate. If you have suffered a financial loss or inconvenience you may be able to claim damages from the firm. Take advice. See *Buying services*.

Disabled access

Complain as above if you have a disabled access problem, for example if a licensed taxi charged you for carrying a guide dog or hearing dog, these should be carried free. Also any newly licensed taxi must be wheelchair accessible from 1 January 2002.

Useful addresses

Metropolitan Police Public Carriage Office
Officer in Charge
15 Penton Street
London N1 9PU
Tel: 020 7941 7800
Email: enquiries@pco.org.uk
Website: www.tfl.gov.uk/pco

Sample letter 85: Complaint about a taxi company

1, Any Street
Anytown
Anyshire
AN1 2YZ

25th June, 2003

Taxi company

Dear Sirs,

Re: Complaint about your Taxi Service

I am writing to complain about your taxi service. The taxi journey in question was on *11th May* at 11pm, being picked up at *Elephant and Castle* travelling to *London Bridge*.

My complaint is that the taxi driver travelled the long way round to my destination and charged me *£3* more than what I would normally expect to pay for this journey. He could not explain why he took this route, and he became very abusive when I questioned the fare. I felt intimidated so I paid it in full, albeit under duress.

I would like to receive an explanation and apology from your firm, in addition to a refund of what I regard as the excess fare. If you do not respond to my satisfaction, I will not hesitate to complain to *Southwark Council*, as I understand they licence taxi firms in your area.

I look forward to your reply.

Yours faithfully,

David Chambers

David Chambers

Telecommunications

Here we deal with all domestic telephone communication services and equipment (home phones, computer internet connections and mobile phones). For telephone advertising see *Advertising*.

Home telephones

If you have a fault you will need to establish whether your equipment is the cause, or the telephone service. If you are unsure the phone service provider may do a fault check on the line, though you may be charged if this proved to be OK.

Before complaining check your legal rights (see *Buying services*). You also need to check the company's Code of Practice, which should set out information such as charges, terms and conditions of service, standards, and complaints procedures. Also check your service agreement. Phone the customer service office if this is not to hand. The complaints procedure may also appear on the back of your bill.

Many concerns might be resolved by phoning. If the complaint is complex, or is not getting resolved stick to the procedure and put the matter in writing.

Mobile phones

If you have a rental agreement, check the terms before complaining. If you bought the phone on a pay as you go basis, you did enter into a contract for goods and services on purchase so you then continue to have a contract for services each time you buy a top up voucher. In this case you may have no written terms but statutory rights still apply (see *Buying goods* and *Buying services*).

If you have a complaint you could start by talking to the trader who sold you the phone, then try the customer services office for the service provider. If you are using Orange or One 2 One you can complain to them direct as you have contract with them as service providers. If you use Cellnet or Vodaphone airtime your contract may be with the service provider, which bought the airtime from them to pass on to you, so complain to them – your trader will confirm who they are.

Internet

If you are having problems getting access to the internet or e mail service on your computer the problem could be the phone line, in which case get in touch with the phone service provider, but the culprit could be your computer (see *Buying goods*).

Alternatively, the problem may be with your **Internet Service Provider (ISP)**. They will have a publicised complaints procedure so check their website. You will probably have to talk to their customer helpline who will help you check that the software has been installed properly and that your computer meets all the necessary specifications to handle this. If they accept that they are at fault you should be able to claim compensation for loss of the service, and a refund of any fees being paid.

Complaining further

Check if the company belongs to an arbitration scheme (some do, such as BT). It may help to get your case referred to this unless you would prefer to sue in the County court (see *Taking things further*). If you are still getting no joy the next step is to contact the **Office of Telecommunications (OFTEL)** – see sample letter 86. This is the government watchdog and one of its tasks is to investigate complaints and exert influence on the provider if necessary. However, they do not help negotiate reductions on your bill. You could also find out from your phone book if there is an **Advisory Committee on Telecommunications (ACT)** in your area. They represent telephone users so they may assist you. Take advice. Alternatively, you could join the **Telecommunications Users Association** as they may act for you.

Other issues

- If you wish to dispute your bill ask for a fully itemised one and use the procedures above (see sample letter 87). To convince the service provider the bill is wrong you may have an uphill struggle but circumstantial evidence may help, for example if you can prove you were not in the house when a call was made. The company will investigate by monitoring their equipment.

- Your bill may be high because someone else in your household may have used unauthorised premium rate services such as chat lines. Complain to the **Independent Committee for Supervision of Standards of Telephone Information Services (ICSTIS)** within six months. An adjudicator will decide whether you should be compensated, and how much, or alternatively may help you negotiate a partial refund from the phone company. This is only likely to be considered for one bill and you will be expected to take more precautions such as arranging call barring in future.

- Some phone tapping is authorised by the Home Office for the police or the intelligence services to carry out surveillance. To complain contact the **Interception of Communications Tribunal.** Unauthorised phone tapping could be challenged in the courts for example under the Human Rights Act – take advice. Certain phone conversations are recorded legitimately, for example enquiries to call centres dealing with queries. Complain if you were not advised in advance (if you find out!)

- If you are refused a phone service only British Telecom (BT) is obliged to provide you with one, so if any other operator refuses apply to them. If they fail to do so, or you disagree with an advance payment and/or deposit they are charging complain on 0800 800 150 or write to your local BT Customer Services Manager. See your phone book or dial 0800 800 150 for the address. If you are still unhappy phone again and ask the manager to review the complaint. Next, ask the same of a more senior manager. If this fails ask about the **BT Complaint Review Service** (0800 545 458) and they will look over the

complaint again. If things are still unresolved complain as above. See also *Credit* as BT may have used a Credit Reference Agency. If they fail to do so or if their charge is unreasonably high complain. Their code of practice covers time taken to install.

- If a BT public payphone lets you down complain to BT, using the procedure above, but phone 0800 661 610 instead. If you can dial out from the phone ring 150 and your call may either be connected for you, or any lost money reimbursed to you or credited to your telephone account if you have one. The **Complaints Review Service** this time will be 0800 252 745.

- If you have been recorded inaccurately in the phone book complain to BT asking for compensation, either financial or free services, using the procedure as above. If **Yellow Pages** have made a mistake complain to them, if they fail to compensate consider taking legal action for breach of contract (see *Buying services*).

- If you are receiving nuisance or malicious calls contact the phone service provider and they may have a procedure to assist. You would be unlikely to be able to use 1471 caller return, as the caller would probably have withheld their number. You could purchase a phone with a caller display facility. Otherwise contact the police and they may authorise the provider to trace the calls if they think a criminal offence is being committed.

Useful addresses

Advisory Committee on Telecommunications (ACT)

England
ACT Secretariat
50 Ludgate Hill
London EC4M 7JJ
Tel: 020 7634 8773
Fax: 020 7634 8924
Email: actsec@acts.org.uk
Website: www.acts.org.uk

Scotland
Secretary to SACOT
28 Thistle Street
Edinburgh EH2 1EN
Tel: 0131 226 7275
Fax: 0131 226 4181
Email: sacot@acts.org.uk
Website: www.acts.org.uk/sacot

Wales
Secretary to WACT
4 The Science Park
Aberystwyth
Ceredigion SY23 3AH
Tel: 01970 636 413
Fax: 01970 636 414
Email: wact@acts.org.uk
Website: www.acts.org.uk/wact

British Telecom (BT)
Website: www.bt.com

Independent Committee for the Supervision of Standards of Telephone Information Services (ICSTIS)
4th Floor, Clove Building
4 Maguire Street
London SE1 2NQ
Tel: 020 7940 7474
Fax: 020 7940 7456
Email: secretariat@icstis.org.uk
Website: www.icstis.org.uk

Interception of Communications Tribunal
P.O. Box 12376
London SW1P 1XU
Tel: 020 7273 4096

Office of Telecommunications (OFTEL)
50 Ludgate Hill
London EC4M 7JJ
Tel: 020 7634 8888
Fax: 020 7634 8845
Email: advice@oftel.gov.uk
Website: www.oftel.gov.uk

Telecommunications Users Association
Woodgate Studios
2/8 Games Road
Barnet
Herts EN4 9HN
Tel: 020 8449 8844
Fax: 020 8447 4901
Email: tua@dial.pipex.com
Website: www.tua.co.uk

Yellow Pages
Queens Walk
Reading
Berkshire RG1 7PT
Tel: 0800 671 444
Website: www.yellowpages.co.uk

Sample letter 86: Requesting an OFTEL investigation

1, Any Street
Anytown
Anyshire
AN1 2YZ

25th June, 2003

OFTEL
50 Ludgate Hill
London EC4M 7JJ

Dear Sirs,

Re: *Star Telecom Company*, Account Number *2342*, and Telephone Number *5256447*

This letter is in reference to my complaint with the above company, which has still not been resolved.

Please refer to the enclosed correspondence relating to this case. My complaint is *that the bill for the month of May is £100 higher than usual and I feel that the telecom company has created this in error.*

I would be grateful if you could look into my claim. It is my understanding that during your investigation my services will not be interrupted.

Please keep me informed on the status of my case.

Yours faithfully,

David Chambers

David Chambers

Enc.

Sample letter 87: Complaint to telecom company

1, Any Street
Anytown
Anyshire
AN1 2YZ

25th June, 2003

Telecom Company

Dear Sirs,

Re: *Star Telecom Company,* **Account Number** *2342,* **and Telephone Number** *5256447*

I received your bill dated *20th June, 2003* regarding the above referenced account.

I am questioning the accuracy of the bill, as it does not appear to be in line with my usage during this period. In particular, the itemised records show that calls were made to *Newcastle and Norwich* on *27th April and 1st June,* but over that period *my home was unoccupied as we were on a family trip to New York.* I can provide evidence of this if required.

Please review and adjust the bill or, if necessary, send someone to test the meter on my line so we can determine its accuracy and settle the bill.

Please respond within 14 days providing the appropriate adjustment or a proposed date by which the test may be conducted. Otherwise, I shall refer this matter to the Office of Telecommunications.

Yours faithfully,

David Chambers

David Chambers

Water and sewerage services

Private companies that have to conform to the same guaranteed standards as published provide all water and sewerage services. For some areas the same company provides both services. Complain if these standards are not kept to, as agreed rates of compensation should be paid to you automatically otherwise you can ask for extra compensation! Follow the complaints procedure set out in their customer code of practice.

The next stage is to take the matter to your local **Customer Service Committee (CSC)**. Phone or email them first if the matter is urgent. Some complaints, see below, may be made direct to the **Director General of Water Services (OFWAT)** – see sample letter 88. For England and Wales, you can contact their head office direct or get in touch with their Customer Service Committee for your area. In Scotland, you need the Water Services Commission for Scotland.

Supply restricted or interrupted?

If your water supply is interrupted for more than four hours you should be given at least 48 hours notice, except in emergencies, and adequate information and compensation depending how long you are cut off. Write off to request this, see sample letter 89. With emergencies, say a burst water main, the company must restore the supply within 12 hours unless the burst is in a strategic main, in which case the company has 48 hours.

Your supply may be restricted due to low water levels (a Drought Order), but do complain if you are not advised of alternative supplies (e.g. a standpipe) or if you are still having to pay extra charges (say, for a sprinkler).

Poor water quality

If the water pressure falls below the usual minimum for an hour or more on two occasions in 28 days, you can claim compensation if you write in within three months of the date of the second time, provided the company was to blame.

If water quality is poor complain as above, then to the **Drinking Water Inspectorate**. The Inspectorate checks that the water companies monitor the quality of water by the book, and if necessary can intervene and prosecute the company. If you suffer any loss or illness as a result of the water quality consider legal action but you would probably need evidence from the Inspectorate. Take advice.

Disputes over the bill

If you dispute a metered water bill first check that the meter reading on the bill is correct or a reasonable estimate, if not send in the correct reading or ask the company to read it and re-bill you. If there is a leak and the leaked water is going through your meter you are liable but the company will let you off and credit your bill if it is the first time, provided you then get the leak repaired. The other possibility is that your meter is faulty. If so, you can ask the company to get an independent tester in to check for accuracy. With some companies you will be charged for doing this if the meter is found to be OK.

To dispute an unmetered bill find out on what basis the company arrived at the bill. If they used a flat rate charge there is not much you can do. If they used banding, or the old rateable value system, it will be worth contesting if you can show that your property should be in a lower band (see also *Council Tax*) or it has changed since its old rateable value was arrived at pre 1990. Take advice.

For sewerage charges check the bill against the company's charges for the year and their charging method, which must be publicised. To dispute land drainage charges appeal to the **Internal Drainage Board,** then to the **Environment Agency** (except where the Agency levied the charge direct, then you can only appeal to them).

Other issues

Is the company being unreasonable about installing a meter, that is are they trying to press you to have one against your will or are denying your request to have one installed? In either situation complain. If you request a meter this usually must be installed within three months and if they fail to do so, you can appeal to OFWAT. If you do not get a meter the company is obliged to offer you an alternative charging system that better reflects your water usage.

- If you are eligible for financial assistance toward your water charges from the company (e.g. due to low income) complain if you think the rules have been applied unfairly, also see *Taking things further* if you feel the rules are discriminatory.

- The company is responsible for any leaking pipes up to and including the stop valve, even where they are inside your boundary. Pipes beyond this are your responsibility, or whoever owns the property you live in.

- If a flooding sewer damages your property you can claim a refund from the company on your sewerage charges for that year, up to £1,000. Alternatively, you may want to consider legal action. However, the company will not be responsible for repairing private sewers, drains, cesspools and septic tanks, as these are the property owner's responsibility (or may be shared with neighbours). You and your neighbours could ask the company to adopt your private sewer and they would then be responsible for it. If they refuse, appeal to OFWAT. In some areas sewer upkeep is delegated to the local authority so you could complain to them as well (see *Local authorities*).

Useful addresses

Director General of Water Services (OFWAT)
Office of Water Services
Centre City Tower
7 Hill Street
Birmingham B5 4UA
Tel: 0121 625 1300
Fax: 0121 625 1400
Email: enquiries@ofwat.gsi.gov.uk
Website: www.ofwat.gov.uk

Drinking Water Inspectorate
Floor 2/A1, Ashdown House
123 Victoria Street
London SW1E 6DE
Tel: 020 7944 5956
Fax: 020 7944 5969
Email: dwi.enquiries@defra.gsi.gov.uk
Website: www.dwi.gov.uk

Environment Agency
Freepost (PO Box 60)
Patchway
Bristol BS32 4YY

Tel: 0845 933 3111
Email: enquiries@environment-agency.gov.uk
Website: www.environment-agency.gov.uk

Water Industry Commission for Scotland
Ochil House
Springkerse Business Park
Stirling FK7 7XE
Tel: 01786 430 200
Fax: 01786 462 018
Email: enquiries@watercommissioner.co.uk
Website: www.watercommissioner.co.uk

Sample letter 88: Requesting OFWAT investigation due to water being unwholesome

1, Any Street
Anytown
Anyshire
AN1 2YZ

25th June, 2003

Office of Water Services
Centre City Tower
7 Hill Street
Birmingham B5 4UA

Dear Sirs,

Re: *Acme Water Company* – Reference Number *10275*

This letter is in reference to my complaint with the above company, which has still not been resolved.

You will see from the enclosed correspondence relating to this case that I am attempting to claim the set amount of compensation that is due to me from the water company. This is due to the fact that they breached the Water Industry Act 1991 for a period of *three* days from *12th June at 4.15pm* to *11.30pm on 15th June, 2003*, by failing to supply me with wholesome water.

I would be grateful if you could look into my claim and if necessary, refer my complaint to the Drinking Water Inspectorate.

Please keep me informed on the progress of my case.

Yours faithfully,

David Chambers

David Chambers

Enc.

Sample letter 89: Requesting compensation for water supply interruption

1, Any Street
Anytown
Anyshire
AN1 2YZ

25th June, 2003

Water Company

Dear Sirs,

Re: Account number *10725*

I am writing to complain about my water supply, which was cut off without notice on *12th June at 4.15pm* and was not reconnected until *5.00pm on 15th June, 2003.*

Your company is in breach of the Water Act 1989 in that it failed to provide my household with a water supply that is sufficient for my domestic purposes.

Please confirm that this interruption was not as a result of a burst main and that I am therefore entitled to compensation under the above Act in the amount of £30, *the latest agreed rate of compensation.*

In addition to this, I am writing to claim damages for losses I have suffered as a result of the water being cut off. These total £50. I have arrived at this figure as follows:

1. Dry cleaning bill for washing clothes - £30
2. Household plants deprived of water - £20

I enclose evidence in the form of copies of receipts for repairs (or replacement items) and reports from contractors, which show that the damage was caused by the disconnection.

I look forward to hearing from you.

Yours faithfully,

David Chambers
David Chambers

Enc.

Index

This index covers the main text, but not address lists.

A

accountants 26
advertisements
    junk mail 260
    misrepresentation 29
    offensive 29
advice services 3, 4, 5, 33
    financial advisers 152, 153, 154
    see also barristers; solicitors
aircraft, noise 202
airlines 36
airports 36
appointments, breaking 69
arbitration 16 *see also individual terms*
assaults 217
    by medical staff 191

B

bailiffs 87
banks
    branch enquiries 40
    losses from 40-1
    ombudsmen 40
barristers 47 *see also* advice services
  solicitors
Benefits Agency 265
bonfires 204
British Gas Transco 123
British Telecom (BT) 289-93
Broadcasting Standards Commission

(BSC) 183
BT (British Telecom) 289-93
building developments 204
    new homes standards 69-72
    and property values 205
building societies
    branch enquiries 41
    losses from 41
    ombudsmen 41
bullying 249-50
burials 120
bus services
    access 50
    lobby groups 50
    London 49, 50
    operators 50
    subsidised 49-50

C

cafés
    bills, disputing 245-6
    damages from 246
    misrepresentations 246
standards 245
Child Support Agency (CSA)
    assessment procedures 77, 78
    payments from 77-8
children 204
    schools 249-52
Citizens Advice Bureaux 3-5
coach services 49-50
Community Legal Services (formerly
  Legal Aid) 275-6
contracts 13 *see also individual terms*
correspondence 10 *see also individual terms*
Council Tax
    bands 82
    overpayments 82

County courts 12
credit
 agency decisions 88-9
 disputing 86
 harassment for debts 87
 hire purchase 87
 holidays paid by 133
 mortgages 86, 153
 ratings 88-9
 time limits 86
cremations 120
criminal records 216
CSA (Child Support Agency)
 assessment procedures 77, 78
 payments from 76-8

D

debts 86-9
dentists 193
discrimination 14, 183
 racism 203, 249-50
drink
 buying 59
 pubs and wines bars 229-30
driving
 accidents
  conditions on the road 96-7
  obstacles in road 96
  people 96
  buses and coaches 49-50

E

electricity
 connection 103-4
 cancelling contract 103
 supplies 104
employment
 arbitration 111-2

changes 109
dismissal 109-11
formal procedures 107-12
health and safety 107, 108
informal procedures 107
minimum wage 108
redundancy 110
rights associations 108
statutory conditions 107, 112
tribunals 109-11
Energywatch 123
environment, formal procedures 204-5
 Environmental Health
  Department 59, 204
estate agents
 negligence 117
 payments 117
 surveyors 284
 trade associations 117
 valuers 284
European Convention on Human
 Rights 14-15
eviction 167
evidence 9 *see also individual terms*

F

flights 36
food
 buying 69
 eating out 245-46
 rail services 234
 school meals 252
funerals 120

G

gardens, overhanging vegetation 203-4
gas services
 health and safety 123

payments 123
supplies 123-4
trade associations 123
government
charters 225
local *see* local authorities
ombudsmen 225-6
politicians 16-7
guarantees 59
guest houses
booking errors 137
losses from 137
prices 137
standards 138

H
health and safety 107-8
gas supplies 123
maintenance by landlords 168-9
health services
dentists 193
National Health Service (NHS)
assaults by staff 191
changing GPs 192
formal procedures 190
hospital discharges 192
informal procedures 188-9
medication errors 191
misconduct 190-1
negligence 190-1
ombudsman 191
psychiatric units 191
rights associations 188
waiting times 192
opticians 193
residential homes 240-1
helplines 4 *see also individual terms*
hire purchase 87

holidays
accommodation 130-1
air travel 36
bankruptcies 132
compensation 132
evidence for 131
national laws and 130
package 130-3
unreasonable clauses 132
hotels
booking errors 137
losses from 137
prices 137
standards 138
Human Rights Act 1998 11-12

I
independent financial advisers (IFAs)
152
injunctions 12 *see also individual
terms*
Inland Revenue
errors by 141
formal procedures 140-1
informal procedures 141-2
overpayments 140-1
taxation 142
insurance services
intermediaries 145-6
loss assessors 146
premiums
quote discrepancies 146-7
time limits 146-7
trade associations 145
unmet claims 147
internet 2, 182, 290
purchases from home 259
investment companies 152-3
losses from 153

J

jobseeker's allowance 266
journalists 17-8, 183-4
judicial reviews 15
junk mail 260

K

knowledge 8-9, 57-8, 108-9

L

landlords
 changing tenancies 168
 eviction by 166-7
 harassment by 167
 health and safety obligations
      169-70
 maintenance by 169-70
 management by 161-2
 of profit-based housing 166
 rent demands 167-8
 of social-based housing 166
LEAs (Local Education Authorities)
      249-52
leaseholders
 management challenges 162-3
 service charges and 162
 tenants' associations 161
libel 15, 180, 181
libraries 3
lobby groups 17
 local authorities 176
 for transport services 50
local authorities 175
 Benefits Agency 265
  ombudsman 266
 correspondence 176
 council tenancies 166-7, 168-70

damages from 176
health services 188-93, 240-1
lobbying 176
Local Education Authorities (LEAs)
      259-52
 ombudsmen 176-8
 social services 270-1
  residential homes 240-1
London Underground Ltd 232

M

mail 221, 222
 junk mail 260
Maternity Pay, Statutory 112
media 17-18
 advertisements 29
 Broadcasting Standards
  Commission (BSC) 183
 discrimination by 183
 internet 2, 182, 259, 290
 obscenities in 183
 press 17-8, 180-1, 183-4
 privacy from 183
 radio 182
 TV 182-3
mediation 16, 201
minicabs
 charges 287
 licences 286
minimum wage 108
mortgages 86, 153
MOTs 98

N

negligence 13-4 *see also individual
 terms*
neighbours
 bonfires 204

gardens, overhanging vegetation
203-4
mediation 201
noise 202
pets 203
noise
neighbours 202
transport 202-3
nursing homes 240-1

O

objectives 8 *see also individual terms*
offers 10-11 *see also individual terms*
Office for the Supervision of
Solicitors (OSS) 273-4
ombudsmen
banks 41
Benefits Agency 265
building societies 41
funerals 120
government 225-6
health 189-90
legal services 273-4
local authorities 176-7
opticians 193
OSS (Office for the Supervision of
Solicitors) 273-4

P

parcel services 221
parking penalties 96
patience 9 *see also individual terms*
PCC (Press Complaints Commission)
181
pensions 153
pets 203
phones
access rights 291

landline 289
line surveillance 291
malicious calls 292-3
mobile 290
payphones 292
police
confiscation of property 217
formal procedures 216-7
informal procedures 216-7
local policies 218
politicians 17
Post Office 221-2
press 17-18, 183-4
defamation 181
inaccuracies 180
Press Complaints Commission
(PCC) 180-1
privacy 183, 184
procedures 10 *see also individual
terms*
pubs
ownership 229
short measures 229
purchases
compulsory 205
from goods traders 33
as contracts 57-8
on credit 86-9
delivery times 59
guarantees 59
knowledge and 57-8
manufacturer enquiries 58-60
overseas 60
Sale of Goods Act 1979
(amended) 57
time limits 58
trade associations 58-9
unsafe goods 59

from home 33
  via the internet 259
  misrepresentations 259
  rights to cancel 258-9
  time limits 259
  trader disappearances 259-60
  unsolicited goods 260
from services traders 33
  breaking appointments 71
  company enquiries 70
  as contracts 70
  refunds of advance payments 71
  small print 70
  trade associations 70-1
  withholding payments 71
  see also individual terms

R
racism 203, 250
radio 182
rail services
  access requirements 234-5
  cancellations 233-4
  charters 232
  delays 233-4
  food 234
  London Underground Ltd 232
  losses from 233-4
  misinformation 234
  restrictions 234
  rights associations 232
  stations 234
residential homes 240
  mistreatment in 241
restaurants
  bills, disputing 245-6
  damages from 246
  misrepresentations 246

standards 245

S
Sale of Goods Act 1979 (amended) 57
schools
  accidents 250
  bullying 250
  choice of 252
  exams 250
  exclusions 251
  formal procedures 249
  Local Education Authorities
    (LEAs) 249. 250, 251, 252
  meals 252
  punishments 251
  special needs 252
  transport 252
  uniforms 252
self-control 10 *see also individual
  terms*
sewerage services
  bills, disputing 298
  leaking pipes 299
  supply, restrictions 297
Sick Pay, Statutory 112
slander 15, 180, 182
Small Claims Track 12-13
small print 70
social security
  Benefits Agency 265
    ombudsman 266
  jobseeker's allowance 266
  payment challenges
    appeals 267-8
    formal procedure 267
    late appeals 267-8
    time limits 268
  statutory pay 112

social services
  formal procedures 270
  informal procedures 270
  residential homes 240-1
solicitors 5
  bills
    court assessments 275
    disputing 275
    remuneration certificates 274-5
  changing 276
  factors beyond control 273
  losses from 276
  Office for the Supervision of
  Solicitors (OSS) and 273-4
  ombudsman 277
  practices 277
  see also advice services; barristers
support 10 see also individual terms
surveyors 284

T

taxation
  errors 141
  payments 141
taxis
  charges 287
  licences 286
telecommunications
  bills, disputing 291
  British Telecom (BT) 290-2
  formal procedures 290-1
  inaccuracies 292
  internet 2, 182, 259, 290
  phones 289-292
tenants
  associations 161
  changing tenancies 168
  eviction 167-8
  harassment 167

  maintenance by 168-9
  in profit-based housing 166-8,
                          169
  rent, overpayments 167-8
  in social-based housing 169-70
tour operators 130-3
Trading Standards 6, 59
TV 180-4

V

valuers 284

W

water services
  bills, disputing 298
  meters 298
  pipes, leaking 299
  quality of water 297-8
  supply, restrictions 297
wine bars, short measures 229